Emergent Science

Emergent Science

Teaching science from birth to 8

Jane Johnston

Routledge
Taylor & Francis Group

LONDON AND NEW YORK

First published 2014
by Routledge
2 Park Square, Milton Park, Abingdon, Oxon OX14 4RN

and by Routledge
711 Third Avenue, New York, NY 10017

Routledge is an imprint of the Taylor & Francis Group, an informa business

British Library Cataloguing in Publication Data
A catalogue record for this book is available from the British Library

Library of Congress Cataloging in Publication Data
A catalog record for this book has been requested

ISBN: 978-0-415-73573-5 (hbk)
ISBN: 978-1-408-23764-9 (pbk)
ISBN: 978-1-315-81551-0 (ebk)

Typeset in 9.5/12.5 Charter ITC Std
by MPS Limited

Printed and bound in Great Britain by
TJ International Ltd, Padstow, Cornwall

Dedication

To Doreen Doggett with love.

Contents

Section 1   Development

List of illustrations

Photographs

Figures

Contributors

Carol Callinan is a lecturer in special educational needs at Bishop Grosseteste University College Lincoln. Her PhD research focuses on how children develop their ideas in science within the classroom environment, how they use multimodal clues and cues to express their knowledge and what this can tell us about how children's ideas develop over time. Carol has degrees in Psychology and Child Studies, has taught Psychology at degree level and has worked with children at both primary and secondary level.

Coral Campbell is an Associate Professor in the School of Education, Deakin University, Australia, where she is the course director of the Graduate Diploma of Teaching. Coral spent 17 years in science laboratories and 13 years as a primary teacher. She has a B. App Sci, B. Ed(post-grad) and a PhD. Her PhD gave an account of the changes that were impacting on the teaching of science in primary schools in Victoria across 1993 to 1999. Coral's research interests are predominantly in the area of how children learn, and experiential and holistic learning, particularly in early years and primary science, technology and environmental education. Her conference presentations and refereed publications relate to these areas. In addition, Coral has contributed several chapters to both a science education book and an environmental education text.

Andrew Johnston is currently a Year 4 teacher at St Mary Magdalene Primary School, Sutton-in-Ashfield, Nottinghamshire. He formerly taught Year 2 children in Lincolnshire and then moved to his current school and taught Year 1 children. His areas of interest are in music education and religious education. He is the coordinator for RE in the school.

Jane Johnston has recently retired as a Reader in Education at Bishop Grosseteste University, Lincoln, where she worked extensively, both nationally and internationally in three distinct areas: early childhood studies, primary science education and practitioner research. She has worked as a primary classroom practitioner, working with children from 5–11 years of age and as a subject leader and programme leader in primary science education and early childhood studies. She has particular interests in children's emergent scientific skills and coordinates the international emergent science research network and is co-editor of the *Journal of Emergent Science* and coordinator for the early years special interest group of the European Science Education Research Association (ESERA). She is the author of many books, chapters and journal articles on early childhood, primary education and science education. In 2006, she was one of the first of five teachers to be awarded Chartered Science Teacher status in the UK.

Maria Kallery is elected Assistant Professor of Didactics of Physics at the Aristotle University of Thessaloniki, Greece. She holds a BSc in Physics, an MSc in Computation and a PhD in Science Education. She has taught prospective primary and secondary science teachers and science classes in secondary education. Her publications include articles in international and European science education research journals, and in collective volumes and books in physics and astronomy for young children. Her research interests include development of teachers' content and pedagogical content knowledge in science, action research, modelling of didactical activities and development of teaching learning sequences.

John Oversby is a science teacher educator with interests in science for all, equity science education, promoting collaboration between teachers and researchers, visualisation, and teacher development. He has taught in schools in Ghana and the UK for 22 years. He has had responsibility for primary and secondary science education courses at Reading University. He is presently coordinator of a Comenius European Network in climate change education, and recently worked on a European project on history and philosophy in science teaching. He is a Board member for the *Journal of Emergent Science* and for the International Organisation for Science and Technology Education.

Beatriz Sena is a Brazilian trained teacher, who works as the Foundation Stage coordinator at the Botafogo site of the British School, Rio de Janeiro. She has extensive experience of leading changes in the early years and in 2011 completed her MA in Education with a thesis that looked at the introduction of provision for children from 2 years of age. Her other research interests include transitions in the early years and she has been able to ease transitions from home to school and through the Foundation Stage.

Sue Dale Tunnicliffe is a zoologist specialising in education, who has taught all ages and at university level. She is a senior lecturer at the Institute of Education, University of London. She was Head of Education at the Zoological Society, an education officer at the BBC and science education adviser to a cultural museum. Her PhD (Kings College) was in Science Education. She has published widely.

Acknowledgements

My love of science began early, when in the 1960s I was part of the Nuffield Primary Science Project, and my desire to be a teacher began a few years later (also in the 1960s) when I experienced (fortunately not first hand) the effect of poor teaching and knew that it should not be like that and that I could, as only an 11-year-old can think, make a difference! My career from a primary child to my present position has not always followed a smooth path, but I have been fortunate in my career to have been at the frontier of both early years and primary science educational developments and have hopefully been able to contribute to educational developments. I am particularly grateful to all colleagues and students, past and present, as well as my family and friends, who have influenced my thinking, challenged my assumptions and supported my love of early years science and who have contributed to the legacy of emergent science.

Introduction

Overview

This book is written to support professionals working with children in the early years (from birth to 8 years of age) in the development of their pedagogical and scientific knowledge and skills. In this introduction we:

- Look at the nature of science and consider what **emergent science** education is
- Identify how stories of science and learning about scientists can enrich science development and learning
- Look at the aims of the book and its target audience
- Consider how to use the book and the pedagogical features incorporated in it
- Look at the **study skills** strand that runs through each chapter of the book and how this can develop readers at different stages of their professional lives.

What is science? What is science education?

Science is often regarded as a body of facts about the biological, chemical and physical world and this implies that scientists know all there is to know about the world we live in. In reality, science is the study of the world and involves exploring and examining theories about the wider world – therefore involving not just biology, chemistry and physics but also elements of geology, geography, astronomy, technology, medicine and more, where they overlap with or share scientific concepts or processes. Views of the nature of science are influenced by social, political, geographical and educational factors, so it is a complex understanding.

Research undertaken in 1998 (Johnston *et al.*, 1998) identified that Finnish teachers were very influenced by environmental concerns because of the shared border with the Soviet Union (later to become Russia) and identified science as about being biology and geography. This was reflected in the **curriculum** for primary children, which was about environmental science – the overlap between biology and geography – and although it was not evident how this had been influenced, it appeared likely to be as a result of the shared history between Finland and Russia, the effect of a shared and changing border and the effects of environmental disasters. These influences included the loss of 13500 square miles of Eastern Karelia to Russia on September 19, 1944 after the signing of a peace treaty with Britain and the Soviet Union, and the Chernobyl nuclear power disaster on 26 April 1986 which affected countries close to the Soviet Union.

By contrast, English teachers in 1998 identified that science was about 'doing science investigations' and this was reflected in the first National Curriculum in science, which emphasised the process of science in primary science education. I suspect that English teachers today would identify science as being about learning scientific knowledge and I fear for the future, with the narrow knowledge objectives in the **National Curriculum** (DfE, 2012). For the English teachers, I suspect that the curriculum was the major influence on their views of science and that this affected their views of science education too. Interestingly, in 1998 the formerly communist European countries looked towards the UK for advice on how to become more practical and skills-based, although they have historically had a view of science as being about knowledge in three distinct areas of biology, chemistry and physics, without taking into account wider environmental issues, probably because environmental concerns are of little importance in a developing country recovering from war. The nature of science is an area that is well recognised as a part of science education (Taber, 2012), but the ambiguity about what it is remains.

It seems that the view of educational professionals on science is bound up in their view of science education and it may be unhelpful to try to tease out the differences. The influence of values on science education has been identified by Fensham (2012), so views of science have influenced comparative tests and the results, in turn, have influenced curriculum developments:

- Trends in International Mathematics and Science Study (TIMSS) undertook comparative tests in discrete areas of science in 1995, 1999, 2003 and 2007 (see TIMSS, 2012).
- The Programme for International Student Assessment (PISA) had a slightly different slant from international comparisons and has tested scientific literacy every three years since 2000 (PISA, 2012).
- Relevance of Science Education (ROSE) went further and aimed to shed light on factors of importance to the learning of science and technology (ROSE, 2012). Results from these comparisons have been used to support the development of attitudes.

The nature of science is very bound up in our understanding of the stories of science – a link between history and science **(see Figure I.1)**. These stories are often ones that give a white, male, northern hemisphere perspective on science, which belies the true nature of science and scientists and perpetuates the image of scientists as white-coated, slightly mad, dishevelled men **(see Figure 3.3)**. Throughout the book, we use stories of scientists that are important to our conceptual focus and the activities for early years children, but also that portray a more rounded view of the nature of science and scientists. So we have included some lesser known, but important ethnic and female scientists and also stories of scientists that illustrate the contentious nature of science and the tensions that existed, and still exist, between science and society and the Establishment, such as the established church and the Royal Society. There are many others missed off this list and, in particular, it still has a northern hemisphere perspective.

One's view of science education appears to depend on whether you are a scientist first or an educationalist first – and if, like me, you are an early educationalist first and a primary scientist second, you will probably find tensions between your pedagogical values and those of other science educators. However, members of the science education community (not well known for their rate of change) have slowly begun to embrace not just primary science, but also emergent science (Johnston, 2008, 2010; Johnston & Dale Tunnicliffe, 2008). Recent years have seen:

- early years science as the first special interest group of the European Science Education Research Association (ESERA) and a strand in their biennial conference;
- the formation of the Emergent Science Network (ESN), which aims to facilitate communication between people interested in emergent science, develop understanding of young

Scientist	Story summary	Relevance to science	Link to chapter
Biology			
Joseph Banks	Sir Joseph Banks (1743–1820) was an English naturalist and botanist who sailed on Captain James Cook's first voyage and discovered many new forms of plants. He is credited with the introduction of the eucalyptus, acacia and mimosa to the Western world and many species of plants bear Banks's name.	Variation and classification Growth	1, 6 and 4
James Barry	James Barry (c 1789–1865) was a Scottish military surgeon who improved the life expectancy after injury and operations by making the link between hygiene and survival after surgery. Although he lived as a man he was thought to have been born female (Margaret Ann Bulkley) but chose to disguise this so he could continue to train and serve as a doctor. He was the first person to perform a successful Caesarean section, where both mother and child survived. His/her peers concealed the evidence of her gender in the belief that a woman could not have been able to practise as a medical surgeon.	Health and hygiene	2 and 9
Marie Curie	Marie Curie (1867–1934) was a French-Polish physicist and chemist, famous for her pioneering research on radioactivity. She was the first person honoured with two Nobel Prizes, in physics and chemistry, and was the first female professor at the University of Paris. Her achievements included a theory of radioactivity and the discovery of two elements, polonium and radium, which ultimately led to X-rays.	Ourselves Life processes and living things	2 and 7
Charles Darwin	Charles Darwin (1809–1882) was an English naturalist who travelled around the world on the *HMS Beagle*. On the voyage he noticed similarities between fossils of extinct animals and living animals and between animals in one part of the world and animals in another part of the world. This led him to develop his theory of natural selection and common ancestry or what we now know as evolution. This is based on the premise that life on Earth is continually evolving and that minor genetic adaptations in animals and plants that support survival are passed on to offspring, and the species change over time to adapt to the environment they find themselves in. Darwin's ideas have been controversial since the day he published them and illustrate the tentative nature of scientific theories, especially when they conflict with the more established views and the need to respect evidence.	Variation and classification (plants)	1, 6
Charles Drew	Charles Drew (1904–1950) was a black American doctor and medical researcher, who developed improved techniques for blood storage. He was important in the formation of large-scale blood banks early in World War II that saved thousands of lives through blood transfusions. He died after a car crash in Alabama when he was a denied blood because of his ethnicity.	Ourselves Life processes and living things	2 and 7

Figure I.1 Scientists and their stories

Scientist	Story summary	Relevance to science	Link to chapter
Carolus Linnaeus	Carolus Linnaeus (1707–1778) was a Swedish botanist who began the main classificatory systems for plants and animals that we still use today. He divided living things into two kingdoms (plants and animals) and each kingdom into phyla, classes and divisions.	Variation and classification of plants and animals	1, 2, 3 and 4
Chemistry			
John and Jesse Boot	John Boot (1815–1860) was a farm worker and untrained English herbalist who founded M & J Boot, Herbalists, using the herbal remedies his mother made. Boot was not trained as a chemist and learned his later profession. His son Jesse Boot (1850–1931) transformed The Boots Company and it became known as the 'Chemists to the Nation'.	Materials and their properties Plants	2, 3 and 4
Humphry Davy	Sir Humphry Davy (1778–1829) was a British chemist and inventor, who discovered several alkali and alkaline earth metals. In 1815 he invented the Davy lamp, which allowed miners to work safely in the presence of flammable gases. Whilst Sir Humphry Davy was credited with the discovery, George Stephenson (1781–1848), an English civil and mechanical engineer, invented a safety lamp separately. Although it was later accepted that this was coincidental, there were many who thought that Stephenson must have stolen the design from Davy, as it was felt that an uneducated man would not have come up with such an educated invention.	Materials and their properties Light	3 and 8
Antoine-Laurent de Lavoisier	Antoine Lavoisier (1743–1794) was a French chemist who named both oxygen (1778) and hydrogen (1783) and put together the first extensive list of chemical elements. He discovered that, although matter may change its form or shape, its mass always remains the same.	Materials and their properties	2 and 3
John Loudon McAdam	John Loudon McAdam (1756–1836) was a Scottish engineer and road-builder. He invented a process for building roads with a smooth hard surface that would be more durable and less muddy by binding stones together using tar. Modern road surfaces are influenced by his process and the word tarmac comes from his name and the tar used in the process.	Materials and their properties	3
Charles Macintosh	Charles Macintosh (1766–1843) was a Scottish chemist and inventor of waterproof fabrics; the mackintosh raincoat is named after him. In 1823, he patented a method for making waterproof garments by using rubber dissolved in coal-tar naphtha for cementing two pieces of cloth together.	Materials and their properties	3 and 9
Physics			
Archimedes	Archimedes of Syracuse (c.287–c.212 BC) was a Greek mathematician, physicist, engineer and inventor, who laid the foundation of hydrostatics, and explained the principle of the lever. He is credited with designing machines, such as the screw pump.	Forces Energy	5 and 9

Figure I.1 (*continued*)

Scientist	Story summary	Relevance to science	Link to chapter
	He died during the Siege of Syracuse when a Roman soldier came across him making mathematical calculations.		
Nicolaus Copernicus Galileo Galilei	Nicolaus Copernicus (1473–1543) was an astronomer and the first person to theorise, from his observations, that the Earth was not the centre of the universe and that it moved around the Sun. Galileo Galilei (1564–1642) was an Italian physicist, mathematician, astronomer, and philosopher who supported Copernicus' ideas and helped improve the telescope. Both Copernicus and Galileo were opposed by the established Church as their ideas were not only controversial but questioned the central part the Church played in everyday life.	Astronomy	7
Benjamin Franklin	Benjamin Franklin (1706–1790) was one of the Founding Fathers of the United States, as well as an author, printer, political theorist, politician, scientist, musician and inventor. As a scientist, he was important for his discoveries and theories regarding electricity. On one occasion, he is reported to have taken a kite out in a thunderstorm, with a key attached to the end of the string and experienced tingling in his hand as the lightning (a form of static electricity) travelled down the string.	Electricity Magnetism	6 and 9
Elijah McCoy	Elijah McCoy (1844–1929) was a black Canadian inventor educated in Scotland. He made a successful machine for lubricating engines which spawned many copies, all inferior to the original, so his invention was called the real McCoy. He patented the design in 1872.	Forces Energy	5 and 9
Isaac Newton	Sir Isaac Newton (1642–1727) was an English physicist, mathematician and astronomer, who is considered to be the father of science. His theories include universal gravitation, the three laws of motion, and light.	Forces Light Astronomy	1, 5, 7 and 8

Figure I.1 *(continued)*

children's scientific development, support professional working with young children and evaluate the impact of emergent science research on early years pedagogical practice;

- the publication of the *Journal of Emergent Science* (JES), hosted by the Association for Science Education on its website, which aims to make research into early years science accessible to **early years professionals**.

These developments and the interest in emergent science are also helping us to understand the nature of science education in the early years, and to overcome misunderstandings about young children's science and the foundation it provides for later scientific development.

The book

The book explores emergent science, by looking at the three aspects; development, the context of that development and early science pedagogies.

Section 1, Development, is made up of three chapters that look at the development of emergent **skills** by exploring the scientific process (Chapter 1), the development of emergent thinking by looking at children's development through Piaget's (1929) cognitive stages and Montessori's (1994) planes of development (Chapter 2), and the development of emergent attitudes by focusing on the child within Bronfenbrenner's (1995) ecological systems theory.

Section 2, Contexts, also consists of three chapters and examines the different contexts in which development takes place in the early years: the home, the educational setting and the **transitions** children face in the early years. Chapter 4, Learning science at home, continues the focus on Bronfenbrenner's (1995) ecological systems theory by considering the child's position in the microsystem in three stages in the early years: birth to 3 years of age, 3–5 years of age, and 5–8 years of age. Chapter 5, Learning science in the curriculum, looks at the history of the **Early Years Foundation Stage** and National Curriculum and considers the possible future impact of changes on young children's scientific development. Chapter 6, Transitions between stages of development, considers transitions in the first 3 years of life from a parent's perspective, transitions from 3 to 5 years of age from a professional's perspective, and transitions from 5 to 8 years of age from a child's perspective.

Section 3, Pedagogy, looks at different pedagogical approaches and their role in emergent science; these are scientific play (Chapter 7), scientific explorations and **discovery** (Chapter 8) and scientific investigations and problem-solving (Chapter 9).

Together, the nine chapters outline everything about emergent science that involves the development of scientific skills, attitudes, understandings and language through concrete, social experiences. Early years children will have some very firm **cognitive** ideas about the world around them, which are the result of a whole range of diverse experiences, even before they formally start school, and in many instances they will be developing knowledge about scientific phenomena but will be unaware of its scientific nature. They will also be developing scientific skills, important in other areas of life and the curriculum, but which together form the unique scientific process that is important to develop in young children if they are to progress in science. Through emergent science experiences, children will also develop an understanding of the nature of science, including the understanding of scientists and the part they have played in our understanding of science **(see Figure I.1)**. An important aspect of early years science is making it relevant to children and their lives, so that science is not seen as a separate part of their lives but as integrated, embedded and intertwined in all aspects of their lives. For this reason, the book makes links with nursery rhymes, stories and story books and scientific concepts **(see Figures I.2 and I.3)**.

The target readers of the book include:

- Initial teacher education students on both primary and early years courses, including PGCE and undergraduate routes;
- Education Studies and Early Childhood Studies undergraduate students;
- Foundation degree students with work-based learning in early years settings and primary schools;
- Professionals working with children in the Early Years Foundation Stage (from early career to leaders);
- Lecturers teaching HE courses in Education Studies, Early Childhood Studies, Early Years Education and Primary Education.

Nursery rhyme	Relevance to science	Link to chapter
Biology		
Mary, Mary, Quite Contrary *I Had a Little Nut Tree*	Growth of plants Environment	2 and 4
Little Miss Muffett	Mini-beasts/variation and classification Environment	1, 6 and 4
Baa, Baa Black Sheep *Mary Had a Little Lamb* *Hickety, Pickety, My Black Hen*	Variation and classification Life processes and living things	3 and 6
Jack and Jill Went up the Hill	Health	2 and 9
Chemistry		
Pease Pudding Hot, Pease Pudding Cold	Materials and their properties	3
Pat-a-cake, Pat-a-cake Baker's Man	Materials and their properties	2 and 3
Physics		
Old King Cole	Music/sound	5
Tom, Tom the Piper's son	Music/sound	5
Twinkle, Twinkle Little Star	Astronomy	7
Dr Foster Went to Gloucester	Weather	8
Three Wise Men of Gotham	Forces (floating and sinking)	1, 2 and 5
Humpty Dumpty	Forces	5

Figure I.2 Nursery rhymes and science links

The book aims to:

- support the development of early understandings, skills and attitudes in science education, drawing upon the author's expertise in primary science and early years education and her successful publishing record in both;

- support students and professionals working with children up to the age of 8 years of age, by providing them with the theory underpinning good emergent science development and practical ideas of how they can provide quality science experiences for the children they work with;

- support students and professionals by identifying how they can develop both personally and professionally.

Study skills

Professional development begins in the undergraduate environment and during initial teacher education, moving through the early career and into the professionals' later career; it does not stop but continues, as all development, throughout the professionals' career. This means that professionals should develop a range of study skills, which facilitate their professional practice and **reflection** on emergent science practice and provision. Within the book, these skills are embedded in reflective and practical tasks **(Figure I.4)**.

Children's book/story	Relevance to science	Link to chapter
Biology		
Carle, E. (1970). *The Very Hungry Caterpillar*. Harmondsworth: Penguin Bradman, T. (1990). *The Little Red Hen*. London: Methuen Children's Books	Life processes and living things	1, 6 and 7
Glori, D. (1995). *The Snow Lambs*. London: Scholastic Publications	Life process and living things	3 and 6
Smallman, C. & Riddell, E. (1986). *Outside In*. Abingdon: Frances Lincoln Children's Books Pearse, P. & Riddell, E, (1989). *See How You Grow*. New York: Barrons Educational Series	Life processes and living things (ourselves)	2 and 7
Baker, J. (1987). *Where the Forest Meets the Sea*. London: Walker Butterworth, N. & Inkpen, M. (1991). *Wonderful Earth*. London: Hodder and Stoughton	Environment	3
Wilson, K. (2007). *Bear Feels Sick*. London: Simon & Schuster	Health and Hygiene	2
Briggs, R. (1970). *Jim and the Beanstalk*. London: Penguin (Picture Puffin)	Variation and classification (ourselves) Growth (plants)	2, 4 and 6
Browne, E. (1997). *Handa's Surprise*. London: Walker Books	Variation and classification (plants)	1 and 4
Sendak, M. B. (1992). *Where the Wild Things are*. London: Picture Lions Peters, A. F. & Coplestone, J. (2007). *Animals Aboard*. London: Frances Lincoln Kaye, G. (1980). *Kassim Goes Fishing*. London: Methuen	Variation and classification (animals)	6
French, V. (2007). *Oliver's Vegetables*. London: Hodder Children's Books Carle, E. (1987). *The Tiny Seed*. London: Hodder and Stoughton	Growth	2 and 4
Chemistry/earth sciences		
Green, M. (1978). *Mr Bembleman's Bakery*. New York: Parents Magazine Press	Materials and their properties	1
Ahlberg, A. (1981). *Mrs Lather's Laundry*. London: Penguin (Picture Puffin)	Materials and their properties	3 and 4
Freedman, C. & Cort, B. (2007). *Aliens Love Underpants*. London: Simon & Schuster	Materials Astronomy (physics)	3 and 7
Carle, E. (1996). *Little Cloud*. London: Penguin Cloke, R. (1989). *Tales of Oaktree Wood. Mandy's Umbrella*. London: Award Publications Wilde, O. (1978). *The Selfish Giant*. London: Penguin	Weather	8
Physics		
Allen, P. (1986). *Mr Archimedes' Bath*. London: Hamish Hamilton	Forces (floating and sinking)	1, 2 and 5
Grey, M. (2005). *Traction Man is Here*. London: Random House Oke, J. & Oke, J. (2004). *Naughty Bus*. Budleigh Salterton, Devon: Little Knowall Publishing Inkpen, M. (1992). *Kipper's Toybox*. London: Hodder and Stoughton Children's Books	Forces	5 and 9

Figure I.3 Stories and science links

Children's book/story	Relevance to science	Link to chapter
McKee, D. (1987). *The Sad Story of Veronica who Played the Violin.* London: Red Fox	Music	3 and 5
Inkpen, M. (1993). *Lullabyhullaballoo!* London: Hodder and Stoughton	Music	3 and 5
Hughes, S. (1985). *Noisy.* London: Walker Books	Sound	5
Hughes, T. (1985). *The Iron Man.* London: Faber and Faber	Magnetism	6
Baker, J. (1987). *Where the Forest Meets the Sea.* London: Walker Butterworth, N. & Inkpen, M. (1991). *Wonderful Earth.* London: Hodder and Stoughton Hindley, J. & Stojic, M. (2004). *Can You Move Like an Elephant?* London: Doubleday	Energy	9

Figure I.3 (*continued*)

Section/ chapter	Title	Study skills
	Introduction What is science and science education? How to use the book	
Section 1	DEVELOPMENT	Reading and reflection
Chapter 1	The development of emergent skills	Selecting and using literature
Chapter 2	The development of emergent thinking	Reflection and analysis
Chapter 3	The development of emergent attitudes	Writing a literature review
Section 2	CONTEXTS	Collecting and analysing primary data
Chapter 4	Learning science at home	Observation as a research tool
Chapter 5	Learning science in the curriculum	Talking and listening as a research tool (incl. questioning)
Chapter 6	Transitions between stages of development	Narrative as a research tool
Section 3	PEDAGOGY	Synthesis and communication
Chapter 7	Scientific play	Synthesis of ideas
Chapter 8	Scientific explorations and discovery	Writing up
Chapter 9	Scientific investigations and problem-solving	Presenting findings
	Glossary	

Figure I.4 **The development of study skills within each chapter of the book**

The order of the study skills in each chapter follows a developmental sequence, which should be helpful for students and professionals who are attempting to develop their expertise and practice. The first set of study skills, in Section 1 of the book, are connected to reading and reflection of reading. Chapter 1 is concerned with the selection and use of literature:

- helping the reader in making appropriate choices in the type of literature – a combination of books, journals, policy documents and web-based sources, with no over-reliance on one type of source;
- reading for understanding;
- making notes on their reading;
- using reading effectively in the development of persuasive arguments, rather than describing it;
- referencing using the Harvard system of referencing;
- using original sources rather than using books cited in other texts.

In order to select and use reading effectively, you need to be very clear what the reading is being used for. Usually, this means having clear questions that need to be answered. These may be SMART (specific, measurable, analytical, relevant and time-related). Questions that are too broad and generic will be unanswerable, especially if you are focusing on a few texts. You need to be clear about how you are going to measure success in finding evidence to answer the questions. You need to pose analytical questions (how, why and so what?) as opposed to descriptive questions (what, when, who?) and understand how the evidence that you will collect will answer them (how relevant the evidence is to the questions). Finally you need a clear timescale for collecting the reading to answer the questions, as it is very easy – and reassuring! – to spend a great proportion of your available time reading and collecting nice bits of information.

In Chapter 2, we focus on reflection and **analysis**. We start by looking at what analysis is: to take something apart or separate in order to illuminate, reveal, uncover, understand, resolve, identify or clarify. We look at how you can analyse events, situations, experiences or reading, revealing what the main factors affecting them are, understanding why someone has acted in a particular way or clarifying issues for further development/action. We also consider deeper analysis that mines data to different depths, understands different perspectives, identifies patterns and chronology of events and illuminates meanings, all of which will help us in our professional practice with children.

In Chapter 3, we focus on what a literature review is and how to write one and develop persuasive written arguments. There is a mistaken view that a literature review should provide a general description of all the writing in a large area (e.g. the development of scientific understandings, skills and attitudes in the early years), rather than a more specific analysis of the literature to help answer posed questions in a narrower and more defined area (e.g. the effect of play on development of understanding of forces). The literature review of any study has two main functions:

1 To set the scene and provide an introduction to the research, through a critical examination of literature in the area;

2 To use the literature to provide a critical analysis to answer the research questions posed.

There are four steps to writing a literature review. The first one is to select appropriate literature, ensuring a balance between different types of texts: professional and academic; books, journals and websites; seminal and recent texts; policy documents and historical documents. The second step is to read and understand the literature and not merely skim-read in the search of juicy quotations. To fully understand a text, you may need to read and reread it and reflect upon it for a while before using it. Step three involves using the analysed ideas in the literature. In order to use the reading effectively, you need to develop a persuasive argument (Toulmin, 1958) and use ideas from the literature to support your thinking or argue against and answer your research questions. Effective use of reading involves making persuasive arguments and using reading to support it, rather than citing reading, as this shows understanding of the issues through analysis of the ideas expressed in the text rather than description.

Section 2 of the book (Contexts) focuses on the collection of primary data, with each chapter looking at a different research tool. Chapter 4 (Learning science at home) focuses on observation as a research tool and through the chapter we look at observation, develop observation skills and so understand processes, events and development. We look at different types of observations, focused, unfocused, participant and non-participant, and at the use of observation schedules. Chapter 5 (Learning science in the curriculum) focuses on talking, listening and questioning as research tools. We can tell a great deal about children by listening to them in a variety of situations. If children talk to us and ask us questions, this information can inform us about their worries, concerns, achievements and aspirations. Evidence collected from children can be a powerful way to find out about them and will help us to make decisions to continue to support them. On its own, listening to children can provide evidence to support our deep understanding; combined and triangulated with other evidence, from observation, narratives, discussions with parents and other professionals, the evidence is more valid and powerful. Chapter 5 also considers the ethos and environment that encourages children to talk and helps us to evaluate our own environment. We also explore the type of adult interaction and the type of questions that encourage children to talk openly and honestly and enable us to gain a better understanding of them and how we can support their development. Chapter 6 (Transitions between stages of development) focuses on narrative as a research tool. In narrative, participants or informants tell a story. These stories are more than anecdotes – they can provide powerful insights into situations and support analysis and **synthesis**. Each chapter in this book contains such stories, sometimes in the form of case studies, exemplars of practice or research. Sometimes the story is told by different participants, triangulating data and getting a more vivid and comprehensive picture of the action, event or situation being described. A story told from different perspectives allows layers of data to be analysed and a more valid (truthful) picture to be revealed. Collecting evidence to support personal and professional development is a scary phase of an enquiry as you cannot rely on the work or support of others. You also need to critique the tools/**methods** and consider the **reliability**, **validity** and **ethics** of the different data collection methods you use and how these methods fit into an overall **methodology**.

This book does not look closely at different research methodologies, but there are many other helpful support texts (see, e.g. Cohen *et al.*, 2011; Oversby, 2012). There are many different methodologies or types of research and each one has its own individual characteristics. You need to understand different methodologies in order to make a decision about which type best describes your research. The types of research which best suit research in emergent science are as follows:

● Action research in which the professional attempts to improve or develop practice in a cyclic way, by planning the next step of action or development as a result of analysis of the previous action or development. This is significantly different from other research methodologies and it needs to be written up in a particular way with each action cycle/ action step showing how it is planned as a result of the analysis of evidence from the previous action cycle/step. You may be attempting to develop children's observational skills **(see Chapter 1)**, or developing role-play in your setting to support emergent thinking **(see Chapters 2 and 7)** and therefore research the effectiveness of your teaching and the children's learning, in a plan-do-review research process.

- Case study research, which involves analysis of a number of specific instances to understand the bigger picture. You may be researching the effect of transition on scientific attitudes by looking at the different perspectives of parents, children and professionals (with each one being a case). Your cases may also be issues or factors affecting transition that emerge from the data, so in research into transition this may be the role of the parents, the curriculum or other settings in the transition **(see Chapter 6)**.

- Correlational research, which considers interrelationships among variables involved in the research. For example, you may research the relationship between the children's achievement and positive attitudes towards science **(see Chapter 3)**, or the relationship between exploratory teaching and learning approaches and the development of emergent thinking **(see Chapter 2)**.

- An evaluation, which would attempt to evaluate the curriculum or an approach. For example, you could undertake a piece of appreciative inquiry into how to develop the school grounds to promote scientific development and understanding of the environment. Appreciative inquiry focuses on positive aspects for evaluation (Cooperrider & Srivastva, 1987; Reed, 2007), through a cycle that aims to discover what is good, to imagine new goals and reaching these collaboratively. Alternately you could undertake an illuminative evaluation (Parlett & Hamilton, 1972), which illuminates the reasons for children's achievement using a particular pedagogical approach **(see Section 3, Pedagogy)** or the factors affecting scientific achievement in the Early Years Foundation Stage or the National Curriculum **(see Chapter 5)**.

- Historical research does not depend on primary data but uses policy documents and research reports to analyse historical trends, or the effect of new developments. This may involve analysis of the changes in the early years curriculum **(see Chapter 5)**.

- Accounts or narratives are types of interpretive ethnography where situations are considered from the participants' perspectives. Professionals may narrate their life stories to help understanding of their attitudes to science **(see Chapter 3)**, or **critical incidents** in a child's life that may have affected his or her scientific development **(see Chapter 4)**.

You may find it helpful to articulate your ideas for your research (questions, methodology, methods and preliminary reading) in a research proposal. A format for this can be found in Figure I.5. Planning your research in this way helps you to firm up your ideas, preparing yourself and giving yourself a greater chance of succeeding in your research – as Dwight Eisenhower (1890–1969) said, 'In preparing for battle I have always found that plans are useless, but planning is indispensable.'

The research methods considered in Section 2 can be used in most of the methodologies described above.

The study skills in Section 3 of the book are connected with synthesis and communication. Chapter 7 (Scientific play) looks at the synthesis of ideas. Synthesis a very important skill that enables you to take analysis from a wide range of primary and secondary evidence (from data you have collected and reading) and put them back together in order to draw conclusions, make sense of the whole, draw inferences producing new ideas or models and identifying implications. Synthesising involves breadth and depth of understanding,

Focus of research. A brief statement about the focus of the research (perhaps with a title or an overarching research question or area).

Research questions. A maximum of three questions that will help you to explore the area or answer your overarching research question.

Methodology. Detail about the type of research you are conducting. You need to read to inform your choice of methodology and how it structures your research from the research questions through to the report. This should not be a theoretical piece on methodology and should focus on what you are doing not what you are not doing.

Sample. An outline of the participants and how you will address the ethical issues of permissions, anonymity and right to withdraw, so addressing the ethics of sampling.

Methods. A critique of the methods to be used to collect evidence to answer your questions. Identify also how you can ensure your research methods are ethical and reliable and that the data collected will be valid. This *must* include reading to support your choices.

Analytical framework. A brief description of how you intend to analyse the data collected using the methods above, the analytical lens that you will use, or how you will sort, code and make sense of the data and overcome any issues of objectivity in analysis.

Ethical statement. This section will be for any ethical issues and issues of objectivity not addressed in the previous sections. You must explain how you have ensured your research adheres to ethical guidelines.

Figure I.5 **Outline of a research proposal**

making links between different analyses and engaging in a deep and critical discussion of the ideas, implication or models of thinking that have emerged from the analysis. In other words, it involves critically discussing the findings from reading and from the data collected. Most importantly, the discussion does not repeat the analysis, but moves forward from it to greater clarity, sophistication of ideas and understanding, using strong arguments that use the data as evidence. In order to create arguments, you need to understand what an argument is and the difference between an argument (an evidence-based belief) and an opinion (a non-evidence-based belief). You also need to know what makes for a good rather than a weak argument; one that provides reasons behind what you are claiming, evidence to support your argument, such as factual data, persuasive language and a counter-argument.

In Chapter 8 (Scientific explorations and discovery), we focus on writing up professional enquiry for a range of audiences. For example, different methodologies (the over-arching type of research you are undertaking), as described earlier in this chapter, will structure the written report, especially if you have undertaken action research or case study research. When you decide your methodology, you need to consider what the research will look like in its final written form and keep this in mind throughout the data collection and analysis process and ensure that the relevant primary data is collected and written up in a form that is appropriate to the type of research. We consider how to write up a thesis, remembering that it is your written thesis that is assessed and so it should show the depth and breadth of your understandings, and remembering also that writing up the research takes far longer than most people envisage. This chapter considers some of the dilemmas you may face when writing up your research thesis and possible solutions to help you perfect your work. In Chapter 9 (Scientific investigations and problem-solving) the study skills section focuses on presenting research, both orally and visually. Oral presentation of ideas and findings helps to articulate understandings and ultimately will help with written communication. Oral communication is an essential element of professional development as well as degree-level work, and individuals who seek an opportunity to speak out and articulate ideas are likely to advantage their personal and professional development. In this book there are plenty of opportunities for large and small group discussions in the reflective tasks and critical discussion boxes (see the next section). The skill of formally presenting ideas orally also needs to be developed, since presentations form a part of assessments both in higher education and in professional life. The skill of oral presentation includes the ability to speak coherently, engage with the audience, referring to notes rather than reading from them, or using notes only as a prompt. An excellent visual and oral presentation will motivate and engage an audience and have a clear sense of purpose. It is easy to spend considerable time making a presentation visually striking and even engaging, but failing to have a clear objective means it is likely to fail in its purpose.

Boxed features

As well as the study boxes, there are other boxed features within the book. Each chapter has a number of reflective tasks and some have opportunities for critical discussions. Many of the reflective tasks relate specifically to the study skills being developed in the chapter and each has three levels: for early career professionals, developing career professionals/teachers and later career professionals/leaders. The chapters also have case studies and these are usually followed by a reflective task to help make sense of the case study. In this way, the case studies are not simply illustrative, but lead to reflective and personal and professional development. The chapters also have activities and key questions to promote understanding in a specific scientific conceptual area and practical tasks. These activities' ideas and practical tasks encourage the reader to undertake some more practical physical activities related to the content of the chapter and are written for those working in the Early Years Foundation Stage, **Key Stage 1** or **Key Stage 2**. They are designed to support application of ideas in practice, and thus support professional developments and thinking. Each chapter has a scientific conceptual focus that underpins the activities and this is identified in knowledge boxes. Finally, each chapter is underpinned by extensive research from experts in science education, and specific current research is summarised in each chapter.

The decision as to which level of task to undertake is one that each individual reader must take and the route through the book will, likewise, be individual. For example, someone in their early career may be a science specialist and so wish to look at tasks designed for those later in their career or even as a leader in science, whilst a lead professional may have little scientific expertise and wish to look at tasks for an early career professional. Reflective tasks for early career professionals build on from their post-16 qualifications and are the sort of task undertaken on initial teacher education programmes. Tasks for those who are developing career professionals or teachers are designed for early years professionals and teachers with extensive experience of working with young children up to 8 years of age. Tasks for lead professionals, head teachers and managers are designed to provide ideas for extending not only their own professional development, but also that of their team/staff through in-service training sessions and staff meetings. They may also wish to incorporate some of the other practical tasks to support the development of professionals in their setting.

We recognise that books of this nature contain many terms and acronyms not used in everyday life. Understanding these terms and what the acronym stands for, as well as being able to use them, are increasingly important in professional life. In the book, the first time that these terms are used, they are highlighted in blue bold in the text and the reader can then turn to the glossary page where the term will be defined and the acronym identified in full.

How to use the book

Like any book of this nature, it is not expected that you will read it from cover to cover, but instead that you will use sections to support particular areas of study or personal and professional development. It is also not designed to be 'dipped into' to find useful quotations to support your work, as this is an unscholarly approach that will not help your personal and professional development. Each chapter stands alone, focusing on a specific aspect of emergent science and should be read and re-read, undertaking the relevant reflective and practical tasks to support deep understanding. The study skills follow a sequence and these may be looked at in order or when the particular skill is being developed by the reader.

We hope that you will enjoy the book and find it useful in your personal and professional development.

References

Bronfenbrenner, U. (1995). The bioecological model from a life course perspective: reflections of a participant observer. In: Moen, P., Elder, Jnr, G. H. & Lüscher, K., eds. *Examining Lives in Context.* Washington DC: American Psychological Association, pp. 599–618.

Cooperrider, D. L. & Srivastva, S. (1987). Appreciative inquiry in organisational life. *Research in Organisational Change and Development*, 1, 129–169.

Cohen, L., Manion, L. & Morrison K. (2011). *Research Methods In Education*, 7th edn. London: Routledge: Falmer.

Department for Education (DfE) (2012). *National Curriculum for Science. Key Stages 1 and 2 – Draft.* London: DfE.

Fensham, P. J. (2012). International Science Education: What's in it for science teachers. In: Oversby, J., ed. *ASE Guide to Research in Science Education*. Hatfield: ASE.

Johnston, J. (2008). Emergent science. *Education in Science*, 227 April 2008, 26–28.

Johnston, J. (2010). What emergent science is telling us about scientific development. *Primary Science*, 111, 3.

Johnston, J., Ahtee, M. & Hayes, M. (1998). Elementary teachers' perceptions of science and science teaching: Comparisons between Finland and England. In: Kaartinen, S., ed. *Matemaattisten Aineiden Opetus ja Oppiminen.* Oulu: Oulun yliopistopaino, pp. 13–30.

Johnston, J. & Dale Tunnicliffe, S. (2008). The emergent science electronic network. *Research Intelligence*, 103, 26.

Montessori, M. (1994). *From Childhood to Adolescence*. Oxford, England: ABC-Clio.

Oversby, J. (ed). (2012). *ASE Guide to Research in Science Education*. Hatfield: ASE.

Parlett, M. & Hamilton, D. (1972). Evaluation as illumination: a new approach to the study of innovatory programmes. Reprinted in: Parlett, M. & Dearden, G., eds. (1977), *Introduction to Illuminative Evaluation: Studies in Higher Education*. Cardiff-by-the-Sea, CA, USA: Pacific Soundings Press and Guildford, UK: Society for Research into Higher Education.

Piaget, J. (1929). *The Child's Conception of the World.* New York: Harcourt.

Programme for International Student Assessment (PISA) (2012). *OECD Programme for International Student Assessment.* http://www.pisa.oecd.org/pages/0,3417,en_32252351_32235731_1_1_1_1_1,00.html. Accessed 7/12/12.

Reed, J. (2007). *Appreciative Inquiry. Research for Change.* London: Sage.

Relevance of Science Education (ROSE) (2012). Relevance of Science Education. Online at: http://roseproject.no/. Accessed 12/7/12.

Taber, K.S. (2012). Teaching and learning about the nature of science. In: Oversby, J. (ed). (2012). *ASE Guide to Research in Science Education.* Hatfield: ASE.

Trends in International Mathematics and Science Study (TIMSS) (2012). Trends in International Mathematics and Science Study. Online at: http://nces.ed.gov/timss/results.asp. Accessed 12/7/12.

Toulmin, S. (1958). *The Uses of Argument.* Cambridge: Cambridge University Press.

Websites and further reading

http://www.ase.org.uk/journals/

Development

Chapter 1

The development of emergent skills

Overview

In this chapter we look at:

- The scientific process and the skills that are part of that process
- What these emergent skills look like in children in the early years and how we can support their development
- Research into the skill of observation by Jane Johnston
- How to select and use literature, as part of the study skills theme
- Practical and reflective tasks that look at the link between social and scientific skills
- Activity boxes on how collections of objects can lead to the development of scientific skills
- Knowledge boxes focusing on gravity and air resistance.

Introduction

Science is a practical and social endeavour, involving the development and use of a range of skills. Some of the skills are generic ones that are of use in other aspects of the children's lives (e.g. observation, interpretation), whilst others are quite specific to **enquiry** in science and other related subjects (e.g. **classification**, handling **variables**). The skills involved in science form part of the **scientific process (see Figure 1.1)**. The scientific process is not fully linear, although it does follow certain stages, beginning with observation and ending with **interpretation** and **communication**. However, at every stage, it may be appropriate to revisit an earlier stage in a more cyclical way. So, for example, children may have observed that puddles dry up in the sun and may begin to explore this further by predicting that bigger puddles will dry faster. They may draw a line around the puddles and see how much they have dried up after one hour. At that stage they may wish to revisit their prediction and compare the speed at which small puddles dry up with that at which big puddles dry up. They may also decide to measure the gap between the drawn lines or extend the time gap between observation and measurement.

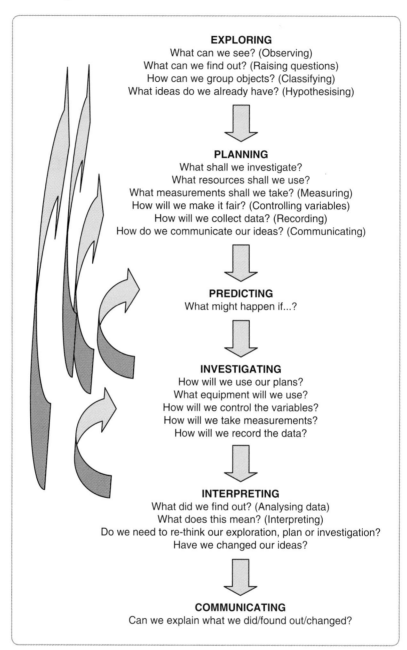

Figure 1.1 The scientific process
Source: Johnston (2005: 32)

They may then try to make sense of their **explorations** and discuss where the water goes to, at which stage they may decide to go back to observing the puddles to focus on this.

Like all practical processes, the scientific process is one that is developed in a holistic way, but that does not mean that individual skills cannot and should not be focused on for specific development. If we leave children to develop skills without focus (by exposure or a kind of osmosis), the probability is that the skill will be underdeveloped. We also need to understand what the skills are and how they develop – in Figure 1.2 the different skills that make up the scientific process are analysed in more detail.

Scientific Skills

Exploring skills

Observing
- Using all senses
- Identifying similarities and differences
- Identifying patterns in and between objects and scientific phenomena
- Interpreting observations
- Interpreting sequences and events in phenomena observed

Raising questions
- Raising questions about scientific observation and phenomena
- Identifying the difference between productive (questions that can be answered through exploration and investigation) and non-productive questions
- Beginning to plan how questions can be answered through exploration and investigation

Classifying
- Sorting objects according to one simple category (categoric criteria)
- Re-sorting objects according to a number of criteria (from simple to more complex, e.g. colour, size, weight, buoyancy, conductivity)
- Classifying objects according to more than one criterion at the same time (e.g. sorting plants according to size and where they grow)

Planning skills

Planning (deciding what can be explored/investigated, what method, what resources, what records to keep)
- Identifying opportunities for exploration and investigation
- Planning explorations and investigations with structured support (planning boards, ladders etc.)
- Adapting plans after discussion with others (analysis of plans)
- Planning with little or no support from teacher

Predicting
- Making predictions about observable scientific phenomena/events
- Making sensible predictions based on evidence
- Seeing incorrect predictions as useful evidence to support future correct predictions

Handling variables
- Identifying key variables (what you are changing [independent variable] and what you are finding out [dependent variable])
- Identifying control variables (what is needed to make investigation fair)

Figure 1.2 A breakdown of scientific skills

- Controlling variables in an investigation (categoric $\Rightarrow$ discrete $\Rightarrow$ continuous $\Rightarrow$ derived)
- Using and controlling larger number of and more complex variables

Hypothesising
- Explaining an event or phenomenon (not necessarily scientifically correctly and not obviously based on evidence or experience)
- Using limited, everyday evidence to explain events or phenomena
- Using scientific ideas/evidence/research to explain events or phenomena

Measuring (e.g. length, mass, force, sound, light, electricity, temperature)
- Measuring using non-standard measures (measuring qualitatively)
- Recognising the need for standard measures
- Using simple standard measures with simple measuring devices (e.g. temperature strips, probes), with support/decreasing support
- Using more complex measuring equipment, with support/without support

Recording skills

Preparing graphs, charts, tables
- Constructing simple pictograms, Venn diagrams etc.
- Constructing more complex charts and graphs (bar charts, line graphs)
- Identifying what types of graphs, charts, tables are the most appropriate for results to be recorded
- Understanding what each graph, table, chart is recording

Writing reports (Question [What were you trying to do?] – Resources [What was used?] – Method [What was done?] – Results [What was found out?] – Interpretation [What does this mean?])
- Describing in one's own words what was done and what has happened
- Using a simple writing structure to support one's ideas
- Constructing one's own reports, with appropriate headings, based on what the exploration/investigation involved

Drawing pictures and diagrams
- Drawing simple observational pictures
- Labelling pictures
- Drawing a sequenced cartoon of exploration/investigation
- Constructing group/pictorial concept maps
- Constructing individual concept maps
- Drawing complex observational drawings
- Amending/adapting concept maps/annotated diagrams

Interpreting skills

Interpreting
- Recognising different ways to present data/record data to support interpretation

Figure 1.2 *(continued)*

- Interrogating graphs, charts, tables (simple ⇒ more complex), with support/without support
- Recognising the difference between specific and generalised interpretations

Analysing
- Describing what has happened in an exploration or investigation
- Using more scientific language in their descriptions/analyses
- Providing own ideas for why something has/may have occurred
- Using previous knowledge and scientific research/literature to analyse why something may have occurred

Concluding
- Identifying what results of explorations or investigations mean
- Identifying what has been learned
- Posing new questions for exploration or investigation
- Making specific or generalised conclusions

Communicating skills

Displaying ideas and results
Presenting ideas and results
Explaining ideas and conclusions

Figure 1.2 *(continued)*

STUDY SKILLS

Selecting and using the literature

In this chapter, the study skills we are focusing on to develop your learning involve the selection and use of the literature. When we select reading, we should try to get a comprehensive understanding of the areas and choose a balance among policy documents, professional texts, research articles and online information. The balance is important, as over-reliance on one type of text will weaken any argument you are trying to make. For example, over-reliance on policy documents merely reiterates government policy and does not show an understanding of the tensions that exist among policy, practice and research. Likewise, over-reliance on web-based texts does not take into consideration the validity of the text and you may be reiterating the subjective view of the author. Over-reliance on research will not help you to consider the implications of the findings on practice and provision and future policymaking.

Effective reading involves understanding the issue you are researching and looking at the objectivity of the author, the argument he or she is making and how that fits in with your thinking and experience. This is critical reading – the first step toward the critical use of ideas from reading. Critical reading involves reading for understanding and reflection on what that reading means in terms of your own practice, your ideas and the current policies in early years education and care. In order to fully understand what you are reading, it needs to be read and re-read, making notes as you go and recording the full bibliographical reference.

In this book we use the Harvard system of referencing, which involves putting the name(s) of the author(s) and the date of publication in the main text, along with page numbers in cases where you use a direct quotation. Full references should be provided at the end of the piece of writing, as follows (note that the punctuation varies slightly from publisher to publisher):

Study Skills (*continued*)

Book: Name, Initial (Year). *Title of Book*. Place of publication: publisher.

Journal article: Name, Initial (Year). Title of article. *Title of Journal*, volume (number), page range.

Chapter in a book: Name, Initial (Year). Title of chapter. In: Name of Editor, Initial., eds. *Title of Book*. Place of publication: Publisher, page range.

At the end of each chapter, you will find references that illustrate how this works in practice.

When reading and referencing reading, you should always use original sources and they should always be read and referenced, rather than citing references that have been used in the book you are reading. This is necessary, not only for scholarly purposes and because it aids understanding, but also because you need to check that the original author and reference are correct.

The notes you make on your reading can be used to support arguments you are making. Effective use of reading involves making persuasive arguments and using reading to support it, rather than merely citing reading, as this shows an understanding of the issues through analysis of the ideas expressed in the text rather than description. This is discussed further in the following chapters. As one's skill of using reading develops, so will the ability to develop critical arguments using the literature.

Study skills tasks

Consult early years policy documents, professional documents and research papers and find references to early years skills in general and scientific skills in particular.

Study skills task level 1

Read the different texts and draw out the main themes and arguments relating to both generic and scientific skills. You may find it useful to put the information into an electronic or paper database with the following headings:

- Reference for the text (using the Harvard system)
- Type of document (policy, professional, research, web page, newspaper, other)
- Claims made within the text
- Evidence base within the text and link to claims being made.

Study skills task level 2

Having created your database, compare and contrast the claims that are being made and add this to your database. Add a further section identifying your own view of the authors' ideas/claims, based on your experience and the evidence from this experience that supports your view.

Study skills task level 3

Using your data base actively critique the claims, questioning assumptions and considering the tensions that exist between policy, practice and research.

Science as a social endeavour involves children in working together, co-operating, as they explore the world around them. They need to develop independence to enable them to follow their own lines of enquiry and to develop inquiry skills and conceptual understandings. These social skills have a close inter-relationship with general and specific **attitudes** that children should be developing to enable them to live and work in social contexts in the world **(see Chapter 3)**.

Observation – the first and most important scientific skill

Observation is an important generic skill for early years children and is recognised by many theorists, including Pestalozzi (1894) and Piaget (1929), and is incorporated into the early years curriculum in the UK (Department for Education, 2012) and other countries (e.g. Ministry of Education, 1996). Professional texts on early years education (e.g. de Bóo, 2006; Covill & Pattie, 2002) and early years science (Johnston, 2005; National Research

Council of the National Academies, 2007) highlight the importance of observation, integral as it is to the development of curiosity and motivation, helping children to remember their **investigations** and solve investigative problems (Grambo, 1994).

Observation begins before birth, as the foetus begins to observe its environment, listening to sounds, identifying changes in its mother's heartbeat, her tone of voice, and stretching, moving and experiencing their tiny world. From birth, children use all their senses to make sense of the world around them and observation supports development in every area (Berk, 2003; Johnston, 2005).

Most of our knowledge about scientific observation comes from older children of primary and secondary school age, although my own research (Johnston, 2009) has indicated that observation in young children is tactile, involving the senses of touch and hearing as much as sight; as they develop they move from broader observations to more specific observations. However, there are always individual children whose observational skills appear more advanced than 'normal'. For example, one 4-year-old child playing in a garden centre role-play area (de Bóo, 2006) engaged in close scrutiny of individual seeds using a digital microscope and lined them up in order of size, observational behaviour that is more characteristic of older children (Harlen & Symington, 1985). As children develop, they begin to focus on the details of their observations (Harlen & Symington, 1985; Johnston, 2005) and events to help them understand how the world works. These early observations are influenced by both personal and taught ideas (Driver, 1983; Duschl, 2000; Tomkins & Tunnicliffe, 2007) as well as interests (Tunnicliffe & Litson, 2002).

Research

Early scientific observations in children under 4 years of age (Johnston, 2012)

Jane Johnston

Research questions
- What does the skill of observation look like in children under 4 years of age?
- How can the skill of observation be supported through social interaction and co-construction?

Research design
The sample involved two groups of children:

1 Six children aged 15 months to 2 years, with two early years professionals, plus the researcher

2 Nine children aged 2–4 years with four professionals and the researcher.

All the children attended a private day nursery in a rural location, which had agreed to support the research. The toys included:

- Moving toys, such as a battery-operated hen that danced while singing, wind-up toys and pull-back cars/helicopter

- Aural toys which made sounds, such as a rattle, a battery-operated chick that cheeped, a megaphone that children could speak through in alien/robot/spacemen voices and a jack-in-the-box

- Toys that involved some operation by the child, such as a ball and hammer set, a wooden frog that makes a frog noise when a stick is pulled across its back, a helicopter (whose propellers move when pushed), a honey bee that 'buzzed' down a pole and 'colour-change' ducks (which change colour when warm)

- Soft toys, such as a large dog, and a sheep rug (that can be worn)

- Other toys, such as a large multifaceted mirror, a magnetic elephant with body parts that can be removed and replaced, and a wooden person (with moveable limbs).

The play session was videotaped, the interactions were transcribed and the types of initial observations made by the children, as well as the number and types of

Research (*continued*)

observations made in the different parts of the activity, were identified.

Four categories of observation were identified:

- Observations containing an affective element, where children show interest through body language, giggles and exclamations, such as 'Whee!'
- Observations containing functional comments or behaviour that focuses on how the toys work
- Observations involving a social element, where children communicate and interact with their peers in the play
- Observations that lead to scientific exploration of the toys.

Further analysis looked at the effect that personal, adult participatory and peer participatory interaction had on the scientific skill of observation (Rogoff, 1995). Robbins (2005) and Fleer (2002) both drew upon these analytical techniques in analysing different aspects of interaction in early years science contexts.

Summary of findings

Most responses in the children were non-verbal. Affective responses took the form of dancing and squealing, although a few children used gestures or rubbed their faces or heads when unhappy or distressed. Their play and observation were solitary (playing alone) and needed greater adult modelling of play or participation in play. Indeed, the youngest children had no verbal social interaction with peers and limited other social interaction, as can be seen from the interaction below between two of the youngest children aged between 15 months and 2 years.

> Boy 1 crouches by the hammering box, picks up the hammer and puts it in his mouth.
>
> Another child comes up to the box and picks it up.
>
> Boy 1 tries to hammer (unsuccessfully, as his motor skills are undeveloped), but continues to play alongside the other child.
>
> The second child takes the box away and Boy 1 picks up the moveable man, drops it and follows the child with the box (with the hammer still in his hand). He drops the hammer and picks it up again.

The older group of children (2-4 years of age) occasionally made a verbal response, such as one child who played quietly and independently with the helicopter throughout the whole time observed and then force-

fully said, 'No!' when he left it and another child picked it up.

Social responses in the youngest age group (15 months to 2 years of age) were initiated by the professionals, who interacted with the toys, saying things like 'Stroke the doggy, stroke the doggy', and gave encouragement to share toys and guidance on the functionality of the toy: 'Push the button' (to show the child how to turn on the dancing chicken toy).

Social interaction involving one girl in the youngest age group (15 months to 2 years) was observed as she took toys to the professional and the professional responded by focusing attention on how a toy worked (e.g. demonstrating how the Jack-in-the-Box works). The professionals asked questions and engaged in ludic play and co-construction of ideas (Siraj-Blatchford, 2009) that linked previous experiences with the current play, e.g. by playing with the ducks and singing 'Four little ducks went swimming one day . . .'.

Older children (aged 2-4 years) initially focused on a broader range of toys and engaged in some social responses with peers, showing them how a toy worked and sharing a toy with, or taking a toy to, another child, although most of their play was solitary. In one example, a boy appeared aimlessly to pick up one toy after another, and had almost peripheral engagement with others, or engaged in parallel or companionship play (Bruce, 2004). Some adult interaction, in both age groups, involved questions that focused on the function of the toys, such as, 'What colour has yours gone?', when looking at colour-change ducks with the youngest children, 'How do you get that one to work?' or 'Push it in', when encouraging a child to turn the dancing chicken on himself.

These older children needed less adult support to initiate observations, although they appeared to benefit from interactions that focused on specific functions or aspects of the toys. One boy engaged in the most functional responses, by looking very intently at different toys (a rattle, the butterfly, the dancing chicken), but self-initiated functional responses were not particularly characteristic of the children observed.

All children responded to aural and moving/operated toys, showing interest and motivation through oral exclamations and laughter and by dancing. A few older children also engaged in ludic (fantasy) and symbolic play (Piaget, 1976), and so the play was analysed again to consider the responses to the aural and moving/operated toys and the ludic and symbolic play. There was an overlap between aural and moving/operated toys, with

Research (*continued*)

the toy responded to most often (and receiving the most affective responses) being the dancing chicken, which was both aural and moving. There was also an over-lap between ludic (fantasy) and symbolic play, which involves children using their existing knowledge about toys in their play.

Implications

The research findings appear to indicate the importance of social interaction as it enables children to negoti-ate social boundaries (Broadhead, 2004) and develop conceptual understandings through cultural mediation (Bruner, 1991). This confirms ideas concerning effec-tive pedagogy for young children as including interac-tion among children, their environment and adults (Vygotsky, 1962). Children should be active participants in their own understanding of the world, exercising some autonomy and developing understanding from experiences that build upon their previous knowledge (Piaget, 1929). They should have opportunities to **scaf-fold** their own and others' learning, with adult support (Bruner, 1977; Stone, 1993). In this way, the research endorses the view that effective pedagogies lead to understandings and sustained shared thinking (Siraj-Blatchford *et al.*, 2002; Siraj-Blatchford, 2009). However, it is unclear if this is a conscious pedagogical approach adopted by professionals working with young children (König, 2009). It may be that this needs to be explored more fully with professionals working with very young children to ensure that they move seamlessly from soli-tary and ad hoc observations, to more socially supported functional and exploratory observations.

Practical and reflective tasks

Early career professional

Set up an activity that allows children to observe and explore. This may involve a collection of objects on a scientific theme (e.g. magnifiers, torches, mirrors, prisms or a set of objects that float or sink) or allow the children to choose what to observe in the outside play area or from within the classroom. Observe what they do and note what type of observation they engage in: solitary, adult participatory or peer participatory.

- How do the different types of observation lead to scientific enquiry?
- Why do you think some types of engagement lead to more scientific enquiry?
- How could you change the way you engage with the children to support observations that lead to scientific enquiry?

Developing career professional/teacher

Set up a role play activity that will support scientific observations. This may be:

- a 'greenhouse' or 'allotment', focusing on growth of plants
- a 'chemist/pharmacy', focusing on materials and their properties
- a 'building site', focusing on forces and structures.

Observe the children's play and note what type of observation they engage in: solitary, adult participatory or peer participatory.

- How do the different types of observation lead to scientific enquiry?
- Why do you think some types of engagement lead to greater scientific enquiry?
- How could you change the way you engage with the children to support observations that lead to scientific enquiry?

Later career professional/leader

Organise a whole school cross-curricular science day, with a focus on activities (explorations, problem-solving and role play) that focus on observation as a skill. These could include:

● Explorations from collections (see examples for early career/student earlier)

● Role play (see examples from developing career/teacher earlier)

● Problem-solving activities, such as finding out: 'Which coat will keep teddy dry?', 'How to make the best bubble?', or 'How to make the best play-dough?'

At the end of the day, lead a staff meeting to evaluate the success of the different activities in promoting observational skills. Consider the following:

● Which type of activities best supported the development of the skill of observation? Why?

● How could the adult interaction be improved to further support scientific observation?

● How will you use these types of activities in the future?

Sorting and classifying

Young children sort in a variety of contexts and sorting a collection of scientific objects can support both mathematical and scientific development. Children's development follows certain stages as indicated in the following extract from Johnston (2005: 40):

> At an early stage of their development, children will put objects into groups, but will be unable to give reasons for the groupings which make sense of their actions. These objects 'go together'

Photograph 1.1 Children observing and sorting

rather than have a shared feature. They possibly recognize a feature which distinguishes them but may be unable to communicate this. A further development is when children use one feature as a basis for grouping. For example, when exploring a collection of toy vehicles a young child may focus on the red vehicles and will then group all the red vehicles together in one group and then all the other vehicles in another group, regardless of colour. At the next developmental stage children will decide upon a single criterion such as colour which differentiates all the vehicles. They will then be able to make several groups, for example, red cars, blue cars, green. As children notice that objects can have more than one property at the same time, they become able to classify them and then to re-classify them because of another criterion. With the vehicle example of cars, criteria could include colours, shape, make, usage, speed and number of passengers. In order to classify objects according to two criteria simultaneously children need to be able to keep two ideas in their minds at the same time. The exploration of a collection of vehicles could lead to investigating the distance travelled by different vehicles down a ramp, covered with different surfaces.

However, like other stages of development (e.g. Piaget's, 1929 cognitive stages; **see Chapter 2**) the stages cannot be assigned to ages, as moving through the stages is dependent on how the individual child is encouraged and supported in sorting. For example, my grandchild was sorting according to colour and shape from about 1 year of age and at 22 months was playing with magnetic letters in her kitchen and finding out what they would stick to, saying, 'Sick' or 'No sick', and she was most disappointed that they would not stick to her mother.

Sorting objects according to their properties can lead to the skill of handling variables in older children, an important skill for later scientific development. Variables come in different levels of difficulty, the easiest being categorical variables, or variables that are easily visible, such as colour or shape. The next levels of difficulty are, first, discrete variables, which are those that can change (e.g. by addition; layers of insulation) and, second, continuous variables that can have any value, such as time or the weight added to a bridge or vehicle. The most complex variable is one that is derived or calculated from more than one measurement (e.g. speed). Young children are unlikely to be able to use derived variables, at least on a regular basis.

In an investigation children need to recognise and control variables. They need to know what the key variables are, what they are investigating (the dependent variable) and what they need to change to find out the result (the independent variable), as well as controlling for all other variables in order to make the investigation fair. So, for example, if they are investigating the effect of water on a growing plant, children need to give plants of the same size different amounts of water (the independent variable), control all other variables (amount of light, type of soil etc.) and measure the growth (this is the dependent variable, because it is dependent on the amount of water given and nothing else).

Young children find the handling of too many variables, and overly complex variables, difficult and yet we often take plants and put them in different places, in different sizes of pot, with different soil types, different amounts of light and a different watering regime, and ask children to deduce from this what plants need to grow. Not only is this a very difficult **concept**, as the most important thing a plant needs to grow (air) is rarely mentioned until they are much older and looking at photosynthesis, but there are too many variables in the investigation, so the children get confused. It is far better to help children in their inquiry by limiting the number and type of variables and thinking through the type of scientific activity they do **(see Chapter 9)**.

CASE STUDY

Sorting of objects by reception-age children

A class of 30 reception children (4 and 5 years of age) were sorting a collection of objects they had found in the outside play area, including feathers, leaves, flowers, seeds, twigs, stones, soil, etc. An initial sort was done according to size, with big objects going in one pile and small ones in another. One of the adults working with them asked how else they could sort them, and the children began to list different ways the objects could be sorted, as follows:

- Colour, shape or size (categoric)
- Whether they grow, float, bounce and so require further exploration
- Whether they come from plants, animals or from on top of or underneath the ground (some groupings of which may overlap, e.g. an acorn may grow on a tree but be found on the ground or buried by a squirrel).

The children then tried to sort and re-sort the objects according to their chosen criteria. The adult introduced sorting hoops to help the children record their sorting.

Reflective questions

1 How could you support younger children (from birth to 3 years of age) in sorting a collection of natural objects?

2 What other collections are suitable for work with young children?

3 How could you extend older children (between 5 and 8 years of age) when sorting and classifying a collection of natural objects?

4 How can sorting and classifying be used to develop learning objectives in other key areas of learning/subjects?

Raising questions

Children are always asking questions, but not all questions are productive, in that they can lead to further inquiry. During scientific explorations and play, children should be encouraged to raise productive questions that lead to inquiry. These can often come from the observational activities described earlier and can lead to children raising questions, especially if they are motivated and encouraged by adults supporting them and also by peer interaction. Sometimes young children's questions can be a pain for professionals, especially if the professionals do not know the answer. Nevertheless, it is important that children feel able to ask questions without fear of ridicule or comment and that adults try to help them answer such questions for themselves. Adults are important role models for children and will support and encourage children in asking questions if they ask questions themselves, do not pretend to know all the answers and show an interest in the questions children raise. In view of this, it is interesting to note that Cazden (2001: 94) found teachers in the UK provide less 'wait time' to allow children to respond to questions than teachers in other countries.

Photograph 1.2 A questioning classroom

There are also pedagogical strategies that will encourage and support children in raising productive questions. These include developing a questioning environment, through the production of interactive questioning displays, the provision of opportunities to question and to listen to the ideas of others, the provision of creative experiences that motivate and inspire awe and wonder in children and help them to look at familiar scientific phenomena, such as echoes, shadows and toys, in novel ways **(see Chapter 3)**. For younger children, the pedagogical strategies can include encouraging them to articulate questions arising from their scientific explorations and encouraging their peers to undertake further exploration or inquiry to answer these questions and perhaps posing new questions for other children to answer. With older children, the pedagogical approaches include encouraging the children to write their questions down on Post-It notes or cards on interactive displays, on flip-charts, white boards or speech bubbles stretched across the classroom on washing lines.

Practical and reflective tasks

Practical tasks
Plan a practical science activity that involves the development of practical skills.

Early Years Foundation Stage
For the Early Years Foundation Stage (EYFS), this could be an exploratory activity where they explore a collection of objects (e.g. different materials, such as play-dough, sand, cornflour

and water, and plasticine) or a scientific phenomenon (e.g. melting, by exploring an ice balloon).

Key Stage 1

For children at Key Stage 1 (KS1), this could involve an exploration of a scientific phenomenon that can lead to simple investigations (e.g. gravitational force, by exploring the way things fall) or a problem-solving activity (such as trying to find which of a selection of papers is the strongest).

Key Stage 2

For children at Key Stage 2 (KS2) this could involve an investigation (e.g. vehicles rolling down a ramp) or a problem-solving activity (e.g. investigating changes in heart rate with exercise).

If your school has children from EYFS to KS2, you could plan the same activity for each phase. For example, children can explore a scientific phenomenon (melting, floating and sinking, falling objects) and the different outcomes can be observed.

Reflective tasks

Observe the children engaged in the tasks and consider the following:

- What skills, both generic and scientific, are the children using?
- How are these skills used in other areas of the curriculum or everyday life?
- How can you support the children in recognising the links between scientific skills and skills used in other areas of life?

Prediction and hypothesis

The difference between a **prediction** and **hypothesis** can be confusing. Predictions are statements made about future events, usually based on prior knowledge (Klemtschy, 2008). Hypotheses are explanations or sets of possible explanations for observed scientific phenomena or events (Wenham, 1993), with recognition of relationships in an event (Quinn & George, 1975). A prediction always looks forward and makes a sensible guess as to what will happen, based on the person's experience or knowledge. For example, we can predict what will happen if we put a toy boat in a water trough, or if we put an ice cube in a warm place, or if we mix washing-up liquid with water. In each case we will use our previous experience to inform our predictions. Young children will probably have experienced washing up the dishes at home and will know that washing-up liquid lathers to produce bubbles. They may have watched ice melting in glasses, or outside in rising temperatures and so will probably predict that the ice will melt. They may know that boats float and so will predict that the toy boat will also float.

If, however, you change the prediction slightly, it can challenge the children's conceptual understanding and make them think **(see also Chapter 2)**. For example, if you give children a collection of objects and ask them to predict which ones will float and which will sink, they will often predict that the 'heavy' things will sink, based on their previous experiences. When they find that not all heavy things sink and that some light things do, they will be encouraged to re-think their ideas and predictions.

A hypothesis can look both backwards and forwards and involves providing sensible explanations for why something happens or why it has happened. For example, children can explain why they think heavy things sink and light things float, or why some things fall faster than others, or why they think an ice cube will melt in a warm place. As with predictions, hypotheses are based on children's prior experiences, which may indicate alternative views of the world: heavy things sink, fall more quickly **(see Chapter 2)**. The link between hypotheses and predictions is made by McComas (1998), who suggested that hypotheses should lead to predictions which can be tested and so support the hypotheses.

In the case study that follows, children had to predict which type of glove, from a range including woollen, rubber, cotton and fur, would keep a piece of ice in the form of a hand (made by freezing a surgical glove filled with water) cold. The children predicted it would be the thin gloves – their hypothesis was that because woolly gloves keep their hands warmer than cotton gloves, the latter would keep the ice hand cool whereas the woollen gloves would melt it.

CASE STUDY

Keeping a hand made of ice cold

Andrew Johnston

At the time of the case study, Andrew Johnston was teaching a Year 2 class in a two-form entry infant school in Lincoln.

My class of Year 2 children (6 years of age) were involved in a science topic on materials and their properties. They started by identifying different materials, discussing where they had come from and if they were man-made or natural, as well as describing the properties of each material. The next steps of our exploration were to investigate how different materials may change under different environments, which may extend to whether the change is reversible or not.

One activity involved the children finding out what would happen if they put different gloves (woollen, cotton, rubber, fur) on an ice hand (made by freezing a surgical glove filled with water). Two children of very contrasting abilities talked about their very different predictions regarding how to keep the ice hand frozen – although both agreed the woolly glove would keep the ice hand warm and melt it. This led to a debate with others and a collaborative effort to find out the answer. It turned out that both children had made errors in their initial predictions and hypotheses and, as a result of the debate, they were able to accurately discuss what materials could be used to keep the ice hand frozen and why.

John, a 7-year-old boy with severe learning difficulties, who is unable to read and write and who has every piece of work differentiated so it can be achieved at his level, was particularly interested in the surgical glove and wanted to know how we got the ice

in there. John told us that ice comes from water that is very cold. We filled up two gloves with water and asked John to tell us where we could put them to turn them into ice. John first suggested the freezer, so we went and put one in the freezer. John then noticed that it was very cold outside and that he had seen ice that morning. He asked if we could put the other glove outside. After 10 minutes he asked if we could check them. We did and the water in the gloves was still not frozen. John told me that more time was needed for it to get really cold. A short while later John wanted to check again. This time, we noticed that in the freezer the water in the fingers of the glove was frozen but the rest wasn't. John said this must be because the palm is thicker and the cold hadn't got to the middle yet. Eventually the glove in the freezer froze, so we took it back to the classroom and compared it with the glove outside.

Other children had now noticed this investigation and it led to a whole class discussion about what had happened. We discussed many possible reasons before another child, Lorna, told us that it gets coldest outside at night because there is no sun to warm us up. It was then suggested that we leave the glove outside overnight and see what would happen by morning. We did this, allowing the investigation to last beyond the normal lesson slot. The children also did the same investigation at home and brought their results in.

Case study (*continued*)

A few weeks later we carried out an investigation where we held different objects in our hands to see how they changed. We started with a chocolate button and discovered that it melted very quickly. We then held a Smartie and discovered that it didn't melt as quickly. This led to a discussion in which one child, Timothy, suggested that the Smartie had a thicker coating that was stopping the heat getting in to melt the chocolate and, referring back to the glove investigation, likening the coat on the Smartie to the glove.

Reflective questions

Early career professional

1 How were the children encouraged to predict and hypothesise in this case study?

2 How could you develop your teaching skills to support children in predicting and hypothesising?

3 How did the experience develop other generic social skills such as cooperation, collaboration and independence?

Developing career professional/teacher

1 How else could Andrew have encouraged prediction and hypothesising in these children?

2 How can you develop the skills of prediction and hypothesising in your next scientific topic?

Later career professional/leader

1 How could you plan science activities in school that encourage children's predictions and hypotheses?

2 How can you plan activities that support children in developing their skills of prediction and hypothesis?

Development in the skills of prediction and hypothesis depends on an ethos that encourages children to identify what they think without fear of ridicule, even if their predictions or hypotheses are later shown to be incorrect. All children, as is the case with adults, like to be correct and sometimes hold on to incorrect ideas even when they have been shown to be false. For example, it is common for young children to think that heavy things sink in water and fall more quickly than light things. When this does not happen, they are often likely to hang on to their ideas and make minor modifications to their hypotheses to explain why their predictions were incorrect.

One group of 4- and 5-year-olds explored how items fell after they were dropped. They had sheets of paper and observed that a crumpled sheet fell faster than a flat sheet and decided that the paper had been made 'heavier' by crumpling. In another enquiry, 7-year-old children tested their predictions about which objects float and which ones sink. Given a small lump of plasticine that sank and a large 'boat-like' piece of plasticine that floated, they decided that the small lump must be heavier. When the teacher suggested that they put the two pieces of plasticine on either sides of a balance, so that the large piece was seen to weigh more, the children decided that the balance 'was broken', as this conflicted with their ideas.

Knowledge box

Gravity and air resistance

Objects fall to the ground when dropped because of the gravitational force acting on them. Gravitational force is the pull on an object due to gravity and this gives the object its weight. It is the same for all objects on Earth (the effect of gravity on a 100 gram mass produces a force of 1 Newton). Weight is a downward force due to the effect of gravity (it is not a measure of the mass of an object). Weight is affected by gravitational force, which is in turn affected by the mass; so the greater the mass the greater, the gravitational force and the weight. Weight is measured in Newtons.

Neither weight nor mass plays a part in the rate of fall, so that a heavy object that is the same shape and size as a light object will fall at the same rate. What makes a difference to the rate of fall is the air resistance (a friction force on objects moving through the air). Thus, an object that has more resistance to the air as it falls, because of its shape and size, will fall more slowly than an object that is compact in shape and size. Because of this, when we scrunch up a piece of paper, it will fall more quickly than when flat. This is why a feather will fall more slowly than a hammer – this was shown during an Apollo Moon walk when both a feather and a hammer were dropped at the same time in the atmosphere of the Moon, with no air resistance, and they both fell at the same rate.

It is also why, in the scenario of a bullet being shot horizontally from a gun at the same time as a bullet is dropped from the height of the gun barrel, both bullets reach the ground at the same time – the vertical forces acting upon the bullets are the same in each case.

See Chapter 9 for further ideas on dropping things.

Children need to understand that discrepancies in their predictions and hypotheses and their enquiry are opportunities, not threats, and can lead to deeper enquiry and scientific understanding.

STUDY SKILLS

Selecting and using literature

Level 1

Find a book that deals with young children's scientific skills and read about one scientific skill. Compare what the book says about children's development in the skill with your own experience and make notes about the similarities and differences.

Level 2

Find two books that deal with young children's scientific skills and read what the authors say about one scientific skill. Compare and contrast the ideas in the books and make notes about the similarities and differences.

Level 3

Find books that discuss children's scientific development in one particular skill and try to find alternative viewpoints in the literature and use these and your own experiences to critique the ideas.

Measuring

As children explore the world around them, there are plenty of experiences that help them to begin to understand measurements. They will begin to recognise differences in temperature in their bath water, whilst eating and drinking, or outdoors at different times of year, and will be told not to touch something hot or wrap up warm when it is cold. They will experience distances and time; it may be a short distance to the shop and take a few minutes to walk, but it may be a long way to visit relatives and take longer in the car. They will know that the car or bus they travel in can go fast or slow and that the speed affects the time it takes to reach their destination. They will recognise that objects can be heavy or light and may have tried to move a big stone and realised that it takes more force to move a big stone than a small one or even a ball of similar size.

They will have experienced floating and sinking through bath play and may have noticed that some objects float while others sink. They will have experienced loud and quiet noises and understood that sound can be muffled when wearing a hat or when they are in another room from the source. They will have experienced electrical appliances and that the cooker or fire can have high and low settings. They will have battery-operated toys and realise that some of these can have different settings. All these experiences will have given them emergent ideas about the world around them **(see Chapter 2)** and they may also have had some opportunities to measure in their own ways, using non-standard measures.

If children start from their observations and begin to measure in their own qualitative ways, this is more likely to help them to understand what they are measuring. This could be a comparison of temperature with their own body temperature, measuring distances with steps, shoes, spans or bricks, or measuring time by counting or putting beads in a jar. For very young children, these experiences will help them as they develop and need to measure using standard measures. This is because the early experiences help them to understand what they are measuring and, without this understanding, the use of standard measuring equipment is meaningless. What does a temperature of 10°C mean if you have no experience of feeling different temperatures?

Practical and reflective tasks

The following are some measurements that are sometimes taken in science:

- Temperature (°C)
- Distance/length/width (cm, m)
- Force (N)
- Mass (g, kg)
- Speed (= distance/time, e.g. m/s)
- Sound (decibels)
- Electricity (volt, amps, ohms)
- Time (seconds, minutes, hours)
- Volume (ml, l).

Rank them in the order of which you feel are easier to understand to which you feel are more difficult to understand.

Early Years Foundation Stage

From the list of measurements, choose those that children in the EYFS will begin to experience and measure. Add any other measurements that are not on the list. For each measurement, consider:

- What are the experiences that will provide opportunities for qualitative measurements?
- How can you support the early experience of measuring?

Set up an activity or provide an opportunity for children to explore one type of measurement. This may be exploring volume of liquid while playing with a tea set, or exploring mass in shop role-play, or exploring time while waiting for an event. Observe and interact with the children during the experience/activity.

- How did you encourage and support the focus on measuring?
- How did the experience/activity support children in understanding measurement and in developing the skill of measuring?
- How could you begin to move the activity further to develop understanding of and skills in using standard measurements and using measuring equipment?

Key Stage 1

From the list of measurements, choose those that are appropriate for children at KS1. Add any other measurements that are not on the list. For each measurement, consider:

- What are the experiences are that will provide opportunities for children to move from qualitative measurements to more quantitative measurements?
- What measuring equipment can support children in KS1 to make and understand measurements?

Set up an activity or provide an opportunity for children to explore one type of measurement and to move from qualitative to quantitative measurements, perhaps with the use of measuring equipment. This may be finding out the height of different towers of bricks (e.g. in role-play of a building site), exploring how the temperature of a drink changes over time or measuring sound while trying to find what material is best for sound-proofing. Observe and interact with the children during the experience/activity.

- How did you encourage and support the focus on moving from qualitative to quantitative measuring?
- How did the experience/activity support children in understanding measurement and developing the skill of measuring?
- How could you develop your role in the activity to support measurement?

Key Stage 2

From the list of measurements, choose those that are measurements appropriate for children at KS2. Add any other measurements that are not on the list. For each measurement, consider:

- What are the experiences that will provide opportunities for children to use measuring equipment to make accurate quantitative measurements?

Set up an activity or provide an opportunity for children to explore one type of measurement and to use measuring equipment to make measurements. This may be finding out the speed of a vehicle rolling down a ramp, the force needed to move an object, or the density of objects and whether they float or sink. Observe and interact with the children during the experience/activity.

- How did you encourage and support the use of measuring equipment without losing understanding of the measurement?
- How does the context of the activity affect understanding of the measurement?
- How could you develop your role in the activity to support measurement?

The context of the measuring activity/experience is important in understanding what the measurement means and, ultimately, the development of the skill. If the experience is out of context with real life and the children cannot see the links between what they are doing and real life, then the subsequent development is likely to be less effective. For example, as part of role-play as gardeners, children may gauge the temperature to see if the weather is okay for the growing plants, measure the amount of water they give plants each day and measure how tall the plants are growing. When baking, children will need to measure the ingredients and then time how long the baking takes and at what temperature. This sets the measurements in real contexts, so giving them meaning, motivating the children and making them more likely to develop measuring skills as well as understanding why they need accurate measurements.

The story of *Mr Bembleman's Bakery* (Green,1978) illustrates the need for standard measures well and can be a stimulus for work in science, mathematics, literacy and technology. Of course, measurements are needed in many subjects (e.g. geography, history, science, technology, mathematics, creative arts and design) and measuring skills learned in a cross-curricular way can be effectively applied in other contexts.

Children do not always measure in the ways we expect and sometimes it is best to allow them to choose how they will measure and then introduce them to other methods. For example, children may choose to measure the distance from their classroom to the playground by using large bricks or paces and they may experience problems with each method (bricks are obstacles and paces can be of different length) before being introduced to a trundle wheel or tape measure. However, unless they have paced the distance out or put bricks down, they may not have a real feel for what the distance is.

> Diarra, a 5-year-old boy, was exploring the volume of two beakers – one tall and thin and one short and fat, but both having the same capacity. He chose to use small pompom balls. He filled up the short, fat beaker with 10 balls, counting each one in. He then took the balls out one at a time and put them into the tall, thin beaker. When he had filled up the beaker with all 10 balls, he looked puzzled and said, 'That can't be right' and started again. He repeated the activity four times, getting increasingly puzzled, as he expected the tall, thin beaker to hold more than the short, fat beaker. After the fourth attempt he looked up and said, 'They are the same!'

I wonder if he would have reached this decision if he had used conventional liquids to measure the volume.

Interpreting

Interpretation is an enquiry skill, used in many areas of the curriculum and in everyday life. As adults, we need to be able to look at evidence and use analysis of that evidence to make informed decisions. For example, if we want to buy a car, we need to look at evidence about fuel consumption, speed, comfort in order to reach a decision about whether the car is suitable for our needs. If the local council decides to use a green field site to build a factory, we need to look at the environmental disadvantages and the social and community advantages in order to make an informed decision, rather than one based on gut instinct.

Acquiring the skill of interpretation starts from a very early age and should be encouraged and supported in order that children can make sense of their enquiry. It is an important skill, as it is the link between skills and conceptual understanding. At

18 months, Polly was playing with magnetic letters on the fridge at home and she decided to see what else they would 'stick' to. She went around the kitchen trying out the magnets on a variety of household objects and her toys. At 4 years of age, Joey was playing in the sandpit and trying to make sandcastles. After some trial and error, he discovered that if the sand was dry or very wet it did not make good sand castles, but that damp sand was good. Ellie, at 8 years of age, undertook a **problem-solving** activity to find out which fabric was best to make a waterproof hat. She tested the different materials and used the evidence to decide which material was the most waterproof.

One of the problems with developing the skill of interpretation is that it is often the part of the science experience that we do not have time for or do not spend sufficient time on. If we are out for a walk in the park and a child makes an observation about the things he or she sees, we need to have time to help the child interpret the observations. If children are undertaking a science exploration or investigation, they need time and support to make sense of their findings, even if this means they have to return to the activity at a later time. We need to give children time to interpret, to discuss their enquiry and to discuss the ideas formulated from their enquiry.

It is in acquiring interpretation skills that children begin to recognise that not everyone has the same ideas as they do and this is an opportunity for discussions involving conceptual conflicts (Hand, 1988) through debate and argument (Naylor *et al.*, 2004). Through these discussions, children begin to understand that knowledge is not absolute and that there may be different interpretations of the same scientific phenomena. There may even be the 'sustained shared thinking' that Siraj-Blatchford (2009) has found supports cognitive development, as part of the process of constructing knowledge and moving to understanding (National Research Council of the National Academies, 2007). How the skill of interpretation supports cognitive development will be discussed further later in the book **(Chapter 2)**.

Recording and communicating

Harlen (2000) suggests that communication is closely linked to interpretation, giving children time to think about their enquiry and their ideas arising. Effective communication is also an important social skill that children will need throughout life. Providing opportunities to express ideas enables children to organise and clarify their thoughts and ideas and to reach a better understanding. **Dialogic teaching**, advocated by Alexander (2008), supports children in making links between their enquiry and new ideas and in recognising that others' ideas are not the same as their own. Dialogic teaching involves sharing ideas and challenging assumptions and is based on the principles that dialogue is (Alexander, 2008: 28):

- collective – so that children and teachers address learning together
- reciprocal – so that each participant in the dialogue listens to others and there is sharing of ideas and viewpoints
- supportive – so that there is clear articulation of ideas without fear or embarrassment
- cumulative – in that it builds on ideas from all participants and these ideas are linked together in a coherent way
- purposeful – so that dialogical teaching and learning has clear educational goals.

In dialogic teaching, teachers and children share ideas on an equal footing (Mercer, 2000) and if the language environment is unequal and weighted in favour of the teacher, then it is 'cognitively restricting' (Alexander, 2008: 14; Barnes, 1976). In this way, effective communication is two-way, socially equal and can support cognitive development (Cazden, 2001). Effective communication does not therefore involve the traditional teacher questioning and child answering. Where communication is seen as social and affective and takes the form of questions by the teacher and answers by the child, it is thought to be less effective than sustained dialogue, which can support cognitive development (Cazden, 2001; Alexander, 2008). However, it may be that communication that is social, emotional and cognitive can be most effective if care is taken to ensure that it engages in 'sustained shared thinking' (Siraj-Blatchford, 2009).

Active social interaction is a common characteristic (Vygotsky, 1962; Siraj-Blatchford *et al.*, 2002) of early scientific learning and appears to be most effective with children learning alongside peers (Bruner, 1991) and teachers (Stone, 1993) in a complex social interaction identified by Rogoff (1995). This involves children learning through social interaction on three 'inseparable, mutually constituting planes' (Rogoff, 1995: 139) – personal, interpersonal and community/contextual – which have been found to be useful in analysing early scientific development (Fleer, 2002; Robbins, 2005).

Recording is a form of communication that makes a more permanent record of the child's enquiry than a dialogue or discussion. It can take a number of different forms and is only one part of the scientific process and, as such, is not always necessary, unless it is a planned outcome of the science activity. Children may draw an observed plant or animal or produce an annotated drawing identifying the main features observed with some explanations. They may make a list or a table of measurements made, or a diagram of what has been measured, with the measurements as annotations. Younger children are more likely to use images, such as drawings, photographs or videos to record, whilst older children are more likely to use symbolic records such as writing or measurements. This does not mean that older children cannot make effective video recordings in the form of TV documentaries, or that younger children cannot create tables or pictograms, or write a poem or song that depicts their findings.

A group of EYFS children can make shaker instruments and use these to create a soundtrack for their favourite book, recorded on a CD. They can record their sorting of collections of objects using sorting hoops in photographs, or video record some role-play. Key Stage 1 children can produce collaborative charts and tables, perhaps using working walls (see the case study that follows). They might produce a cartoon of their scientific enquiry (this has an advantage of sequencing the enquiry but using few written words) or an environmental poster encouraging others to look after the school grounds. Key Stage 2 children might produce a television programme about their findings from an investigation, or produce a piece of drama or song recording their knowledge about the Earth and universe, forces or some other scientific conceptual area.

It is important that the form of recording:

- actually helps to support the development of the learning objectives as identified by the teacher, so that it supports the planned development;
- is not always literacy-based so that every science activity becomes a literacy activity, thus disadvantaging children who may have good scientific skills but poor literacy skills;
- is not added on as a time filler or justification of work undertaken, but is a meaningful addition to the activity.

Children will need to be helped to choose appropriate forms of recording to best communicate their ideas, findings etc., but as they develop, it is appropriate to give them more autonomy in their choice. Sometimes their choices are better than the obvious ones that teachers might advocate and I never cease to be amazed by their creative ideas. They will particularly need help in recording using tables, charts and graphs (Goldsworthy & Feasey, 1997), so that they can move from simple pictograms to more complex graphs, choose the scale for graphs and so on.

CASE STUDY

Recording using a working wall and class book

One Year 1 class of 5-year-old children were using the story of *The Very Hungry Caterpillar* (Carle, 1970) as a stimulus and they had a story sack to re-tell the story. They used a working wall (see photograph below) to record their work in a cross-curricular way and also created a class book, with each child writing one page using the computer (see photographs to the right).

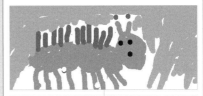

One sunday morning the egg popn and a came a very hungy cater piller ,

Reflective questions

Early career professional

- How does a working wall or a class book record children's scientific understanding?

- How does a working wall or a class book promote collaborative skills?

- How could you use a working wall or class book in your own teaching?

The caterpillar wasnt hungry any more and he wasnt a LittiL any more he wasnt a big fat caterpillar.

Photograph 1.3 A working wall based on *The Very Hungry Caterpillar*

Source: after Carle (1970)

He nibbled a hole and pushed his way out and he was a beutifull buterfly.

Photograph 1.4 Pages from a class book based on *The Very Hungry Caterpillar*

Source: after Carle (1970)

Case study (*continued*)

Developing career professional/teacher
- How can you promote the skills of recording, communicating through use of a working wall or class book?
- How could you improve **collaboration** through recording?
- What other ways could you communicate science findings and promote collaborative skills?

Later career professional/leader
- How can you use working walls to communicate scientific understanding between classes and to parents?
- In what other ways could you develop skills of recording, communication and collaboration throughout the school?

ACTIVITIES AND KEY QUESTIONS

To promote observation and classification

Allow children to observe, sort and classify a collection of objects according to their own criteria. Collections can include:

- Seeds, which can be sorted according to shape, size, colour, the way they are dispersed
- Animal pictures, which can be sorted according to physical similarities such as teeth, horse-like, cats, fur, claws, flies etc. **(see also Chapter 6)**
- Moving toys **(see also the research box at the start of the chapter)**, which can be sorted according to whether they spin, are electrical, magnetic, jump, need winding up and so on
- Sweets that can be sorted according to colour, shape, whether they are soft or hard, have wrappers, melt in the hand and so on.
  Key questions: How else can you sort them? How can you put an object in two groups?

To promote prediction and hypotheses (see Chapter 9, page 219)

- Which gloves will keep the ice hands in the surgical gloves cold? Children investigate whether woollen, cotton, rubber and furry gloves keep ice-filled surgical gloves cool or melt them.
  Key question: What will happen if you put the different gloves on the ice hands?
- What clothes does Teddy need for his holidays? Children pack a suitcase of clothes suitable for a warm/cold/wet holiday.
  Key question: Why does Teddy need these clothes for his holiday?
- What wrapping paper is strongest? Children investigate which Christmas wrapping paper is the strongest. They can use any method they choose but have access to 10 g masses.
  Key question: Which paper do you think will be the strongest? Why?
- How can we stop our shoes slipping? Children investigate a range of shoes with different soles to see which one is the least slippery.
  Key question: Which shoe is the least slippery? Why? How can we make our shoes less slippery?
- How can we free the bears/minibeasts from the ice? Children work out how to free small teddies or minibeasts stuck in ice. They have salt, warm water and a hairdryer to hand to help them.
  Key question: How do you think we can free the bears/minibeasts?

Activities and key questions (*continued*)

To promote observation and interpretation

- What happens when you pour hot water over sugar and margarine (both in clear bowls and with an adult doing the pouring for safety reasons)?
  Key question: What is the difference between the two?

- How does a Cartesian diver work? (see Photograph 5.1 A Cartesian diver)
  Key question: Why do you think the diver goes up and down?

- Why is this plant sick?
  Key question: What do you think the plant needs?

- What happens when we heat water?
  Key question: Where do you think the water is going?

References

Alexander, R. (2008). *Towards Dialogic Teaching: Rethinking Classroom Talk*, 4th edn. York: Dialogos.

Barnes, D.R. (1976). *From Communication to Curriculum*. Harmondsworth: Penguin.

Berk, L.E. (2003). *Child Development*, 6th edn. Boston, Mass: Allyn & Bacon.

de Bóo, M. (2006). Science in the early years. In Harlen, W., ed. *ASE Guide to Primary Science Education*. Hatfield: ASE, pp. 124–132.

Broadhead, P. (2004). *Early Years Play and Learning: Developing Social Skills and Cooperation*. London: RoutledgeFalmer.

Bruce, T. (2004). *Developing Learning in Early Childhood*. London: Hodder & Stoughton.

Bruner, J.S. (1977). *The Process of Education*, 2nd edn. Cambridge, MA: Harvard University Press.

Bruner, J.S. (1991). The narrative construction of reality. *Critical Inquiry*, 18(1), 1–21.

Carle, E. (1970). *The Very Hungry Caterpillar*. Harmondsworth: Penguin.

Cazden, C. (2001). *Classroom Discourse: the Language of Teaching and Learning*. Portsmouth, NH: Heinemann.

Covill, M. & Pattie, I. (2002). Science skills – The building blocks. *Investigating*, 18(4), 27–30.

Department for Education (DfE) (2012). *Statutory Framework for the Early Years Foundation Stage. Setting the Standards for Learning, Development and Care for Children from Birth to Five*. London: DfE.

Driver, R. (1983). *The Pupil as a Scientist*. Milton Keynes: Open University Press.

Duschl, R. (2000). Making the nature of science explicit. In: Millar, R., Leach, J. & Osborne, J., eds. *Improving Science Education: The Contribution of Research*. Buckingham: Open University Press, pp. 187–206.

Fleer, M. (2002). Sociocultural assessment in early years education: Myth or reality? *International Journal of Early Years Education*, 10(2), 105–120.

Fleer, M. (2007). *Young Children: Thinking about the Scientific World*. Watson, ACT; Early Childhood Australia.

Goldsworthy, A. & Feasey, R. (1997). *Making Sense of Primary Investigations. Revised edn. revised by S. Ball*. Hatfield: Association for Science Education.

Grambo, G. (1994). The art and science of observation. *Gifted Child Today Magazine*, 17(3), 32–33.

Green, M. (1978). *Mr Bembleman's Bakery*. New York: Parents Magazine Press.

Hand, B. (1988). Is conceptual conflict a viable teaching strategy?: the students' viewpoint. *Australian Science Teachers Journal*, November 1988, 34(4), 22–26.

Harlen, W. (2000). *The Teaching of Science in Primary Schools*, 3rd edn. London: David Fulton.

Harlen, W. & Symington, D. (1985). Helping children to observe. In: Harlen, W, ed. *Primary Science: Taking the Plunge.* London: Heinemann, pp. 21–35.

Johnston, J. (2005). *Early Explorations in Science*, 2nd edn. Buckingham: Open University Press.

Johnston, J.S. (2009). How does the skill of observation develop in young children. *International Journal of Science Education*, 31(18), 2511–2525.

Johnston, J. (2012). The development and support of observational skills in children aged under 4 years of age. *Journal of Emergent Science*, 3, 7–14.

Klemtschy, M. (2008). *Using Science Notebooks in Elementary Classrooms.* Arlington, VA: National Science Teachers Association Press.

König, A. (2009). Observed classroom interaction processes between pre-school teachers and children: Results of a video study during free–play time in German pre-schools. *Educational & Child Psychology*, 26 (2), 53–65.

McComas, W.F. (1998). The *Nature of Science in Science Education.* Dordrecht: Kluwer.

Mercer, N. (2000). *Words and Minds: How We Use Language to Think Together.* London: Routledge.

Ministry of Education (MOE). (1996). *Te Whãriki early childhood curriculum*. Wellington, New Zealand: Learning Media.

National Research Council of the National Academies (2007). *Taking Science to School. Learning and Teaching Science in Grades K to 8.* Washington, DC: The National Academies Press.

Naylor, S., Keogh, B. & Goldsworthy, A. 2004. *Active Assessment: Thinking, Learning and Assessment in Science.* Sandbach, Cheshire: Millgate House.

Pestalozzi, J.H. (1894). *How Gertrude Teaches her Children* (translated by Lucy, E. Holland and Frances C. Turner). Edited with an introduction by Ebenezer Cooke. London: Swan Sonnenschein.

Piaget, J. (1929). *The Child's Conception of the World.* New York: Harcourt.

Piaget, J. (1976). 'Mastery Play' and 'Symbolic Play'. In: Bruner, J., Jolly, A., & Sylva, K., eds. *Play – Its role in Development and Evolution.* Middlesex: Penguin.

Quinn, M.E., & George, K.D. (1975). 'Teaching Hypothesis Formation'. *Science Education*, 59, 289–296.

Robbins, J. (2005). 'Brown paper packages'? A sociocultural perspective on young children's ideas in science. *Research in Science Education*, 35(2), 151–172.

Rogoff, B. (1995). Observing sociocultural activity on three planes: Participatory appropriation, guided participation, and apprenticeship. In: Wertsch, J.V., Del Rio, P. & Alvarex, A., eds. *Sociocultural Studies of Mind*. Cambridge, UK: Cambridge University Press, pp. 139–164.

Siraj-Blatchford, I. (2009). Conceptualising progression in the pedagogy of play and sustained shared thinking in early childhood education: A Vygotskian perspective. *Educational & Child Psychology*, 26(2), 77–89.

Siraj-Blatchford, I., Sylva, K., Muttock, S., Gilden, R., & Bell, D. (2002). *Researching Effective Pedagogy in the Early Years.* Nottingham: DFES.

Stone, C.A., (1993). What is Missing in the Metaphor of Scaffolding? In: Forman, E.A., Minick, N., & Stone, C.A, eds. *Contexts for Learning; Sociocultural Dynamics in Children's Development.* New York: Oxford University Press, pp. 169–183.

Tomkins, S. & Tunnicliffe, S.D. (2007). Nature tables: Stimulating children's interest in natural objects. *Journal of Biological Education*, 41(4), 150–155.

Tunnicliffe, S.D. & Litson, S. (2002). Observation or imagination? *Primary Science Review*, 71, 25–27.

Vygotsky, L. (1962). *Thought and Language.* Cambridge. MA: MIT Press.

Wenham, M. (1993). The nature and role of hypotheses in school investigations. *International Journal of Science Education*, 15, 231–240.

Chapter 2

The development of emergent thinking

Overview

In this chapter we look at:

- The development of early years conceptual understanding or **cognition** in science; and emergent scientific thinking, using Piaget's (1929) cognitive stages and Montessori's (1994) planes of development
- Research into children's understanding by Sue Dale Tunniclife and Maria Kallery
- Reflection and analysis, as part of the study skills theme
- Practical and reflective tasks that explore children's thinking at different ages and that use one's own experiences in combination with reading to analyse issues
- Activities and activity boxes on exploring the environment, floating and sinking, solid, liquid, gases and ourselves
- Knowledge boxes focusing on floating and sinking and changing materials.

Introduction

Our knowledge of the way young children think – that is, the development of their conceptual understanding or cognition – has a long history, with science at its heart.

For example, Piaget's (1929) theory of cognitive development was initially developed by observing his own children and led to his ideas about how children move from intuitive ideas to more scientifically accurate ideas in stages (Piaget, 1950). Montessori's observations of children with special cognitive needs revealed all children as little scientists exploring and mastering the world (Montessori, 1994). Government reports, such as the Plowden Report (DES, 1967: 242), have also focused on science, advocating an approach to scientific learning that begins by 'initial curiosity, often stimulated by the environment the teacher provides, leads to questions and to a consideration of what questions it is sensible to ask and how to find the answers'.

In this chapter we will look at how children's cognition, their conceptual development or thinking skills develop, using Piaget's (1929) stages of development and making links with other theories and with practical tasks to help us consider children's thinking at different stages. We will also be exploring the study skills of reflection and analysis.

STUDY SKILLS

Reflection and analysis

In this chapter, we are focusing on reflection and analysis. Later in the book, we will look at developing analytical frameworks to make sense of the data collected **(see Section 3)**.

What are reflection and analysis?

Reflection involves the ability to think about actions and ideas and leads to **reflective practice**, an important part of all professional practice, whereby professionals engage in a continuous cycle of reflection and change (Schön, 1983). A further development of reflective practice is **reflexive practice**, a more dynamic process of meta-reflection, which involves the professional in reflecting on the consequences of reflection and action.

Analysis means to take something apart in order to illuminate, reveal, uncover, understand, resolve, identify or clarify. It is a bit like playing pass the parcel, in that each layer reveals something new and tells you a bit more about what is in the middle of the parcel. In analytical practice, you analyse events, situations, experiences or reading and begin to reveal the main factors affecting them; you begin to understand why someone has acted in a particular way; or you begin to clarify the issues for further development/action. It might also help to think of it in terms of a lottery scratch card, where you scratch away a layer to reveal what's underneath. In the same way, analysis involves scratching beneath the surface of reading, ideas and observations to help us understand them. We may be trying to understand why something has happened or why a certain idea is held.

Analysis also involves exploring alternative explanations or perspectives, such as looking at a situation from a scientific, adult or child's perspective. When analysing an observation, a situation, or data of any kind, we are attempting to understand what is happening, why individuals react in certain ways and according to certain situations. We look underneath the obvious and attempt to reveal why something happens and to resolve problems and clarify purposes and intentions. Through analysis, we aim to identify the main factors/issues/components of ideas or actions.

One way to ensure you are being analytical rather than descriptive is to make sure that you are asking yourself (and answering) analytical questions. Analytical questions ask how and why and so what, whereas descriptive questions ask when and where and what.

As you develop your analytical skills, you should aim to look more deeply at events, situations and evidence, and begin to identify the different layers of analysis. This may mean looking at a situation from a number of different perspectives, and perhaps getting evidence from different parties. This deeper analysis is a bit like mining to different depths, encountering different types of soil, rocks and evidence of life across the centuries. It is also like sorting a collection of objects in different ways, so that you get a better understanding of the collection as a whole and of the individual objects. Layers of analysis may reveal a chronology or history, as, for example, in looking at the history of cognitive development. In this context, the layers may involve a number of questions about cognition:

- How is cognition affected by the development of skills and attitudes?
- Why do some children struggle to develop thinking skills?
- How do teachers support cognitive development?

Together these build up to form a holistic and informative picture of how children develop their emergent thinking.

Deep analysis also involves looking at the data collected in order to identify patterns that will help you not only to understand but also to support. For example, you may identify pedagogical approaches that are effective in developing children's thinking, or in helping children to modify their ideas in the light of evidence, which may help you to develop your professional understanding of children's cognitive development and your skills in supporting them. For further reading on analysis, see Johnston (2012).

The young child

We will start from birth, although we know that children explore and develop some understanding of their world while still in the womb – we know, for example, that they recognise and react to sounds. From birth, children are involved in Piaget's (1929) sensorimotor stage or Montessori's (1994) first plane. This is the stage/plane of great development. At first, children are instinctive and have a number of simple reflex responses that help them to survive – sucking, swallowing and reacting to stimuli, such as a stroke on the cheek, helps them to find food, while the ability to grip firmly stops them falling from their mothers and is a primitive reflex action as seen in apes and monkeys.

As children develop, they become more aware of the immediate world around them, recognising faces and becoming aware of the fact that objects that are removed still exist, but their immediate needs still dominate. As they become more mobile and begin to explore the world around them, they also begin to develop intuitive ideas and undergo striking physical and psychological, as well as cognitive, changes (Montessori, 1967). Montessori notes that children at this stage have extremely absorbent minds that enable them to assimilate different cognitive information from exploration using all their senses, and are developing language and beginning to develop concepts (emergent thinking). Montessori (1967) also observed periods of special sensitivity to particular stimuli, or 'sensitive periods', during which children:

- acquire language
- begin to order the world around them
- develop sensory refinement
- take an interest in small objects
- develop social behaviour.

All of these can help with the development of emergent scientific thinking.

Language development and thinking

Language development is a feature of both Montessori's (1967) first plane and Piaget's (1929) second stage of development, the pre-operational stage. This stage is divided into two sub-stages: symbolic and intuitive. In the symbolic sub-stage, language becomes important in mental imagery and understanding of the world. This theory was subsequently built on by Vygotsky (1962), so that a strong inter-relationship between language and thought is thought to exist; so that as children speak, they are able to articulate their ideas, which, in turn, supports their thinking and consolidates their ideas.

At the intuitive sub-stage, language continues to develop and supports thinking and mental imagery, although children's perceptions dominate their thinking and they show a lack of reversibility, being unwilling to change their ideas. This may mean, for example, that children think a tall, thin beaker holds more than a short, fat one (see Chapter 1). They may also think that changes in shape mean differences in quantity or mass. When exploring how things fall to the ground, children at this stage develop the intuitive idea that heavy things fall faster than light things. When faced with evidence to the contrary (e.g. a screwed-up piece of paper that falls faster than a flat piece), they are likely to decide that screwing the paper up makes it heavier.

Ordering the world and thinking

Children order the world around them so that they can make sense of it. There are four types of order:

- Spatial order, where everything has its place ('I am in the garden because I am sitting on the grass')

- Social order, where the child learns to recognise others and develops emotional attachments **(see Chapter 3)** as well as social skills **(see Chapter 1)**
- Sensory order, where children learn to distinguish between the qualities of objects and sort according to texture, colour, shape and so on **(see also the skill of sorting and classifying in Chapter 1)**
- Temporal order, associated with routine and rhythm.

Steiner's educational methods (Steiner, 1996) are closely linked to the idea of temporal order, and advocate a natural rhythm of daily and weekly expansion and contraction where nothing is rushed (Oldfield, 2001). For example, daily rhythm may include creative exploration of the world, which allows expansion, followed by tidying up and circle time (a contraction time). Outdoor play time (expansion time) might be followed by a story (contraction time). A weekly rhythm involves set routines, so there is no uncertainty or surprise for the children. The rhythm of education is also assured, with the first seven years of life being about informal learning (Steiner, 1996).

Developing sensory refinement and taking an interest in small objects

Children order their sensory inputs and explore similarities and differences in the sensory input between objects and the environment. They also take a special interest in small objects. On a trip to the zoo with my granddaughter (aged 18 months) she loved the small monkeys, small mammals and reptiles, but did not seem interested in the elephants, giraffes and large apes. Younger children seem to focus on the smaller picture and not the bigger one. They may look for patterns in nature, recognising similarities in colour, shape and size. Rosie (a 2-year-old) would play with small stones in the garden and line them up in

Photograph 2.1 A young child focusing on small objects

order of size. She then picked up all the 'red' ones. Roxie (3 years old) was 'gardening' and planting seeds in a trough. She decided to put all the small seeds at one end of the trough and all the bigger seeds at the other end. Montessori (1994) observed that children from 3 years of age are likely to independently concentrate on activities for long periods of time

CASE STUDY

Exploring in a garden

A nursery class of 3-year-old children had access to an environmental garden. There was a small bed off a gravel path with a log pile and plants to attract wildlife. A group of children were exploring the garden. Jessie squatted on the path and made piles of stones of different colours: red, blue, brown. She enjoyed looking at how the sun made some of the stones sparkle. Harry and Joe carefully moved the logs to find woodlice and watched how they moved quickly to hide again under the logs. Sacha and Ravi found leaf skeletons and a feather and took them back to the professional. She suggested that they use a magnifier to look at them and then put them under the digital microscope so they could see the patterns of the leaf skeleton and the feather barbs magnified on a large scale and projected on to a screen.

The professional then suggested to some of the children that they look for other patterns in the garden. Harry and Joe noted the patterns on the logs and the professional gave them some paper and a wax crayon and showed them how they could make a rubbing of the pattern of the bark. Harry felt the bark with his fingers and then felt the wax rubbing he had made. 'It's the same,' he said. Jessie then made a rubbing of the stones on the path and the pavement outside the school entrance. Meanwhile, Sacha had moved on and was collecting all small objects that were red. He found a stone, a leaf, a fallen petal and a ladybird.

Reflective questions

1 How do you think the activity enriched the children's sensory input and added to their conceptual understanding of the world around them?

2 What are the advantages of allowing children to take the lead on their explorations?

3 How else could the professional support the children's conceptual understanding of the world around them?

Early career professional/student

1 How can you change your teaching approach to enable children to be more independent in their exploration?

2 How do you think this will support their conceptual development?

Developing career professional/teacher

1 What do you think is the relationship between sensory input, thinking and autonomy?

2 How can you increase opportunities for children's choice in sensory input in your teaching?

Later career professional/leader

1 How can practice in your setting be developed to provide children with greater autonomy in their exploration?

2 How can you evaluate the effect of this on conceptual understanding?

and called this 'normalisation'. Normalisation often arises spontaneously and can positively affect cognition.

Developing social behaviour

The importance of **social development** was discussed in the previous chapter and the link between thinking and social interaction is well recognised (Bruner, 1991; Rogoff, 1995; Siraj-Blatchford, 2009; Stone, 1993; Vygotsky, 1962). As children interact with others, they develop social skills, language skills and thinking skills, and children who are deprived of social interaction are likely to be less socially confident, have poorer language and be less well developed cognitively. Effective cognitive development can occur when adults interact sensitively with children, encouraging active social participation and 'sustained shared thinking' (Siraj-Blatchford, 2009: 77), scaffolding learning (Stone, 1993) and providing opportunities for children to interact and learn alongside peers (Bruner, 1991), discussing their ideas and seeing that these are not necessarily the same as those of others.

In the following research, talking with children was an important means of eliciting their ideas about health, injury and first aid, and also what had influenced their thinking. There is also evidence (Alexander, 2010; EPPE, 2002, 2003; Siraj-Blatchford *et al.*, 2002) that formal early years settings that achieve the best outcomes tend to view social and cognitive development as complementary and recognise that early education can benefit language development and support socialisation (EPPE, 2003).

Research

Teddy bear first aid – what young children know about health and first aid

Sue Tunnicliffe (2007)

As children mature, many of them acquire a greater knowledge of anatomy, albeit it atomistic – i.e. 'the heart' and 'the stomach' are taught, but the understanding of their systems and how they inter-relate is lacking. However, there is little work on the knowledge of first aid amongst young people. As children develop, they acquire more first aid knowledge but become more focused on themselves and less compassionate (Tunnicliffe, 2007). If meaningful first aid is to be incorporated into the formal curriculum in relevant subject areas, particularly science, which embraces first aid theory, it is necessary to elicit the knowledge and beliefs that young children hold.

Research question
What knowledge and beliefs do young children hold about health, injury and first aid?

Research design
Individual interviews with 28 children were conducted at the start of a visit to a children's learning area in a foundation wing of a school. The interviews were begun in the family room off the wing. Each child was given a teddy bear to hold and was encouraged to talk about similar toys they had at home. They were then asked what they needed to do to make sure the toys were healthy. They were also asked where they had learned about the things they were suggesting.

The individual interviews were followed by a role-play partnership between the researcher and each child. They went round the learning area together, looking at and talking about eight 'injured' teddy bears, which were placed around the room. There was a variety of injuries, simulated separately on eight identical 'bears'. At each 'accident' the child was asked what could be done to help 'Teddy' and where they had found out about their suggested actions. Their responses were recorded at the start of the individual interviews. Some children (apparently the less able) tailed off in concentration towards the end of the interview.

Research (*continued*)

Summary of findings

The children said they had learnt about keeping healthy both at home and at school, although six shrugged and said, 'I just know' (see Table 2.1).

Table 2.1 Source of learning about keeping healthy

Where did you learn?	No. of responses
At school	11
At home	11
Just know	6

The children were asked individually what they could do to keep healthy. There were three main categories of their answers:

1 Have comfort

2 Take actions

3 Eat foods.

The breakdown of the responses is shown in Table 2.2. Actions ranged from washing hands to going on holiday!

Table 2.2 Categories of activity children said to do to keep healthy (responses are not mutually exclusive)

Category (no.)	No. of responses	Comments
Comfort (9)	1	Keep warm
	2	Give a cuddle
	3	Stay in bed
	3	Sleep
Actions (9)	1	Washing hands
	7	Recreational activities (swim, play)
	1	Going on holiday
Food (18)	15	Eat
	3	Breakfast

Many children said you had to eat to keep healthy and three were more specific, saying, 'Eat breakfast'. When asked what foods were healthy, they mentioned a range of items (Table 2.3).

Injured teddies and how we might help

The children focused on the task of considering the injured teddy bears, recalling and answering but displayed displacement actions whilst talking, as follows:

Table 2.3 Actions to keep healthy

Eat healthy foods (N = 26)	Detail of which foods are healthy
8	Apples
3	Vegetables
4	Pizza
5	Pasta and cereals
6	Dairy products (two milk, two chocolate)

- Fiddling
- Dressing/undressing the teddy
- Went on a teddy hunt around the classroom
- Jumped about all the time and would not be still.

Several of the children were not keen to join in and the activities were voluntary. A few children appeared resentful at being asked to leave an activity they were enjoying and other children were uncommunicative. A few girls hardly spoke and this was explained (by conversations with teacher/assistants) as responses to strange situations; these were the children who engaged in some of the distraction techniques. One girl was an elective mute, who nodded or shook her head but uttered no sounds.

Four themes emerged as categories of responses after a read/re-read process of analysis of the transcripts and these were not mutually exclusive:

- Don't know
- Tell an adult
- Care by cuddling
- Treatment.

Most children based their 'treatment' on what they knew from home or their own injuries. The children only really knew about cuts and bleeding, which they all seemed to have sustained. Children who understood the term 'burn' were only those who had sustained one. The children recalled their own experiences and a few came up with a course of action informed by the cause, such as the poisoned teddy bear – two children said the poison needed to be taken out of him. This, incidentally, would not be the appropriate action in the case of a caustic substance which is capable of burning, such as washing soda, as this would cause further chemical burns on exit from the oesophagus, but their **reasoning** showed some insight.

Research (*continued*)

Responses categorised into the four main themes

1 Don't know – no experience or did not comprehend
2 Tell an adult
   a Mother/teacher occasionally
   b Call doctor
   c Take to doctor
   d Call an ambulance

When asked, the children did not know how to use the telephone to call for help. 'Call the doctor' or 'Take to doctor' was almost a mantra.

3 Care for teddy
   a Give him a cuddle
   b Make him better
   c Give him a cake
   d Give him another teddy.

4 Treat injury/situation
   a An imaginary response
   b No knowledge
   c Experiential
   d Instructional knowledge was evident from some children who had been told what to do, such as tell an adult
   e Pragmatic – one boy, in particular, was very pragmatic and for the broken leg scenario, remarked: 'Cut it off.'

The children had had some first-hand experience of accidents they themselves had had, mainly cuts and a few burns. Treatment most often was 'put on plaster', or occasionally a 'bandage'.

Implications

The responses of the children indicate compassion and concern for the injured others and they intuitively suggested medical treatment, even though they did not have any real understanding of health. Moreover, in their ideas of helping, assistance and keeping healthy, there were indications of altruism and concern.

The findings provide a base on which effective teaching could be developed for life skills and language as well as science, first aid and health education.

- The understanding of keeping healthy was minimal and focused on food, largely inappropriate foods.
- The children did not know how to use the telephone and the school is now going to ensure that this is taught.
- Children who had experienced an injury knew more about treatment.
- Language was an impediment. Unless children had experience of an injury, they did not understand some words, such as burn or unconscious. These had to be explained first.

However, the data shows that young children are aware of injuries and their treatment and are capable of reasoning within their experience and common sense. If every child really does matter (Department for Education and Skills, 2003), helping them feel safe, but able to help in case of an incident, is part of their educational entitlement. Furthermore, action in emergencies can be incorporated into a developmental sequence across the curriculum to provide them with fundamental first aid knowledge and competencies which can contribute to the well-being of society.

Practical and reflective tasks

Find out about children's ideas on health, illness, injury and first aid. This can be:

- stimulated by a story such as *Bear Feels Sick* (Wilson, 2007), or the story of Dr James Barry (Johnston and Gray, 1999) about a medical doctor during the Crimean War who made the link between hygiene and survival after surgery and who turned out to be female;
- a discussion of their experiences when sick and what treatment they underwent;
- a teddy bear simulation, as described by Tunnicliffe in the preceding research box, giving children an opportunity to discuss their ideas with each other.

Make a note/record the different ideas that the children have about health, illness, injury and first aid. Analyse the ideas and see if you can group them into categories similar to those used by Tunnicliffe, or use your own categories.

Early career professional

● How do the children's ideas on health, illness, injury and first aid differ from adult/scientific ideas?

● How have these ideas emerged from the children's experiences?

● How do you think you could move the children's ideas closer to adult/scientific ideas?

Developing career professional/teacher

● What is the gap between the children's ideas and those you wish them to hold?

● What experiences do you think will bridge that gap?

● How can these experiences cater for all the different ideas that the children have?

Later career professional/leader

● How closely linked are children's ideas to their experiences?

● What type of experience appears to have the most influence on the children's ideas: books/ stories, first-hand experiences, practical play activities or discussion/hearing about others' ideas and experiences?

● What impact does this analysis have on your future planning to develop children's ideas?

The developing child

In Piaget's (1929) third stage of cognitive development, the concrete operational stage, and Montessori's (1994) second plane of development, children's thinking develops further and they begin to coordinate ideas, making links between ideas as well as reason. During this stage, their thinking becomes more rational and adult-like. In Piaget's (1929) theory, scientific understanding occurs through building up of mental structures called schemas (mental representations) and operations (combinations of schemas) as a result of experiences. Cognitive development occurs in a specific order (invariant functioning), but is affected by different experiences and so children's thinking will vary (variant functioning) depending on their experiences. As a result, it is sensible to give children as many opportunities and practical experiences as possible to support their thinking skills. This is also because developing children are able to think logically if they can physically handle the object that they are thinking about, and so what they think is affected by what they experience. Scientific experiences enable children to construct, develop, modify or change their intuitive ideas (Driver, 1983; Scott, 1987).

In this way, the development of emergent thinking is about challenging existing ideas through practical engagement and modifying existing ideas, or even radically changing ideas, as well as adding to and extending existing ideas. Practical experiences can include observation, exploration, play and social interaction, although this is by no means an easy process, as developing children are unlikely to change their intuitive ideas unless there is persuasive evidence and, even then, will resist change.

With developing children, ideas about themselves can be developed as part of a theme entitled 'Ourselves', which could start by looking at their outside bodies. The children could make a passport **(see Figure 2.1)** and make a record of their details. The details in the passport can be changed to suit the planned learning outcomes (e.g. it could include personal measurements, observable features or favourite activities). The information could be recorded electronically, as a personal database, so that a photograph could be taken using a digital camera and added to the database and details added electronically. Class information could be added to a spreadsheet and graphs of eye or hair colour, height, favourite colour or how high the children can jump could be plotted based on all members of the class.

My best friend is..........................

I like to

My favourite colour is

My favourite food is

My passport

This is me

My name is..........................

I am.................years old

My hair is.....................................

My eyes are.......................................

I am...tall

My feet are size...

I can jump, skip, run, swim, play football

I live in this house with my family

Figure 2.1 A passport for the developing child (if copied onto A4 paper it can be folded to make a book)

The theme could also look at the inside of the body through a body mapping activity, where children put outlines of the main organs (brain, heart, stomach, intestines) onto an outline of a human body. Alternatively, they could pin three-dimensional organs made of fabric on to an apron and hat with Velcro, or use a scientific torso borrowed from a secondary school. Most children of this age tend to focus on the digestive system, with more than 20 per cent of children's drawings showing the whole digestive system (Reiss & Tunnicliffe, 2001), a much higher percentage than any other bodily system.

Reiss & Tunnicliffe's (2001) research showed that, as they got older, children appeared to know more organs and started indicating their relative position within the body and to each other. Some children described the function of the parts; for example, Year 6 children called tubes the 'food tube' and the anus the 'pooh hole'; a Year 2 child used the labels 'pooh bit' and 'food tube', indicating that they knew the function and location of these parts.

Further work on the theme could focus on children's understanding of skeletons, which is the focus of research undertaken by Tunnicliffe and Reiss (1999) as outlined in the following box.

Research

Children's ideas about skeletons (Tunnicliffe & Reiss, 1999)

Sue Tunnicliffe

Surprisingly few studies have looked at children's understanding of skeletons. Most of the work in this field that has been done has only involved children's understanding of human skeletons.

Research question
What are students' understandings of the structure of animal (including human) skeletons?

Research design
A cross-sectional approach was used, involving a total of 161 students from six different age groups (ranging from 5 to 20 years old) from a primary school, a secondary school and a college of higher education in the south of England.

On separate occasions, the students were presented with a single dead specimen of a brown rat (*Rattus norvegicus*, stuffed), a starling (*Sturnus vulgaris*, stuffed), a herring (*Clupea harengus*, fresh*) and an edible crab (*Cancer pagurus*, fresh). On each occasion the students were then asked to draw what they thought was inside the specimen when it was alive.

Students were not examined under formal examination conditions but were told not to copy one another's work. On the final occasion, the students were asked to draw what they thought was inside themselves. Students were given 10–15 minutes to complete each drawing.

The findings focus on the information provided by the students about the animals' skeletons. The same researcher (S. Tunnicliffe) carried out all the primary fieldwork; M. Reiss carried out the secondary and undergraduate fieldwork.

Repeated inspections of the completed drawings allowed the construction of a seven-point scale, with levels ranging from 1 (no bones) to 7 (comprehensive skeleton, i.e. backbone, skull, limbs and ribs in the case of vertebrates).

Summary of findings
After the drawings had been obtained, they were sorted through repeatedly, in an attempt to arrange them in an order which it was felt reflected different levels of biological understanding. No notice was taken of the students' ages in determining this order. Eventually, the following order for the vertebrates was agreed:

Level 1 – no bones

Level 2 – bones indicated by simple lines or circles

Level 3 – bones indicated usually by 'dog bone' shape and at random or throughout body

Level 4 – at least some bones shown in their appropriate positions

Level 5 – at least two types of bone indicated in their correct positions (e.g. backbone and ribs)

Research (*continued*)

Level 6 – definite vertebrate skeletal organisation shown (i.e. backbone, skull and limbs and/or ribs)

Level 7 – comprehensive skeleton (i.e. backbone, skull, limbs and ribs).

A separate scale was devised for the crab.

To the children, the skeleton was initially a series of disjointed bones, but ribs were salient and some children (e.g. those in Year 6) indicated the backbone. Among the few Year 9 pupils, two showed the backbone and cranium, one showed disjointed bones and one said she did not know.

The students' knowledge of human skeletons was significantly better than their knowledge of the rat, bird and fish skeletons and very significantly better than their knowledge of the crab skeletons. In England, where this study was carried out, such taxon-specific knowledge is probably largely a reflection of the anthropomorphic

bias in today's curriculum: almost no non-human animal structure and function, sadly, is currently taught to 5- to 16-year-olds.

The analysis suggested that, as expected, older students have a better knowledge of skeletal structure. However, even among the undergraduates (who were biology specialists) only some 10 per cent attained level 7.

Implications

This work has clear implications both in terms of ways in which schools might better encourage pupils to know about and understand the structure of organisms other than themselves and in terms of ways in which extra-school sources of scientific information, such as zoos, science centres and museums, might help. Reiss and Tunnicliffe (1999) believe that children learn about the body as units, which they gradually piece together.

Social experiences, language and the development of thinking

Intellectual independence and social organisation are characteristics of Montessori's (1994) second plane. She identified that developing children tend to work and socialise in groups and, in this way, social experiences continue to affect the development of thinking. As children develop, they become less egocentric and more inclined to listen to the ideas of others, although this is a slow process and one that involves careful and sensitive interaction. Dialogic teaching (Alexander, 2008) is an approach that can utilise social and language development to assist thinking (Johnston, 2011). Dialogic teaching is collective – children and teachers address learning together and reciprocally, so that each participant in the dialogue listens to others and there is a sharing of ideas and viewpoints. Children should be able to articulate their ideas without any fear or embarrassment and this requires a supportive learning and teaching environment.

At this stage of development, children should be beginning to link their ideas with those of others, on an equal footing (Mercer, 2000) and in a coherent way, and beginning to develop simple arguments (Toulmin, 1958) more characteristic of older children (Erduran, 2012; Osborne *et al.*, 2004). If classroom dialogue is more teacher-dominated than child-dominated, consisting of teachers' questions and children's answers, this is thought to be 'cognitively restricting' (Alexander, 2008: 14) and less supportive of cognitive development (Cazden, 2001).

The effectiveness of talk in developing scientific understanding is a common theme in many early years research findings (Johnston, 2011; Kallery *et al.*, 2009; Tunnicliffe, 2007). Kallery *et al.* (2009) (see also the research box on floating and sinking later in this chapter) found that, in teaching about floating and sinking, formal didactic, teacher-led approaches tended to be unsuccessful in supporting understanding and that children needed to make cognitive and verbal links between their exploratory findings and scientific phenomena.

Tunnicliffe's (2007) research outlined earlier in this chapter identified that children's understanding of keeping healthy was enhanced by interaction and talk and led to an improved vocabulary of health and safety. Johnston's (2011) research looking at children's talk indicated that the balance of adult, peer and contextual support needed to be different for different ages, with more adult support in children under 2 years of age and greater peer support in older children. For children at this stage, adults are still needed to lead, encourage and challenge, but the children should be exercising more autonomy and using prior knowledge in their scientific dialogue (see also Siraj-Blatchford *et al.*, 2002). This seems to require professionals who are not only aware of the importance of the complex balance between adult, peer and contextual support, but who will facilitate oral and social interaction, building on the rich and varied language opportunities found in the home and ensuring that formal settings do not restrict language development (Wells, 1987).

STUDY SKILLS

Reflection and analysis

Level 1

The first step in developing analytical skills is to reflect on a situation or experience and answer analytical questions. Analytical questions ask how, why and so what, whereas descriptive questions ask when, where and what?

Look at the questions below and decide which ones are analytical and which are descriptive:

- Do you use science in your everyday life?
- Why is scientific understanding important for young children?
- Do you think that science is an important part of the school curriculum?
- How can early years settings improve the scientific understanding of children in their care?
- What are the main factors affecting scientific understanding in young children?

Level 2

The next step in developing analytical skills is to raise analytical questions after reflection. Remember that analytical questions ask how, why and so what and involve detailed answers.

Read about Piaget's cognitive development in this chapter or by reading chapter 4 in Johnston and Halocha (2010). Considering your own experiences, raise some analytical questions that you can answer about the development of emergent thinking.

Level 3

Deeper analysis involves uncovering layers of analysis or exploring different perspectives. This might involve looking at the history of an incident (what came before and what afterwards), patterns of behaviour, issues or factors affecting behaviour or new ideas or thought resulting from reflection.

Read Piaget's ideas about cognitive development (1929, 1950). Consider what experiences influenced his beliefs. Consider, too, what we now know from research and experience that has added to our understanding of the way children think.

Practical and reflective tasks

Practical tasks

Put a collection of scientifically related objects on a table or on the floor for children to explore, e.g.:

- objects connected to the scientific concept of light, such as torches, mirrors, prisms, coloured acetate sheets and objects to make shadows;
- objects connected to growth, such as seeds, germinating seeds and growing plants;

- a collection of solids, liquids and gases;
- a collection of moving toys (see Johnston, 2009, and the research box in Chapter 1).

Allow the children to explore the collection and engage in dialogue with them. You may wish to make a video or audio recording of the interaction, as this can allow deeper analysis.

If possible, try the activity with children of different ages, either within an age group or across different stages of development (Early Years Foundation Stage, Key Stage 1, Key Stage 2).

Reflective tasks

- Was there a balance in the interaction between adults and children?
- How could this balance have been improved?
- How did the interaction and dialogue support the children's emergent thinking?
- How could you improve your part in the interaction to encourage peer talk and support cognitive understanding?

Research

Introducing floating and sinking in pre-school, employing 'collaboratively' developed activities

Maria Kallery

Aim of the study

This study aimed to test the effectiveness of a teaching intervention that introduces children aged 4–6 years to the phenomenon of floating and sinking. The activities have been designed with specific learning objectives that take into consideration children's alternative explanations reported in literature (e.g. Dentici *et al.*, 1984; Selley, 1993) and were developed collaboratively by a researcher and early years teachers using **action research** processes.

Design and description of activities

The design of the activities used the 'density approach', even though the term 'density' itself is not directly used but is replaced by concepts that indicate descriptive elements of it. This allowed floating and sinking objects to be considered from the viewpoint of size, mass/weight, shape and solidness/hollowness (see also Havu-Nuutinen, 2005). As the density is a characteristic physical property of each individual substance and the one that makes each different material behave differently in the water, the activities' objective was to enable children to link the evidence resulting from their experimentation with objects bearing specifically designed characteristics (size, shape, material) to the idea explaining this evi-

dence (Kallery *et al.*, 2009), shifting their attention from the objects to the material of which these are made (see also Selley, 1993).

The intervention included two units of activities. The activities of the first unit dealt with solid bodies; in each activity, one of the variables shape, size (volume) or material was differentiated, while the rest were kept constant. The activities of the second unit used hollow bodies in combination with solid ones made of the same material, thus allowing a simultaneous comparison of the behaviour in the water of hollow and solid objects made from the same material. Before the start of the activities, the concept of 'hollowness' and the content of the hollow objects (air) were discussed.

In addition to the experiments, children worked on solving the problem of 'how to make float a solid object made of a material that sinks'. Using plastic materials, children worked on constructing hollow bodies and testing their behaviour in water in order to understand the relationship between the size of the bodies' cavity and their ability to float. Lastly, the experiences gained from all the activities were linked to everyday situations and experiences.

The approach to learning can be characterised as socially constructed, in the sense that the teacher's role is

Research (*continued*)

central to explanation of the scientific concepts, children collaborate with peers, sharing opinions and knowledge, and adults and children work together. Within this learning context, whole class and group discussions were considered one of the most important aspects of the activities.

Activities' development procedure
The activities were developed collaboratively by a researcher with a background in physics and the didactics of science, who also served as a facilitator (R/F), and six early years teachers. The work of the group proceeded as follows: the R/F initially designed the activities and presented to the teachers; the teachers implemented them and used action research processes to optimise classroom practices and gather information, which in turn was used by the group for the revision and final shaping of the activities. These processes were cyclical and included the most basic steps: acting-recording, reviewing-reflecting, acting (Dick, 1997). Teacher review and reflection took place in group meetings and was facilitated by the R/F. Group work led teachers to joint decisions on handling common problems and resulted in alterations to the activities as initially designed.

Teacher preparation
Previous research has shown that in many cases the theoretical explanations provided by science teachers who are not specialists are very similar to the alternative perceptions held by children (Kallery & Psillos, 2001). Additionally, an epistemological analysis of typical didactical activities adopted by early years teachers in the study of floating and sinking in pre-school classes revealed that the lessons were fragmentary in character and failed to promote scientific reasoning and understanding of the phenomenon (Kallery *et al*, 2009). Thus, prior to the implementation of the activities, the R/F introduced the concepts and phenomena to be taught in group meetings, presenting the teachers with knowledge that was necessary for responding successfully to the implementation of the activities and answering their questions on the topics of the activities.

During the preparatory pre-implementation stage, the group also dealt with methodological issues such as possible ways of handling children's questions depending on their type (e.g. Harlen, 1996; Kallery, 2000), and the avoidance of personification when answering children's questions or explaining and introducing scientific issues, as personification is often used by teachers in these cases, either consciously or unconsciously (see Kallery & Psillos, 2004). According

to Piaget (1951), use of anthropomorphism can foster subjectivity in young children.

Implementation and assessment
Activities were implemented by the six early years teachers of the work group in their own public school classes (classes were multi-age) as part of the regular pre-school week timetable in a sample of 104 children. Teachers audio-recorded and transcribed the lessons, which were analysed by the R/F.

Activities were assessed by the teachers at least 2 weeks after implementation. Concept cartoons were used for the assessment (Keogh & Naylor, 1999). Children were invited to judge each cartoon character's argument and express their opinion. Children's opinions were audio-recorded by the teachers and analysed by the R/F.

Summary of findings
Qualitative analysis of the lesson protocols, which was validated by 'member checks' (Guba & Lincoln, 1981), revealed that while children's original ideas matched those reported in the literature, during the activities, the children dissociated solid bodies' floating or sinking from their size and from their weight and gradually came to hold the material they were made of as being 'responsible' for the whether the bodies floated or sank.

C: Yes, these have the same shape and same size but have different material and will do different things [meaning will behave differently in the water].

C: Yes, no matter how heavy they are, all of them sink if they are of play-dough. Those of wood stay up.

C: It is the material that decides what they do, just like if it was their teacher!!

With regard to the hollow objects, the children understood the role of the air-filled cavity in the bodies' behaviour in water:

C: See teacher, the glass goes down. The jar has air inside; it is jailed in there and does the job [meaning it makes it float].

The results of the assessment revealed the following:

Solid bodies
- 90% of the assessed children dissociated floating or sinking from the weight of the bodies. Judging the cartoons' arguments the children stated clearly that heavy bodies will float if they are made of a material that floats.

- 88.5% of the assessed children dissociated floating or sinking from the size of the bodies. Children supported

Research (*continued*)

the view that a body, no matter how small it is, will sink if it made of a material that sinks in the water.

Hollow bodies

- 78% of the assessed children were able to differentiate between the behaviour in water of a solid body made of a material that sinks and the behaviour of a hollow body made of the same material. They expressed the view that the air-filled cavity of the hollow body is what makes the difference to its behaviour.

Conclusions and implications

The results of the evaluation indicate that high percentages of children have met the learning objectives of the activities. The findings of the lessons analysis also reveal that children's attention was gradually shifted from the objects to the materials of which they were made. This is a desirable and promising step for children of these formative ages, since this way of thinking will serve as a foundation for later, more sophisticated scientific reasoning concerning the phenomenon. The encouraging results of the present learning study can be attributed to the design of the activities and the instruction materials and approach as well as to the teacher preparation. In the methodological part both the collaborative development of the activities and the action research processes proved very useful for shaping the activities and for preparing teachers for a more effective implementation.

The present work outlines an approach and also tests its effectiveness in real classroom settings with a population whose age falls within a critical span, with encouraging results. Within the limits of the present study, the current findings suggest that this approach can have a wider application for the initiation of very young children in fundamental concepts and phenomena of science in general.

References

Dentici, A. Grossi, M, Borghi, L, DeAmbrosis, A, & Masara, C. (1984). Understanding floating: A study of children aged between six and eight years. *European Journal of Science Education*, 6(3), 235–243.

Dick, B. (1997). *Action Learning and Action Research*. Online at: http://www.scu.edu.au/schools/gcm/ar/arp/actlearn.html. Accessed: January 2007.

Guba, E.G. & Lincoln, Y.S. (1981). *Effective Education*. San Francisco, CA, Jossey-Bass.

Harlen, W. (1996). *The Teaching of Science*, 2nd edn. London: David Fulton.

Havu-Nuutinen, S. (2005). Examining young children's conceptual change process in floating and sinking from a social constructivist perspective. *International Journal of Science Education*, 27(3), 259–279.

Kallery, M. (2000). Children's science questions and ideas provide an invaluable tool for the early years' teacher. *Primary Science Review* 61(Jan/Feb), 18–19.

Kallery, M. & Psillos, D. (2001). Pre-school teachers' content knowledge in science: their understanding of elementary science concepts and of issues raised by children's questions. *International Journal of Early Years Education*, 9(3), 165–179.

Kallery, M. & Psillos, D. (2004). Anthropomorphism and animism in early years science: Why teachers use them, how they conceptualise them and what are their views on their use. *Research in Science Education*, 34, 291–311.

Kallery, M., Psillos, D. & Tselfes, V. (2009). Typical didactical activities in the greek early-years science classroom: do they promote science learning? *International Journal of Science Education*, 31(9), 1187–1204.

Keogh, B. & Naylor, S. (1999). Concept cartoons, teaching and learning in science: an evaluation. *International Journal of Science Education*, 21(4), 431–446.

Piaget, J. (1951). *The Child's Conception of the World*. Savage, MD: Littlefield Adams.

Selley, N. (1993). Why do things float? A study of the place for alternative models in school science. *School Science Review*, 74(269), 55–61.

Practical and reflective tasks

Early Years Foundation Stage

The story book *Mr Archimedes' Bath* (Allen, 1986) can be used as a stimulus to present the idea that different objects will float or sink and displace water to different degrees. You can then set up an exploration so children can explore floating, sinking and displacement. You can use a water trough or tank of water or even a bucket, paddling pool or sink. Give the children a variety of objects of different shapes, sizes and density to explore and encourage them to sort the objects into those that float or sink, allowing them to come up with any other categories they may choose.

Question the children and elicit their ideas on floating and sinking, encouraging them to make generalised statements about why things float or sink. At this stage of development, children are likely to have intuitive ideas about floating and sinking, based on their experiences, such as, for example, heavy things sink and light things float.

- What alternative ideas did the children hold about floating and sinking?
- What further experiences could help them develop, modify or change their ideas to make them scientifically more accurate?

Key Stage 1
You could look at floating and sinking as part of role-play at the seaside. Part of the outside or inside play area could be set up as a seaside with a sandpit (perhaps with a plastic sheet covered with sand), a water trough, paddling pool, water tank and a collection of seaside objects (bucket, spade, nets, and so on). These objects can include some that can be used for floating and sinking, such as large and small shells, floats (swimming and fishing, both large and small), containers (buckets) and even some common rubbish that can be found in the sea (pop bottle, nappy, plastic bag).

Ask the children to sort the objects into those they predict will float and those they predict will sink and ask them to explain why (hypothesise). Then ask them to test the objects and see if they were correct. At this stage of development, children are very likely to have developed simple theories about heavy things sinking and light things floating and are likely to hold on to these even in the face of contradictory evidence, providing some reason why new evidence is contrary to their own ideas. Question them about contradictions in the evidence and challenge their alternative ideas in a sensitive way.

- How did your questioning or challenges affect the children's alternative ideas?
- What further experiences could help them develop, modify or change their ideas to make them scientifically more accurate?

Key Stage 2
For older children you could start with a problem-solving activity such as making a boat out of card, wood or plasticine that can hold 'passengers'. You could give them different types of wood (each of equal size) but with different density (balsa, pine, mahogany), and use Blu-tac or plasticine 'passengers'. They could use card to make different-shaped boats and add marble 'passengers'. They could mould plasticine into different shaped boats, trying to make it float and use marble 'passengers'.

Alternately, you could provide them with a collection of objects (e.g. aluminium foil, a lemon, plasticine, a sponge) to see if they can make the ones that float sink and the ones that sink float.

- How does the problem-solving activity challenge their ideas about floating and sinking?
- What further experiences could help them develop, modify or change their ideas to make them scientifically more accurate?

A follow-up activity could be to explore what happens when you put a lemon pip, raisin or peanut into a glass of fizzy water or lemonade. Try it yourself, predicting what you think will happen and then trying to explain what you observe.

Photograph 2.2 Children exploring floating and sinking

Knowledge box

Floating and sinking

Objects float or sink depending on whether their density is greater or smaller than water or the liquid in which they are placed. Density is defined as the mass of an object per unit volume, or how much matter is squashed into its volume (density = mass/volume). If the object is more dense than water, it will sink; if less dense than water, it will float. Oil will float on water as it is less dense. Ice will float, partly under the water, as it becomes less dense on solidifying; water expands when freezing so becomes less dense. However, salt water is more dense than plain water and so objects that sink in plain water might float in salt water (this is why we float more easily in salty sea water).

For more knowledge about forces, see Chapter 5.

The more developed child

The formal operational stage is Piaget's last cognitive stage and is characterised by children thinking abstractly, i.e. using their minds rather than their hands. As they develop cognitively, children begin to be able to group, separate, order and combine ideas in their minds, solving mental problems. Although **abstraction** is more common in older children and adults, children are able to undertake some quite complex mental problems at earlier ages (Bruner *et al.*, 1956), although some adults are never able to achieve logical, abstract thought.

As children mature and have a variety of scientific experiences, they develop mental models of the world that are stored in their long-term memory and can be accessed as needed. If their experiences challenge existing ideas about the world and how it works, they may add to their ideas or modify them or sometimes even change these ideas. Direct teaching about scientific phenomena may hinder, rather than help, cognitive development, as children can move from intuitive ideas to synthetic ideas (ideas modified or changed as a result of direct teaching but which are still scientifically inaccurate). For example, 7-year-old Andrew (see Johnston, 2005), when faced with heavy things that floated and linking his knowledge of heavy boats that float on the sea, decided that when things are light they float, when heavy they sink and when very heavy they float again.

Children's intuitive ideas about growth often include the view that a plant or animal starts as a miniature version of the adult (**see Figure 2.2**; Russell & Watt, 1990), and teaching about growth using seeds and eggs may not dispel this, as they cannot see inside the seed or egg easily.

At this stage of development, children are likely to have a wider set of experiences from which to draw on and these can influence their ideas. So children with great experience of growth through living on a farm or growing food on an allotment are likely to have more sophisticated ideas about growth than other children at the same stage. It may be that these experiences play a part in the factor theories of cognitive development, although whether the experience or the ability comes first is difficult to determine.

Factor theories were initially identified by Spearman (1927) and developed by Thurstone and Thurstone (1941) and became popular with Gardener (1983). These recognise that there are a number of different factors affecting cognition. Gardener identifies eight of them:

1 Bodily-kinaesthetic or using the body to solve problems and express ideas and feelings

2 Interpersonal, or the ability to gauge moods, feelings and needs

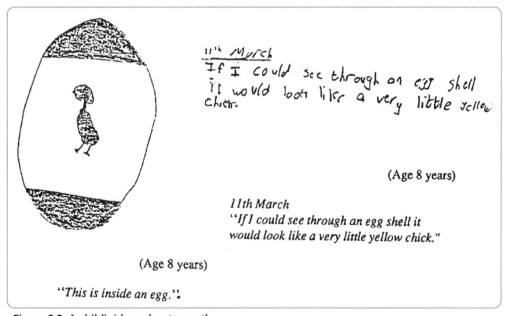

(Age 8 years)

11th March
"If I could see through an egg shell it would look like a very little yellow chick."

(Age 8 years)

"This is inside an egg.":

Figure 2.2 A child's ideas about growth
Source: Russell & Watt (1990: 28)

47

3 Intrapersonal, or the ability to use knowledge about themselves

4 Linguistic, or the ability to use words, oral or written

5 Logical-mathematical, or the ability to understand and use numbers and reason well

6 Musical

7 Naturalist intelligence, or the ability to organise and classify both the animal and plant kingdoms, as well as showing understanding of natural phenomena

8 Spatial, or the ability to perceive the visual-spatial world accurately.

These **intelligences** have captured the interest of many professional and been surrounded by much myth and claims. Gardner himself has attempted to clarify the many issues arising out of his theory (Gardner, 1999). In particular, he believes we should consider how experience and contextual influences affect and promote cognitive development.

It is therefore important that professionals supporting cognitive development start with the children's own ideas and encourage them to develop their own scientific ideas. This can be achieved by the provision of quality experiences, adult support and encouragement, and challenges to help them re-think their ideas. It may be that professional support and encouragement in the development of mental models can help not only in specific scientific understandings, but also in generic thinking skills throughout their lives. When children develop a mental model, they find their own ways of expressing a scientific phenomenon (Bliss *et al.*, 1992; Oversby, 2012), rather than being given an analogy that may lead to alternative conceptions, which are hard to challenge. Mental models are more effective if they develop from a wide range of activities that encourage the children to think for themselves. In the early years, this will involve professionals in challenging the children's ideas and getting them to test out their simple hypotheses, facilitating discussion of their ideas so they can compare them with the ideas of others, and encouraging them to make causal links between phenomena and their ideas.

It is also important that children are not pressurised to develop their ideas at an artificial rate. This may mean adapting cognitive learning objectives to match individual learning needs or removing artificial obstacles that stand in the way of the developing child (see Shayer & Adey, 2002), so that children are allowed to develop in their own way and at their own rate and are not affected by theoretical notions of cognitive development.

CASE STUDY

Young children have intuitive ideas about materials and they are initially guided in their ideas by their senses (Harlen, 2012) and everyday experiences (Johnston, 2005). For example:

- They do not think that air has mass.
- They think gas is a fuel, rather than a state of matter.
- They think liquid is something specific, such as washing up liquid, rather than anything in a liquid state.

Case study (*continued*)

- They think solid is synonymous with 'hard', so salt and play-dough are not solids.

In this case study, a group of 8-year-old children explored different materials in order to develop their understanding of states of matter. They started by exploring different balloons filled with air, water and ice and seeing how heavy they were, how they floated or not and what happened when they were dropped. They then moved on to testing different substances and seeing what happened when they were mixed together. The substances included:

- a collection of solids including cornflour, salt, sugar, plaster of Paris, jelly powder (powder that, when mixed with water, makes a jelly), artificial snow, wallpaper paste (with no fungicide), bicarbonate of soda
- a collection of liquids including a large jug of water, vinegar, colour-change bubble bath, oil, lemon juice.

The children decided to mix each material with a little bit of water and noticed that:

- the salt and sugar 'disappeared';
- the cornflour was 'a little bit hard and a little runny';
- the plaster of Paris went 'hot', the jelly powder went 'wobbly, like jelly';
- the snow was 'cold and bigger';
- the wallpaper paste was 'gooey';
- the oil 'floated';
- the bubble bath 'changed colour'.

They also mixed some of the other materials together and noticed that:

- the bicarbonate of soda when mixed with vinegar 'fizzed';
- when lemon juice was added to the bubble-bath and water it 'changed colour again'.

They recorded the results of the tests in a table on a white board and later the professional encouraged them to tell the rest of the class what they had found out. She presented the children with some scientific terms (melting, solidifying, dissolving, floating) and they provided a definition for each one and decided if they had examples of any of them. Finally, she asked them if any of the changes that they had made to the materials were fixed or could be reversed.

Practical and reflective tasks

Early career professional
- What do you understand by the following terms: dissolve, melt, solidify, solution, chemical change, physical change, viscous liquid? Write a definition for each.
- How do you need to develop your own understanding in order to effectively support children's cognitive development?
- How could the professional develop the children's thinking so they have a more developed understanding of materials and how they can change?

Developing career professional/teacher

- What scientific understandings do professionals need to effectively support children's cognitive development about materials? Identify how you can develop those understandings.
- What further experiences could the professional use to develop understandings of materials?
- Try out some of the ideas with children in your class. How effective were you at developing their understandings?

Later career professional/leader

- What staff development do professionals in your school need in order to support children's cognitive development about materials? How will you access this?
- How could professionals evaluate their teaching and formatively assess the children's understandings of materials?
- Set up an activity with children for all classes in your setting and as a group evaluate staff understandings and teaching and assess children's understandings of materials. How does this identify future staff development needs? This activity can be set in a number of contexts (see, for example, Johnston, 2005, 2010), such as a potions lesson from Harry Potter (Rowling, 1997), a chemist shop, a science laboratory.

Photograph 2.3 Children exploring materials and their properties

Knowledge box

Changing materials

There are two types of changes that occur in materials, physical and chemical change. Physical change is when materials change state (e.g. from a liquid to a gas or a solid to a liquid) and is reversible. Some materials may appear to be in one state when they are actually in another – for example, glass or pitch appears solid but over long periods of time will run like a liquid. These are called viscous liquids. Cornflour mixed with water forms a type of viscous liquid that will run through your hand but will appear solid under pressure.

Chemical change is where the material changes by combining with another material to form a new material or through decomposition, e.g. when it rusts or combusts. Both these changes involve energy. Energy used to heat water will, at 100°C, be used to change the state from liquid to gas, rather than raise the temperature (this is called latent energy). Plaster of Paris, when mixed with water, re-forms into gypsum and releases heat energy.

Some materials mix together but do not change, becoming instead a mixture. Salt and sugar dissolve (form a solution with water) but do not change state or substance and the process can be reversed (the salt and sugar crystals can be recovered when the water evaporates).

Further activities on mixing and changing materials (baking activities) can be found in Chapter 1.

ACTIVITIES AND KEY QUESTIONS

To promote understanding of ourselves and others

- Outside our bodies – explore with children the way they look at and compare themselves with others in the class and in other parts of the world **(see Figure 2.2)**.
  Key question: What are the similarities and differences between you and others?

- Body mapping (see the section on the developing child)
  Key question: What does the brain/stomach/heart do?

- Listen to your heart using a stethoscope and then jump up and down for 5 minutes before listening again.
  Key question: What happens to my heart after exercise?

- Put a photo album and family photographs and baby photographs in the home corner. Children can explore the family photographs and put them into the photo album. Children can also add the photographs to a family tree on the wall of the home area.
  Key question: Who is the eldest/youngest? How can you tell the people are in a family/ related?

- Set up an exploratory table that includes things for the children to feel, smell, taste, see and hear. You could focus on one of the senses for each day of the week. Ideas for the table for each sense are:
  - Feeling – fabric squares (woolly, furry, plastic, cotton), plastic mirror, trays of cornflour and water, cornflour, salt, play-dough, plasticine, finger paint

> **Activities and key questions (*continued*)**
>
> - Smelling – small amounts of play-dough with added essential oils (lavender, peppermint, eucalyptus, rose)
> - Tasting – slices of fruit (try some more exotic fruits as well as ones the children will have tasted before)
> - Seeing – objects of different colours and shades of colours and coloured sorting hoops, mirrors, magnifying glasses, binoculars
> - Hearing – sound lotto games, musical instruments, stethoscopes, funnels, large plastic tubes.
> **Key questions:** What does it feel like? What can you see/hear/taste?

References

Alexander, R. (2008). *Towards Dialogic Teaching: Rethinking Classroom Talk*, 4th edn. York: Dialogos.

Alexander, R. (ed.) (2010). *Children, their World, their Education: Final Report and Recommendations of the Cambridge Review*. London: Routledge.

Allen, P. (1986). *Mr Archimedes' Bath*. London: Hamish Hamilton.

Bliss, J., Mellar, H., Ogborn, J. & Nash, C. (1992). *Tools for Exploratory Learning Programme End of Award Report: Technical Report 2. Semi Quantitative Reasoning-Expressive*. London: University of London.

Bruner, J.S. (1991). The narrative construction of reality. *Critical Inquiry*, 18(1), 1–21.

Bruner, J.S., Goodnow, J.J. & Austin, G.A. (1956). *A Study of Thinking*. New York: Wiley.

Cazden, C. (2001). *Classroom Discourse: the Language of Teaching and Learning*. Portsmouth, NH: Heinemann.

Department of Education and Science (DES) (1967). *Children and their Primary school. A Report of the Central Advisory Council for Education (England) Vol. 1: Report*. London: HMSO.

Department for Education and Skills (DfES) (2003). *Every Child Matters*. London: DfES.

Driver, R. (1983). *The Pupil as a Scientist*. Milton Keynes: Open University Press.

Effective Provision of Pre-school Education (EPPE) (2002). Measuring the Impact of Pre-School on Children's Cognitive Progress over the Pre-School Period. *The EPPE (Effective Provision of Pre-school Education) Project Technical Paper 8a*. London: Institute of Education.

Effective Provision of Pre-school Education (EPPE) (2003). Measuring the Impact of Pre-School on Children's Cognitive Progress over the Pre-School Period. *The EPPE (Effective Provision of Pre-school Education) Project Technical Paper 8b*. London: Institute of Education.

Erduran, S. (2012). The role of dialogue and argumentation. In: Oversby, J., ed. *ASE Guide to Research in Science Education*. Hatfield: ASE.

Gardner, H. (1983). *Frames of Mind: The Theory of Multiple Intelligence* 2nd edn. London: Heinemann.

Gardner, H. (1999.) *The Disciplined Mind: Beyond Facts And Standardised Tests, The K-12 Education that Every Child Deserves*. New York: Simon and Schuster.

Harlen, W. (2012). What do we know about learners' ideas at the primary level? In: Oversby, J. (ed). *ASE Guide to Research in Science Education*. Hatfield: ASE.

Johnston, J.S. (2009). How does the skill of observation develop in young children. *International Journal of Science Education*, 31(18), 2511–2525.

Johnston, J. (2005). *Early Explorations in Science, 2nd Edition*. Buckingham: Open University Press.

Johnston, J. (2010). A topic approach in Key Stage 1 – an example. In: Kerry, T., ed. *Thematic Teaching for the 21st Century*. London: Routledge.

Johnston, J. (2011). Children talking; teachers supporting science. *Journal of Emergent Science* 1, 14–22.

Johnston, J. (2012). Analysing data. In: Oversby, J., ed. *ASE Guide to Research in Science Education*. Hatfield: ASE.

Johnston, J. & Gray, A. (1999). *Enriching Early Scientific Learning.* Buckingham: Open University Press.

Johnston, J. & Halocha, J. (2010). *Early Childhood and Primary Education; Readings and Reflections* Maidenhead: Open University Press.

Kallery, M., Psillos, D. & Tselfes, V. (2009). Typical didactical activities in the Greek early years science classroom: do they promote science learning? *International Journal of Science Education*, 31(9), 1187–1204.

Mercer, N. (2000). *Words and Minds: How we Use Language to Think Together.* London: Routledge.

Montessori, M. (1994). *From Childhood to Adolescence*. Oxford, England: ABC-Clio.

Montessori, M. (1967*). The Absorbent Mind.* New York: Delta.

Oldfield, L. (2001). *Free to Learn. Introducing Steiner Waldorf Early Childhood Education.* Stroud, Gloucestershire: Hawthorn Press.

Osborne, J., Erduran, S. & Simon, S. (2004). *Ideas, Evidence and Argument in Science*. (IDEAS) Project London: Kings College London.

Oversby, J. (2012). Modelling as part of a scientific investigation. In: Oversby, J. (ed). *ASE Guide to Research in Science Education.* Hatfield: ASE.

Piaget, J. (1929). *The Child's Conception of the World.* New York: Harcourt.

Piaget, J. (1950). *The Psychology of Intelligence*. London: Routledge and Kegan Paul.

Reiss, M.J. & Tunnicliffe, S.D. (2001). Students' understandings of human organs and organ systems. *Research in Science Education*, 31, 383–399.

Rogoff, B. (1995). Observing sociocultural activity on three planes: participatory appropriation, guided participation, and apprenticeship. In: Wertsch, J.V., Del Rio, P. & Alvarex, A., eds. *Sociocultural Studies of Mind*. Cambridge, UK: Cambridge University Press, pp. 139–164.

Rowling, J.K. (1997). *Harry Potter and the Philosopher's Stone.* London: Bloomsbury.

Russell, T. & Watt, D. (1990). *Primary SPACE Project Research Report – Growth*. Liverpool: Liverpool University Press.

Schön, D. (1983). *The Reflective Practitioner, How Professionals Think in Action*. London: Temple Smith.

Scott, P. (1987). A *Constructivist View of Teaching & Learning Science.* Leeds: Leeds University.

Shayer, M. & Adey, P (eds.) (2002). *Learning Intelligence. Cognitive Acceleration Across the Curriculum from 5 to 15 Years*. Buckingham: Open University Press.

Siraj-Blatchford, I. (2009). Conceptualising progression in the pedagogy of play and sustained shared thinking in early childhood education: A Vygotskian perspective. *Educational & Child Psychology*, 26(2), 77–89.

Siraj-Blatchford, I., Sylva, K., Muttock, S., Gilden, R., & Bell, D. (2002). *Researching Effective Pedagogy in the Early Years.* Nottingham: DfES.

Spearman, C. (1927). *Abilities of Man.* Basingstoke: Macmillan.

Steiner, R. (1996). *The Education of the Child and Early Lectures on Education.* New York: Anthroposophic Press.

Stone, C.A. (1993). *Contexts for Learning; Sociocultural Dynamics in Children's Development.* New York: Oxford University Press: 169–183.

Thurstone, L.L. & Thurstone, T.G. (1941). Factorial studies of intelligence. *Psychometric Monographs* No.2. Chicago: University of Chicago Press.

Toulmin, S. (1958). *The Uses of Argument.* Cambridge: Cambridge University Press.

Tunnicliffe, S.D. (2007). No time to teach life saving skills? Essential first aid within biology lessons. *Journal of Biological Education*, 42(1), 3–4.

Tunnicliffe, S.D. & Reiss, M.J. (1999). Students' understandings about animal skeletons. *International Journal of Science Education*, 21(11), 1187–1200.

Vygotsky, L. (1962). *Thought and Language.* Cambridge. MA: MIT Press.

Wells, G. (1987). *The Meaning Makers.* London: Hodder and Stoughton.

Wilson, K. (2007). *Bear Feels Sick*. London: Simon & Schuster.

Chapter 3

The development of emergent attitudes

Overview

In this chapter we look at:

- **Affective development** in the early years, or the development of emergent attitudes, using Bronfenbrenner's (1995) ecological systems theory
- Research into stories and motivation by John Oversby
- Writing a literature review, as part of the study skills theme
- Reflective tasks involving analysis of affective development in policy, professional and research texts
- Practical tasks and activity boxes focusing on exploring materials and their properties and on promoting sensitivity to and responsibility for the living world
- A knowledge box focusing on materials and their properties.

Introduction

This chapter begins with a case study from which emergent attitudes are identified – these are then explored more deeply later in the chapter.

CASE STUDY

Working with wool: washing, dyeing, carding and spinning

A class of 7-year-old children visited a farm and watched a sheep being sheared. The farmer gave them the fleece and they took it back to school to explore and use in various ways.

Back in school, the children worked in small groups and each child was given a pair of surgical gloves and a handful of the fleece to look at more closely. The children removed any bits of debris from the fleece and used a hand lens or digital microscope, attached to a computer, to observe anything found in the fleece more closely. (Note that gloves are needed for health reasons in case there are any bacteria on the fleece, but care also

Case study (*continued*)

needs to be taken to ensure that children with allergies to wool or lanolin are protected during this activity.)

The children washed the fleece in detergent to clean it and remove oils, which floated on the surface of the water. Once clean, they used natural materials to dye the wool, by boiling (under supervision) a pan of water with the natural dye and the fleece added (King, 2000: 6–7).

The different colours can be achieved by using the following:

- Blue colours:
  - Blackberries
  - Elderberries
  - Sloe berries
  - Blueberries
  - Marjoram flower buds.
- Yellow colours:
  - Marigold
  - Onion skins
  - Stinging nettles
  - Lily of the valley leaves.
- Red colours:
  - Madder roots
  - Sorrel roots
  - Red cabbage leaves.
- Green colours:
  - Apple bark
  - Bracken
  - Privet leaves
  - Tomato leaves and stems.
- Beige colours:
  - Dock leaves
  - Heather
  - Lichen
  - Crushed pine cones.
- Brown colours:
  - Crushed and soaked walnut shells
  - Elder leaves
  - Dock leaves.

The resulting dyed fleece was dried on a washing line outside the classroom door; a hairdryer could have been used to dry it more quickly, or different washing,

dyeing and drying methods could have been compared. When the fleece was dry, the children carded the wool (see Bird & Catherall, 1977) and made some simple spindles to enable them to spin it **(see Figure 3.1)**. The spun wool was then used to knit or weave. Those who chose to weave made simple card weaving 'looms' **(see Figure 3.2)**. If weaving, you can use raw wool or strips of fabric as well as the spun wool.

Through the activities the children developed scientific knowledge and understanding of the life of a sheep, where wool comes from and how it can change through washing, dyeing, carding and spinning (life processes and living things; materials and how they change). They were able to make links between the wool their jumpers are made of and a sheep's fleece (one child went home and told her parents with great glee: 'Wool comes from a sheep!'). They also developed exploratory

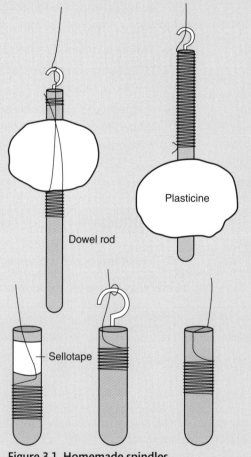

Figure 3.1 Homemade spindles
Source: Bird & Catherall (1977: 32)

Case study (continued)

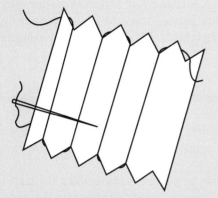

Figure 3.2 A simple card weaving 'loom'
Source: Bird & Catherall (1977: 32)

skills, particularly observational and reflective skills. Most importantly, they were highly motivated, engaged throughout and had a sense of achievement through an outcome they had created. Indeed, woven wall hangings were put on walls as decorations at home and knitted squares were made into a snuggle blanket that was displayed on the wall in the class and then used as a snuggle blanket in the story/library area of the class.

Reflective tasks

Early career professional
- What attitudes were the children developing in the activities described?

- Why are these attitudes important in the success of the activities?
- How can you improve your planning to support the development of attitudes?

Developing career professional/teacher
- Can you group the attitudes that could be developed in the case study to those that motivate children to explore and learn and those that support reflection and thinking?
- What do you consider to be the main attitudes that affect learning?
- How can you develop motivational and reflective attitudes in your teaching?

Later career professional/leader
- Can you group the attitudes that might be developed in the case study to those that motivate children to explore and learn, those that support social engagement, those needed for practical work and those that support reflection and thinking?
- How do you think the development of attitudes is linked to the development of skills and understandings?
- How can your school/setting support the development of attitudes throughout the school?

What are attitudes?

In everyday life we use the term 'attitude' in a vague way or in relation to how we feel about something or affective responses. However, attitudes are more complex than that and can be said to have three components (the tri-component view of attitudes, as in the ABC model of attitudes): affective, behavioural and cognitive.

Affective attitudes are those that are linked to emotions and emotional development, e.g. enthusiasm, timidity, negativity, animosity, and include those attitudes needed to motivate children to explore the world around them. **Behavioural attitudes** are those that can be seen in behaviours, such as cooperation, collaboration, tolerance, aggression, assertiveness, flexibility, independence, perseverance, caring, leadership, responsibility and tenaciousness, and are closely linked to social skills. **Cognitive attitudes** are ones that are needed in the development of knowledge and understanding, such as curiosity, respect for evidence, thoughtfulness, reflection, tentativeness and questioning, and are closely linked to interpretation from enquiry. The relationship between the affective, behavioural and cognitive is complex, so that what you think is a direct result of how you feel and how you behave, and how you behave is a result of how you feel and what you think. Ajzen's (1991) Theory of Planned Behaviour recognises that attitudes combine with subjective norms (perceived expectations) and perceived control to influence a person's actions and so acknowledges the complexity of the attitude–behaviour link and an attitude–intention–behaviour sequence.

Affective attitudes

Affective attitudes are those that influence the way we feel about science and science education and learning in general. In the preceding case study, the children felt good about both the process and the product of their activity. This is an important element in creative activities, such as when children use their imagination in play and also when they can see situations from another person's perspectives.

Activities to explore the fleece of sheep can be stimulated by reading the story of the *Snow Lambs* (Glori, 1995), allowing the children to put themselves into the position of the child whose sheepdog is missing and to experience the joy of finding the missing lamb. Cassius, a 3-year-old child in a nursery class, was read the story by the professional working with him and he later used parts of the story when he took a stuffed sheepdog, rounded up another child dressed up as a sheep, made a box into a kennel and put out food and water for the dog, patting him and saying: 'Good dog – he likes it when we say that.' In this way Cassius showed an understanding of the role of a sheepdog and the needs of the dog and empathised with the dog's need for praise.

Other books, such as *Wonderful Earth* (Butterworth & Inkpen, 1991) for younger children and *Where the Forest Meets the Sea* (Baker, 1987) for older children, can stimulate learning about the natural environment and link to behavioural and cognitive attitudes such as respect for living things.

Children need to be motivated to want to learn and explore the world around them, including the everyday scientific phenomena they experience. Motivated children feel good about themselves and are curious about the world around them, initiating enquiry, with enthusiasm, from their observations and questioning what they observe. Curiosity and questioning have cognitive elements and so the link between affective and cognitive attitudes is evident when children embark on a scientific exploration. Although very young children display curiosity about their world, they can become less curious as they get older. This may be for a number of reasons. Sometimes they are discouraged from being too curious, in the interests of health and safety. Modern children are often less able to take the initiative and explore for themselves because modern life can be overly rushed and over-supervised (Elkind, 2001). This is felt to be seriously damaging to their emotional development (Palmer, 2006) and can adversely affect their scientific development. Some children are reticent by temperament and this can cause difficulties when trying to encourage exploration. However, a child's reticence may disguise an innate curiosity. For quiet children, or those lacking in self-confidence, transitions from home to carers, to new classes and new schools can adversely affect their development, as their reticence may result in a lack of curiosity and inhibit their explorations and scientific development.

Other children may have been discouraged from being too curious by adults or previous experiences. For example, many eager young children (often boisterous boys) may have had their enthusiasm curbed. If over-zealous curiosity is suppressed it may result in the child deciding not to be curious or, at least, overtly curious in the future. As we discovered in Chapter 1, very young children can spend long periods of time observing and exploring and it is demotivating to prevent them from doing this. Despite this, we rush them from one experience to another in our hurried curriculum and outside lives (Elkind, 2001) and so adversely affect their motivation and development. Older children and those who have been allowed more autonomy and to make decisions about what interests them, as well as dictating the pace of their explorations, can sustain their interest for longer periods of time, and it is often at this stage that they begin to ask a multitude of questions that are seemingly impossible to answer.

Affective attitudes will determine the way we feel about scientific activity. This is complex, as scientific attitudes are not a single construct and can be affected by many factors (see the section on 'Factors affecting attitudes' later in this chapter). Fraser (1981) identified seven separate constructs which together contribute to the way we feel about science:

1 Whether we see that science has social implications or plays a part in our lives and society
2 Whether we see scientists as 'normal' individuals, or are influenced by stereotypical images as portrayed by the media **(see Figure 3.3)**
3 The way we feel about scientific enquiry, or whether we enjoy enquiry
4 Whether we have the attitudes (affective, behavioural and cognitive) needed to be scientific
5 Whether we enjoy science
6 Whether science is a leisure interest
7 Whether we are considering science as a career.

In the early part of this century, research into attitudes in science proliferated (e.g. Bricheno *et al.*, 2001) and seemed to indicate that children have positive attitudes towards science, although their interest in science did not affect their choices for further study and their attitudes later in life. In more recent research (Oversby, 2012), attitudes are less overt and incorporated into work on the nature of science (Taber, 2012). The basic

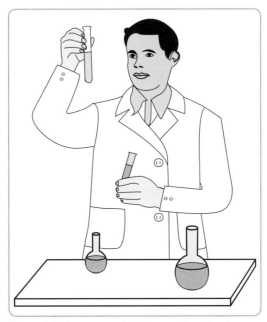

Figure 3.3 A stereotypical image of a scientist

view, however, is unchanged: positive attitudes towards science are needed for both the individual child and also for society. For individual children, a positive attitude helps them to see the part science plays in their own lives and also supports their scientific development throughout their lives. Negative attitudes lead to poor achievement and hamper children throughout their lives. Positive attitudes, on the other hand, lead to a greater understanding of science and scientific literacy, i.e. the ability to apply science in enquiry (OECD, 2003).

In society, science and technological development are essential components in economic growth and environmental sustainability and so it is important that children develop positive attitudes towards science and understand the part it plays in their lives. Nevertheless, the increase in scientific literacy throughout society over the last few decades does not appear to have had a significant effect on attitudes towards science (Fensham, 2001).

STUDY SKILLS

Writing a literature review

Writing is not something that merely happens at the end of the research process, but is an important and integral part of the process itself. Writing should accompany each step in the process and should begin at the earliest opportunity. It is important that reading and collecting reading do not become an excuse to avoid writing. Writing and reorganising writing help to clarify thinking, make writing less difficult and thus support the research process. As writing progresses, a logical structure will emerge. It is very important in the writing process to keep accurate references of your reading, to avoid wasting time and effort and having to abandon useful reading simply because it cannot be located.

The structure of the literature review is often in three parts: introduction, main body and conclusion. The introduction should present the area of research, perhaps providing an overview of the area and key issues and setting the context for the review. This may involve an historical overview of events in the area leading up to the present day. The main body of the review will include the main milestones in the development of major concepts, influential studies and analysis of past research. If the area is well researched, there can be some sorting of research for relevance, and the focus can be narrowed to studies closest to the research area being undertaken. If the area is under-researched, there may be a need to make links between the current problems and research in similar areas or with different age groups. Both too much and too little research are problematic, but either can lead to a good and critical review. In this way, the gap in the research and how the current research fills that gap can be identified.

Reflective tasks

In writing the review, consider the criteria by which it will be judged. One important criterion will be the selection of the literature and whether it matches the scope and purpose of the review. The literature selected should comprise a balanced coverage of the available texts and include the most recent and most relevant research studies. All the reading needs to be well referenced. The review will also be judged by whether the order, themes and ideas are logically sorted and deeply critiqued and whether it moves seamlessly from the general to the specific, identifying the place of the current research in the overall area. A third criterion will be your ability to summarise and interpret the literature, so that the review provides a justification for current research questions posed.

Look at some writing you are engaged in and consider the following questions:

- How well does your work summarise and interpret the literature?
- How well does your writing address the research questions?
- How well does your work make links among policy, practice and research?
- Have you provided a deep and analytical critique of literature? How?
- How accurate are your references? Check, as there are always some errors in every piece of writing.

Behavioural attitudes

Behavioural attitudes are those that affect social behaviour and social skills. They include attitudes such as **cooperation** (working alongside others), **collaboration** (working with others), taking responsibility for one's actions, respect for others (including living things), being independent in one's exploration, and persevering when a scientific activity does not work in the expected way.

Formal and informal learning settings require children to be able to work and play with others, and whatever science experiences we set up for them (e.g. observations, explorations, role-play, problem-solving activities) require them to work either with or alongside other children. Play can be useful in supporting social development (Bruner *et al.*, 1976; Broadhead *et al.*, 2010; Johnston & Halocha, 2010). Young children will play alongside each other (parallel play) before they begin to play cooperatively and often need to be encouraged or to have opportunities provided to enable them to play and cooperate, and this involves allowing them to explore relationships, make friends, fall out and so on (Broadhead *et al.*, 2010). Broadhead's (2006) research identifies that children's play helps professionals to come to a better understanding of how friendship and relationship are integral to learning.

Opportunities for the development of behavioural attitudes and social development in general can be more difficult as children mature, as scientific experiences are formalised and opportunities to explore social boundaries and learn from behavioural mistakes do not come along as often. In addition, we sometimes expect children to be able to cooperate or even collaborate in scientific enquiry without any support or previous experience. As we know, many adults find it difficult to work with others!

CASE STUDY

Ice balloons

A class of 4-year-old Reception children were sitting on a carpet in a circle and the teacher passed around an ice balloon (a balloon filled with water and then frozen) wrapped in layers of newspaper. As the children passed the balloon around, they described what it felt like and unwrapped one layer. Lizze said the parcel was 'heavy', Hopeton that it was 'big' and, as it was unwrapped, Mary said it was 'cold' and Lawrie that is was 'wet'.

Once the balloon was unwrapped, the children were given balloons, one for each group of four, and they were asked to work together to explore the balloon. Lizzie, Hopeton, Mary and Lawrie were working together and at first the ice still had the balloon stuck to it. Hopeton noticed that the balloon was 'torn and not stretchy' and Lizzie that it was 'frozen on the outside'. Mary noticed that the balloon was 'see-through' at the edges but not in the middle. Lizzie said it looked as though a 'frozen hedgehog was stuck inside'. Hopeton said it was his turn now and he wanted to see but Lawrie said 'we need to share'. The teacher agreed and told the children to look and listen very carefully as she put salt on the ice balloon. All four children got very excited as they heard the ice crack and saw 'sparks'. 'Listen to that!' said Lizzie and Mary said it sounded like her 'rice crispies'.

The teacher encouraged the children to take turns to listen with a stethoscope and then Hopeton noticed the ice had 'cuts in it', as the salt had melted rivulets in the surface and made it look 'pretty'. He used a magnifying glass to look at these more closely and then let the others have a look as well. Lawrie noticed that a small mound of salt had frozen on the surface of the balloon and all the children felt it.

Reflective tasks

Early career professional

- What are the affective and behavioural attitudes seen in the children?
- How did the affective attitudes influence the behavioural attitudes?

Case study (*continued*)

- How could you develop your own teaching to support the development of both affective and behavioural attitudes?

Developing career professional/teacher
- How could you develop more collaboration between the children?
- How could the affective elements of the activity support greater collaboration?
- How could you modify/extend the activity so that affective attitudes support the development of independence?

Later career professional/leader
- How could you use an ice balloon activity to develop other behavioural attitudes, such as independence, perseverance and respect for others?
- How does the affective aspect of the activity affect general behaviour?
- How can your school/setting support the development of behavioural attitudes throughout the school?

Further activities with ice balloons

Early Years Foundation Stage (EYFS)
- Allow the children to explore the ice balloon and encourage them to ask questions about the balloons.
- Let them explore the difference between ice-filled, water-filled and air-filled balloons when in a water trough or when dropped outside. Ask them what they notice about the different balloons.
- Let them explore what happens when an ice balloon is put in water and how the ice melts and changes when left in the water.
- Liquid paint or food colouring can be dripped on to an ice balloon after sprinkling with salt and the resulting patterns observed.
- A coloured ice balloon (made by adding a few drops of paint before freezing) can be put in water and the children asked what they think will happen or is happening to it.

Key Stage 1
- Children can be encouraged to raise questions about the balloons and these can be put on washing lines across the classroom or on a working wall. They can be encouraged to answer their own and each other's questions.
- Children can work in groups and set questions for the next group to answer. They can bring their findings to a whole group discussion after the exploration and new questions can be set for the group to answer through exploration.
- Children can explore what happens if they leave an ice balloon on a tray on a table, what happens when it is in water and what happens when it is dropped and then compare the results.
- Torches can be used to explore how light passes through ice.
- The ice balloon can be used to explore friction by sliding it across different surfaces.

Key Stage 2
- Children can raise investigable questions that they can then begin to answer through enquiry.
- Use thermometers to measure the temperature of the outside of the ice balloon. Drill a hole in the balloon and compare the temperature inside the balloon.
- Put ice on the balloon and see what happens to the temperature.
- Carry out an investigation to see what happens to the temperature of the balloon over time. Record the results on a class chart on a working wall.
- Set up opportunities for children to discuss the findings of their investigations and encourage the development of argument, using evidence from their investigations.

Knowledge box

Material and its properties

When water freezes, it changes state from a liquid to a solid. Solid water (like other solids) has a crystalline structure with regular patterns to the atoms. The molecules of solid water vibrate to and fro, alternately attracting and repelling. In liquid water the molecules vibrate as in solid ice but are free to move among other molecules and can therefore take any shape.

When water is heated up to 100°C, it begins to change state from a liquid to a gas. In a gas, the molecules are much further apart than in solids and liquids. The molecules move at high velocities, colliding with each other, and are free to expand to fill any vessel and can be compressed into smaller containers. These changes of state involve latent energy used to change the state and not the temperature. When you put salt on ice, you change the temperature at which it changes state and so the temperature will continue to lower until it reaches about 12°C (this is when water is at full salinity) and then the salt water will refreeze. This is why salt is not put on roads in very cold climates as the ice will melt and then refreeze leaving black ice.

When water freezes it also expands – hence pipes with frozen water often burst. The first part of an ice balloon that freezes is the outside (as with ice cubes taken out of the freezer too soon) and this expands leaving a clear, transparent outside of the ice balloon. The inside of the balloon freezes last and cannot expand easily because of the frozen exterior. If the outside is thick, the inside may be an opaque ball of ice that is denser than the outside and sometimes there are radiating spikes of air coming out of the ball. If the outside ice is thinner, the pressure from the expanding freezing middle will create cracks and fissures within the outside layers of the ice balloon.

Element. A substance which cannot be split into simpler substances (e.g. oxygen, hydrogen and carbon).

Atom. The smallest part of an element. All atoms of an element are identical but different from atoms of another element (oxygen is made up of oxygen atoms O, hydrogen is made up of hydrogen atoms H and carbon is made up of carbon atoms C).

Molecule. Groups or compounds of atoms of various elements which, when in numerical proportion, make up new materials (e.g. water is made up of two hydrogen atoms and one oxygen atom, H_2O, and carbon dioxide is made up of one atom of carbon and two of oxygen, CO_2).

Practical and reflective tasks

Early career professional
Look at some current or older policy documents such as the EYFS curriculum (Department for Education, 2012), *Excellence and Enjoyment* [Department for Education and Skills (DfES), 2003a] or *Every Child Matters* (DfES, 2003b) and consider what they have to say about the importance of attitudes for learning. Compare these with your own experiences and write a short paragraph that identifies the main arguments.

- How well does your writing summarise and interpret the literature?
- How well does your work make links between policy and practice?
- How accurate are your references?

Developing career professional/teacher
Use policy documents as for the 'early career professional' and also professional books to see how affective development influences scientific development. Write a paragraph that identifies the tensions that exist between policy and professional practice.

- How well does your work summarise and interpret the literature?
- How well does your work make links between policy and practice?
- Have you provided a deep and analytical critique of literature? How?
- How accurate are your references?

Later career professional/leader

Use policy documents, professional books and research articles to develop persuasive arguments to answer the question: What is the link between affective development and scientific development? Write a page that identifies the tensions and ambiguities that exist among policy, professional practice and research.

- How well does your work summarise and interpret the literature?
- How well does your writing address the research question?
- How well does your work make links among policy, practice and research?
- Have you provided a deep and analytical critique of literature? How?
- How accurate are your references?

Cognitive attitudes

Cognitive attitudes are those that support the development of cognition **(see Chapter 2)**. These attitudes include curiosity and questioning, which also have an affective element (as discussed earlier), whilst others such as respect for evidence can be linked to behavioural attitudes as children learn to develop respect for the ideas of others as well as the evidence collected. Other cognitive attitudes include thoughtfulness, reflection and tentativeness. One affective and cognitive attitude is creativity, which is acknowledged throughout education (Beetlestone, 1998; Compton *et al.*, 2010; DfES, 2003) as being important in development and learning, as it involves making links or connections and taking intellectual/cognitive 'risks'. In this way creative early years science involves children in making links between scientific phenomena and thinking outside of the box. The Creative Little Scientists project (Creative Little Scientists, 2012) identified how teaching and learning using **inquiry-based science education** (IBSE)and approaches that foreground creativity (creative approaches) can enhance learning through common synergies such as:

- play and exploration
- motivation and affect
- dialogue and collaboration
- problem-solving and agency
- questioning and curiosity
- reflection and reasoning.

This helps to illustrate the links among affective, behavioural and cognitive attitudes.

Research

The Creative Little Scientists research project

Creative Little Scientists: Enabling Creativity through Science and Mathematics in Pre-school and First Years of Primary Education is a 2-year European Commission 7th Framework project, involving early years science and mathematics experts from Bishop Grosseteste University College Lincoln, UK, the Institute of Education, UK, the Open University, UK, the University of Eastern Finland, Artevelde University

---

Research (*continued*)

College in Belgium, Goethe University Frankfurt, the University of Minho in Portugal, the National Institute for Laser, Plasma and Radiation Physics in Romania, and the Université de Picardie Jules Verne, France, the University of Malta, and is led by academics from Ellinogermaniki Agogi in Greece.

The research was carried out in nine European countries, chosen because they represent a wide spectrum of educational, economic, social and cultural contexts, as well as a wide spectrum of practices regarding science and mathematics education in general, science and mathematics education in early years, and creativity in education. The project involved the construction of four literature reviews on:

- Science and mathematics in the early years
- Creativity in the early years
- Teacher education
- Comparative education.

These were used to write the conceptual framework for the project. The project then produced a review of policy across Europe, a questionnaire to schools, fieldwork in schools and the identification of directions for teacher training. More information about the project can be found at **http://www .creative-little-scientists.eu.**

Objectivity, an integral part of fair testing, is a very important cognitive attitude in science because, without it, the development of scientific skills, concepts and knowledge is impaired. In order for children to successfully interpret data in an unbiased way, they need to be objective. This is difficult for many adults, as well as children, especially in a society and educational system that sees success as getting correct answers; of course, science itself is not about correct answers **(see the Introduction)** but instead is a critical examination of theories about the world. When children and teachers are judged on their achievement in narrow cognitive areas of learning, as assessed by national tests, it is hardly surprising that children and adults do not see uncertainty as success and may attempt to modify results.

Harlen (2000: 78) identifies respect for evidence, however contradictory, as 'being central to scientific activity'. However, some people find it difficult to accept evidence that differs from what they expected and will sometimes provide explanations that align the evidence with their own thinking **(see Chapter 2)**. For example, a child who thinks that heavy things fall faster to the ground than light things, when presented with conflicting evidence such as a screwed-up sheet of paper versus a flat sheet, will often believe you have made the paper heavier by screwing it up. Older children will change results of scientific enquiry to fit their ideas. In one example of this (see Johnston, 2005), children investigated whether air has mass by seeing what happened to the point of balance on a stick when one of two balloons attached to the end of the stick was inflated. When the inflated balloon dropped, they decided the original point of balance was incorrect; their intuitive idea was that inflating a balloon makes it lighter. In this case, the evidence did little to help them change their ideas. We can help children to become more objective by encouraging them to evaluate their findings, discuss their ideas with others and begin to see contradictory evidence as opportunities and not threats.

As children examine evidence, they need to be sensitive to the ideas that others hold. Discussion, debate and dialogue may identify the different views that children hold and all partners in the discussion (adults and children) need to be sensitive to these alternative views **(see also Chapter 2)**. It is often the case that some children's ideas may appear bizarre

Photograph 3.1 Exploring whether air has mass

to an adult yet make perfect sense to them and, in some cases, they show more creative thought than the more adult way of thinking. For example, in solving problems, children often think of solutions that are quite appropriate and better than those that adults come up with (see the following Practical and reflective tasks box). They also need to develop a degree of tentativeness so they do not always see their ideas as correct and others as incorrect, even in the face of persuasive evidence to the contrary. Children need to be willing to consider evidence from alternative viewpoints and to change their ideas in the light of evidence.

Practical and reflective tasks

Practical tasks
Try out some problem-solving activities with children. In each case, give the children a problem to solve, ask them questions to support the problem-solving and challenge their thinking, and provide time for discussion about their findings.

Early Years Foundation Stage
For children in the EYFS you could pose the following problems:

- Make a plasticine boat that floats. How many marbles can you get in your boat?
- Make a waterproof hat for teddy or make an umbrella. What makes the hat/umbrella waterproof?
- Make a balancing teddy using half a table tennis ball filled with plasticine and a cut-out teddy on a straw **(see Figure 3.4)**. How can you get the teddy to stay upright?
- Make a musical instrument. How can you make different sounds?
- Make a bridge. Whose bridge will hold the most weight?

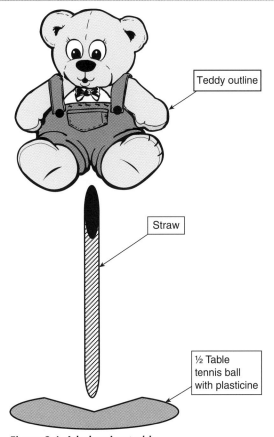

Figure 3.4 A balancing teddy

Key Stage 1

- Make a climbing man.

- Make a 1-minute timer. How could you make it time for longer (2 minutes)?

- Make a periscope so you can see round corners. How does the periscope work?

- Make a kaleidoscope. How does the kaleidoscope work?

- Which glove keeps our hands warmest/or an ice hand cold? **(See Chapter 1)** Why does the woolly/cotton/rubber glove keep the hand cold/warm?

Key Stage 2

- Make a helicopter. How can you make it fall faster/slower **(see Figure 3.5)**?

- Make a marble maze. The marble must travel through a table-top maze without being touched. Who can make the slowest marble maze?

- Make an electrical/magnetic game. How does your game work?

- Can you make a device to see around corners?

- Make a tall newspaper tower. What is the tallest tower you can make with five sheets? What is the tallest tower which will balance a ball on top?

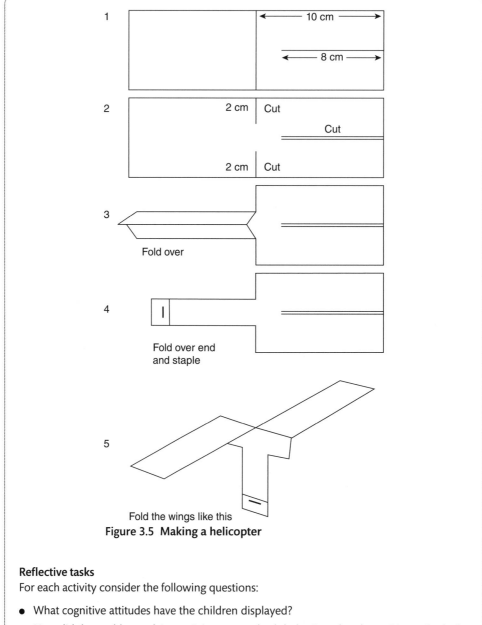

1

10 cm

8 cm

2

2 cm | Cut

Cut

2 cm | Cut

3

Fold over

4

Fold over end
and staple

5

Fold the wings like this

Figure 3.5 Making a helicopter

Reflective tasks

For each activity consider the following questions:

- What cognitive attitudes have the children displayed?
- How did the problem-solving activity support both behavioural and cognitive attitudes?
- How could you improve both cognition and the development of cognitive attitudes in further activities?

It is also necessary that children are sensitive towards and take responsibility for the world in which they live (Harlen, 2000), so they do no harm to the living world by, for example, picking plants, removing animals from their habitats or dropping litter. They need to realise that their actions can and do affect the world they live in. Activities involving exploration of the environment can help to support sensitive attitudes to the environment and foster a sense of responsibility towards plants and animals **(see Chapter 2)**. For more ideas about activities and key questions to promote sensitivity to and a responsibility for the living world, see the box at the end of the chapter.

Research

Using a philosophical mirror to see primary science activities in a new perspective

John Oversby

Introduction

Primary children regularly and frequently engage in philosophical questioning, exploring their world to answer questions such as: Why are some beetles beautiful? Is it better that we cooperate and respect each other? Sometimes the philosophical basis of the question remains implicit, and sometimes the discussion is extended by the teacher, such as asking why the children think it might be better to get along with their peers. I wish to take the latter approach to some scientific activities, and indicate how a subtle change in the question asked might lead children to some philosophical insights. This kind of thinking was prompted by my involvement in the European History and Philosophy in Science Teaching (HIPST) project. I was more concerned with helping children to understand how they were thinking, with considerable success among 11-year-old children. I am convinced they have application with even younger ones.

Classifying or induction

Induction as a philosophical procedure means taking many instances and creating a generalisation. Imagine children testing the electrical conductivity of different materials, using a simple circuit of wires, a battery and a light bulb. Of course, the pattern of conductors and non-conductors (whether the bulb lights or not) is quite easy to establish once they have got the hang of using the equipment. This is not quite induction yet, since they are replacing a narrative description with simple shorthand (conductors and insulators) as a form of classifying. However, providing different metallic objects as the only conductors may lead them into an inductive generalisation (it is the metals, or shiny things, that let the bulb light).

Care must be taken to help the children appreciate that this is so only for the selection the teacher has provided, and that an exception may be found later (a pencil lead is a good exception for this). I have found that many

children appreciate having a word (induction) for what they have just done, rather intuitively. Teaching them about the limitation of this process (it is so only for the things we have investigated) is an important part of the philosophising process.

In the European project we dealt with inducing the chemical concept of 'acid'. This particular example is probably outside the primary curriculum but the principles may well be applicable.

The value of induction is that it can be followed by deduction. Having found that metals let the bulb light (are conductors), they can begin to predict, by deduction before testing, that another example (such as the stirrup of an earring) may well be a conductor. Induction works best when many instances are available, as inducing from only one or two examples is not a strong induction. However, induction is always shaky, since there remains the possibility of an exception. Deduction depends on how well the induction process has been carried out.

Other examples of induction include reptiles having scales and birds having wings, or that foods rot and decay when left in the ground. Again, provision of many examples leads to stronger induction, and then to stronger deduction. An interesting illustration of the problem of not studying all examples is to look at mammals. Exclusion of humans leads to the induction that mammals have hair, and this can be explored with examples of exotic mammals to demonstrate induction. I have found it helpful to mention from time to time that they are now inducing, or deducing, as appropriate. Introducing humans as an example of a mammal (the naked ape, as Desmond Morris describes us) shows the limitation of inducing, a very important point, but it is also an excellent way of dealing with the issue of all mammals having hair, as a limitation of philosophy.

It is valuable for the teacher to make clear how much s/he thinks this is important, by making informal assessments of children's understanding (hands up with eyes closed in response to a question, such as showing

Research (*continued*)

a picture of an exotic mammal and asking whether they can be sure it is a mammal).

Idealisation and simplification

In the European project, this aspect featured the concept of an ideal acid. The principles have been transformed in the following for other examples. My favourite example of this process concerns the idea of a dog. Show a picture of a dog to the class and ask what it is (avoiding the likely response of a knowledgeable child naming the exact breed). After the response 'a dog', they can discuss (in groups or as a class) how they know. Collection of 'dog features' on observation only will produce a list of features. We can guess what this is likely to include (hair, four legs and ears). Pictures of other animals with these features will press the point of distinguishing a dog from similar mammals. Indeed, showing pictures of different breeds of dogs shows how much variation there is among all the animals that we categorise as dogs. Introduce the idea of an imaginary 'ideal dog' which has all the essential observable features of a dog. This construction of the essential elements of 'dog' uses the process of simplification, leaving out all the unimportant differences. This 'ideal dog' can then be used to deduce whether another instance is a dog. This example can, of course, be extended.

Other examples include:

- Types of food, e.g. vegetables
- Flowers
- States of matter, e.g. gas, liquid, solid
- Types of material, e.g. rock or metal.

Measuring

The final aspect in this interpretation of the European project is the idea that scientists measure. We found that 11-year-old children, when asked why scientists measure, simply said: 'Because they do!' However, we found that graduate scientists said much the same thing!

Measuring is a central part of much scientific activity, yet the reasons for doing it are rarely made explicit, not least in philosophical terms. It seems that scientists measure to enable meaningful comparison between different researchers working in different places, to establish patterns of behaviour and identify where these patterns break down, to test theories quantitatively, especially outside the normal range of working, and to explore concepts by creating instruments to measure.

We focused on the history of temperature measurement to explore the idea of what is temperature. Responses from both 11-year-olds and graduate scientists hardly got beyond 'hot and cold'. For readers of this chapter, my best understanding is that temperature measures intensity of heat (it is independent of quantity of material, unlike heat itself), and determines which way heat will move (hot to cold) and how fast it will move (it moves faster if the temperature difference is larger).

In the 17th century, scientists from the Royal Society were challenged to see if the fixed points for standardising thermometers (of the liquid in glass kind) were really fixed, as part of making thermometry reliable. There are issues of safety for children working on this. Beakers of boiling water must be secured to avoid knocking over. Thermometers are best fitted with a long string loop for lowering into boiling water, to avoid scalding. Children must be warned of the dangers of touching hot equipment. Nevertheless, with suitable precautions, children can work safely in these contexts and enjoy an element of controlled danger! Many of them, after all, are often close to, or helping with, cooking at home where boiling liquids abound. Working safely does not mean avoiding all risk – otherwise life could become very boring indeed.

One of the activities concerned de Luc's exploration of whether the temperature of boiling water in a container was the same at all points, and whether it was the same if a glass or metal container was being used. A steel saucepan can be used alongside other suitable containers for checking. De Luc found that there was a variation in what different people counted as boiling (first bubbles, a rolling boil, or a fierce boil) and that the boiling temperature varied throughout the liquid, and depended on whether it was heated from the side or the bottom. In school, a hot plate can be a suitable heater but remember to secure the container to avoid spillages of boiling water.

The outcome of this was that a standard procedure had to be specified to ensure that everyone was doing the same thing. De Luc suggested passing steam into the water until the temperature stopped changing, and specifying the length of the thermometer to be immersed. This is why you may see, on the back of long mercury-in-glass thermometers, 160 mm, which indicates the depth at which the thermometer should be immersed standardisation. De Luc also investigated different liquids in the thermometer. He took three: one with mercury, one with brandy, and one with light paraffin. Each one was standardised at the steam and ice points and a scale was marked off. When they were put into warm water, the mercury thermometer read 50, the

Research (*continued*)

brandy read 42, and the water read 29, on the Celsius scale. So the liquid mattered, and they wondered which, if any, was correct. Eventually, it turned out that none was exactly right!

This exploration of what should have been a straightforward task illustrates the problem of finding out what temperature really is, and how the creation of thermometers helped scientists to understand the idea a little better.

Factors affecting attitudes

There are a number of important influences on children's attitudes which can affect the way attitudes develop and how they may change. In looking at these influences, we will look at Bronfenbrenner's (1995) ecological systems theory **(see Figure 4.1)**. In this theory, the microsystem is the closest system to the individual child and involves the child's immediate surroundings: their immediate family, their immediate carers and the community in which they live and play. The microsystem influences the way a child feels, behaves and thinks and so children whose microsystem displays positive attitudes are likely to be encouraged through positive reinforcement. Gender differences due to the microsystem's influence can play a part in developing and reinforcing attitudes, so a boy may be more likely to be encouraged to persevere and explore scientific phenomena and a girl may be more likely to be encouraged to be sensitive to the environment. As children develop, they are more likely to develop social relationships with other children whose attitudes are congruent with those of their family. The development of attitudes towards science is thought to occur early (Smail, 1984) and be affected by the toys children are given and then reinforced through interactions with others as they develop.

The next system is the mesosystem, which is once removed from the individual child and involves interactions among different parts of the child's microsystem – home, school, childcare, family – which affect the child's social and psychological development. If the attitudes from the child's home and family do not resonate with those of the school, this can lead to dissonance. Festinger's (1957) cognitive dissonance theory indicates that when behaviours and attitudes are not compatible there is cognitive dissonance and this is unpleasant. It can stimulate a change of attitudes, especially where the child can think about the cause of the problem and behaviours are reinforced in school. For example, a child may come from a family of smokers and learn through school and interaction with others about the health effects of smoking. They may develop a respect for the environment and learn not to drop litter and encourage their family to recycle and compost.

In early years settings, affective, behavioural and cognitive attitudes can be developed in a number of ways. Children in the EYFS can play with or explore a range of materials, such as trays of sand, cornflour, cornflour and water, homemade play-dough (see the Activities and key questions box that follows), artificial snow, soap flakes and jelly. Children find this tactile activity very motivating and can spend long periods of time playing with the materials; on one occasion, a 3-year-old in a nursery spent an hour playing with dry cornflour and the ecstatic look on his face showed the affective nature of the activity. Older children can make their own play-dough, adding scents, flowers or sparkles. Lavender essence and lavender flowers can be very calming, frankincense and stars can be appropriate at Christmas and rose water and rose petals in the summer. I have made and used scented play-dough successfully with children with special educational needs and those with behavioural problems. Indeed, many of the activities below will support affective attitudes and motivate children. Where children explore cooperatively, they will develop good behavioural attitudes, and where they discuss what they feel and find out about the materials, they will also develop cognitive attitudes. However, care needs to be taken as some children do not like to get messy and others may worry about being reprimanded for messing up their clothes, causing some dissonance between home and school. In these cases, the gap between home and school can be bridged by the use of aprons, a parent workshop to experience school activities and the learning that they support and/or parent newsletters.

ACTIVITIES AND KEY QUESTIONS

To promote understanding of materials and their properties

Early Years Foundation Stage

- Sand play – in the sand tray or in a role-play of the seaside encourage children to sieve sand, pour it through funnels or a sand wheel, make sandcastles and compare wet and dry sand **(see Chapter 2)**.
  Key question: What do you think will happen when you...? Is wet or dry sand better to make castles? Why?

- Water play – children explore what happens when they add a range of materials (including bath bombs and colour-change bubble bath, coloured ice balloons) to a water trough as part of water play.
  Key questions: What do you think will happen when you . . . put this in the water/stir the water? Why do you think that has happened?

- What clothes does Teddy need for his holidays? Children pack a suitcase of clothes suitable for a warm/cold/wet holiday.
  Key question: Why does Teddy need these clothes for his holiday?

Key Stage 1

- Children can make play-dough and explore how the ingredients change as they mix or heat it. To make the play-dough, mix 2 cups of plain flour, 1 cup of salt, 2 cups of water, 2 tablespoons of oil, 2 teaspoons of cream of tartar and I dessertspoon of powder paint or a few drops of food colouring. Cook the mixture over a medium heat, stirring continually to prevent sticking, until the play-dough comes away from the sides of the pan.

- Play-dough exploration. Children explore what happens when they add essence of lavender, lavender flowers, rose essence and rose petals or small stars/glitter to play-dough.
  Key question: What do you think will happen when you mix the play-dough/add the stars?

- Ice balloon exploration. Children can explore what happens to an ice balloon when it is sprinkled with salt, put in water, compared with a water- or air-filled balloon.
  Key question: What do you think will happen when you put salt on the ice balloon/put the ice balloon in water?

- Explore how black pens are made up of different colours by doing some chromatography. Cut up strips of blotting paper or other absorbent paper and put a line of black pen in the middle. Dip one end in some water and watch the colours emerge.
  Key question: What have you found out?

> ### Activities and key questions (*continued*)
>
> **Key Stage 2**
>
> - Explore/investigate different soap powders/liquids and how good they are at removing stains.
>   **Key questions:** What is the best powder/liquid? Why?
> - Explore/investigate a range of paper towels to see which is the strongest/most absorbent/soft?
>   **Key questions:** Which is the 'best' paper towel? Why?
> - Use colour-change bubble bath or red cabbage water (made by cooking red cabbage and keeping the water) to test for the acidity or alkalinity of different substances. Acidic substances (lemon juice, vinegar) will go red and alkaline substances (bicarbonate of soda) will go blue.
>   **Key question:** What have you found out?

The exosystem indirectly influences children's attitudes through informal support from the extended family (grandparents, aunts, uncles), friends, neighbours, workplace, church and community ties, as well as more formal support, such as community and welfare services. Cultural values can have a very large influence on early attitude development (see Berk, 2009), especially where the values of home and the child's identity conflict with the values of the educational setting (Siraj-Blatchford, 2000). Again this can cause cognitive dissonance and slow scientific development, especially where there are cultural conflicts between the views of the family and scientific views. For example, some religious beliefs on the birth of the universe, sex and relationship education may create challenges for children (see Broadhead *et al.*, 2010). Another influence in the exosystem is the media, which often portrays images of science and scientists in stereotypical ways **(see Figure 3.3)** that can be unhelpful to children who do not know anyone in their own lives who looks like a stereotypical scientist or who behaves in ways as portrayed in the media.

The macrosystem is the system furthest removed from the individual child and involves cultural values, laws, customs and resources, which affect the support children receive in the microsystem. In this way, you would expect that a multicultural society that advocates equality regardless of race, culture or gender would support the development of positive attitudes. In the same way an educational system that does the following is more likely to nurture positive attitudes:

- puts the child in the centre of the learning experience;
- does not proscribe what science is;
- gives the professional some autonomy on how to achieve scientific learning outcomes;
- encourages teachers and children to develop scientific understandings and skills;
- allows children to experience the awe and wonder in the world.

The possibilities of conflict and dissonance in each system can be seen above and these illustrate how behaviour can be affected by attitudes (Ajzen's, 1991). Both Festinger (1957) and Petty and Cacioppo (1979) identify that dissonance can be a factor for behaviour change, through cognition. Petty and Cacioppo (1996) identify two possible routes to attitude change. The central route theory suggests that attitude change occurs when we think about the content and are swayed by the strength quality of arguments, whilst the peripheral route theory suggests that attitude change occurs when we are persuaded by non-content cues, such as the behaviour of others, without thinking.

CASE STUDY

Exploring music

A class of 5-year-old children were read the story *Lullabyhullaballoo!* (Inkpen, 1993).* This motivated them to make their own musical instruments, using junk resources:

- Card, plastic metal and wooden boxes, which make good sound boxes to resonate the sound
- Beans and rice for shakers
- Cling film or empty plastic bags to make drums (be careful to supervise their use)
- Balloons
- Bottle tops that can be added to shakers

- Empty drink cans or bottles that can be filled with water to different levels and with water of different temperatures. You can blow across the open top of the bottle to make a noise . . .
- Art straws or pieces of hollow bamboo which can be cut to different lengths as pan pipes or whistles
- Rubber bands of various sizes, which can be put around boxes to make stringed instruments
- Squares of wood and nails that can be hammered in and hit with a beater.

The Sad Story of Veronica who Played the Violin (McKee, 1987) can be suitable for older children

Photograph 3.2 Children exploring music

Case study (*continued*)

The children worked in groups, as a band, and each child made a different instrument, ones that they could shake, hit, pluck, blow and so on. Once they had made their instruments, they created some music to accompany the story of *Lullabyhullaballoo!* Later they performed for the rest of the class and explained how each instrument made its sound and whether it could make a sound of a higher or lower pitch.

Reflective tasks

Early career professional

- What knowledge and understanding, skills and attitudes can be developed through the activity?
- How could you further support affective, behavioural or cognitive attitudes through the activity?
- Try out some ideas and evaluate the effect on children's attitudes.

Developing career professional/teacher

- Reflect on your planning for science and see how you can develop scientific knowledge and understanding, skills and attitudes in a coherent cross-curricular way.
- In future planning, consider how you might support affective, behavioural or cognitive attitudes through the activity.
- Evaluate the teaching and learning to reflect on the impact the development of attitudes has on other aspects of learning.

Later career professional/leader

- With colleagues, reflect on the long-term schemes of work for your setting and consider how they can be modified to develop scientific knowledge and understanding, skills and attitudes in a coherent cross-curricular way.
- Consider how you can support affective, behavioural or cognitive attitudes through the experiences you provide for children.
- Try out one of the plans for each year group and evaluate the teaching and learning to reflect on how the development of attitudes impacts on other aspects of learning and behaviour.

ACTIVITIES AND KEY QUESTIONS

To promote sensitivity to, and a responsibility for, the living world

- Explore the local environment. Close your eyes and listen, smell and touch things in the environment.
  Key question: What can you hear/smell/see/feel?

- Set up a pet shop with stuffed toys as pets. Make sure the animals are cared for and kept in the correct conditions.
  Key question: How should we look after the different pets?

- Use the small world play farm to explore the conditions that different animals need to be kept in.
  Key question: What does the cow/horse/sheep need to live?

- Look for signs of living things (plants and animals) in the environment. Look above the ground (on buildings, in trees, on plants, at ground level and under rocks and below the surface of the soil). Take care not to harm any plants and animals.
  Key question: What do the animals/plants need to live and grow?

- Visit a pond and look at the different types of life in and around the pond. Do some pond-dipping but make sure all the wildlife is returned safely afterwards.
  Key question: Why should we return the animals to the pond?

> **Activities and key questions (*continued*)**
>
> ● Sand play. In the sand tray or in a role play of the seaside, encourage children to sieve sand, pour it through funnels or a sand wheel, make sandcastles and compare wet and dry sand **(see Chapter 2)**.
> **Key question:** What do you think will happen when you...? Is wet or dry sand better to make castles? Why?

References

Ajzen, I. (1991). The theory of planned behaviour. *Organisational Behaviour and Human Decision Processes*, 50, 179–211.

Baker, J. (1987). *Where the Forest Meets the Sea.* London: Walker

Beetlestone, F. (1998). *Creative Children, Imaginative Teaching.* Buckingham: Open University Press.

Berk, L.E. (2009). *Child Development*, 8th edn. Boston, MA: Pearsons.

Bird, J. & Catherall, E. (1977). *Teaching Primary Science. Fibres and Fabrics.* London: Macdonald Educational.

Bricheno, P., Johnston, J. & Sears, J. (2001). Children's attitudes to science. In: Sears, J. & Sorensen, P., eds. *Issues In The Teaching Of Science.* London: Routledge.

Broadhead, P. (2006). Developing an understanding of young children's learning through play: the place of observation, interaction and reflection. *British Educational Research Journal*, 32(2), 191–207.

Broadhead, P., Johnston, J., Tobbell, C. & Woolley, R. (2010). *Personal, Social and Emotional Development.* London: Continuum.

Bronfenbrenner, U. (1995). The bioecological model from a life course perspective: reflections of a participant observer. In: Moen, P., Elder, Jnr, G.H. & Lüscher, K., eds. *Examining Lives in Context.* Washington DC: American Psychological Association, pp. 599–618.

Bruner, J.S., Jolly, A. & Sylva, K. (1976). *Play: Its Role in Development and Education.* Harmondsworth: Penguin.

Butterworth, N. & Inkpen, M. (1991). *Wonderful Earth.* London: Hodder and Stoughton.

Compton, A., Johnston, J., Nahmad-Williams, L. & Taylor, K. (2010). *Creative Development.* London: Continuum.

Creative Little Scientists (CLS) (2012). *Creative Little Scientists: Enabling Creativity through Science and Mathematics in Pre-school and First Years of Primary Education.* Online at: http://www.creative-little-scientists.eu. Accessed 8/12/12.

Department for Education (DfE) (2012). *Statutory Framework for the Early Years Foundation Stage. Setting the Standards for Learning, Development and Care for Children from Birth to Five.* London: DfE.

Department for Education and Skills (DfES) (2003a). *Excellence and Enjoyment. A strategy for primary schools.* London: DfES.

Department for Education and Skills (DfES) (2003b). *Every Child Matters.* London: DfES.

Elkind, D. (2001). *The Hurried Child. Growing Up Too Fast Too Soon*, 3rd edn. Cambridge, MA: Da Capio Press.

Fensham, P. J. (2001). Science Content as problematic – issues for research. In: Behrendt, H., Dahncke, H., Duit, R., Gräber, W., Komorek, M., Kross, A. & Reiska, P. (2001). *Research in Science – Past, present and future.* Dordrecht, The Netherlands: Kluwer.

Festinger, L. (1957). *A Theory of Cognitive Dissonance*. Stanford, CA: Stanford University Press.

Fraser, B. (1981). *Test of Science Related Attitudes: Handbook*. Victoria, Australia: Council for Educational Research.

Glori, D. (1995). *The Snow Lambs*. London: Scholastic Publications.

Harlen, W. (2000). *The Teaching of Science in Primary Schools*, 3rd edn. London: David Fulton.

Inkpen, M. (1993). *Lullabyhullaballoo!* London: Hodder and Stoughton.

Johnston, J. & Halocha, J. (2010). *Early Childhood and Primary Education: Readings and Reflections*. Maidenhead: Open University Press.

Johnston, J. (2005). *Early Explorations in Science*, 2nd edn. Buckingham: Open University Press.

King, H. (2000). *Dyes and Decoration*. Oxford: Heinemann.

McKee, D. (1987). *The Sad Story of Veronica who Played the Violin*. London: Red Fox.

Organisation for Economic Cooperation and Development (OECD) (2003). *The PISA 2003 Assessment Framework – Mathematics, Reading, Science and Problem Solving Knowledge and Skills*. Online at: http://www.oecd.org/dataoecd/46/14/33694881.pdf.

Oversby, J. (ed). (2012). *ASE Guide to Research in Science Education*. Hatfield: ASE.

Palmer, S. (2006). *Toxic Childhood. How the Modern World is Damaging our Children and What we Can Do about It*. London: Orion.

Petty, R.E. & Cacioppo, J.T. (1979). Issue involvement can increase or decrease persuasion by enhancing message-relevant cognitive responses. *Journal of Personality and Social Psychology*, 37(10), 1915–1926.

Siraj-Blatchford, J. (2000). Promoting equality and citizenship. In: de Bóo, M., ed. *Science 3-6 Laying the Foundations in the Early Years*. Hatfield: ASE.

Smail, B. (1984). *Girl-Friendly Science: Avoiding Sex Bias in the Curriculum*. York: Schools Council/Longman.

Taber, K.S. (2012). Teaching and learning about the nature of science. In: Oversby, J. (ed). (2012). *ASE Guide to Research in Science Education*. Hatfield: ASE.

Contexts

Chapter 4

Learning science at home

Overview

In this chapter we look at:

- Bronfenbrenner's (1995) microsystem in looking at the importance and effect of good home/setting partnership
- Research into multimodality by Carol Callinan and John Sharp
- Observation as a research tool, as part of the study skills theme
- Practical and reflective tasks that look at home–school partnerships and analysing non-verbal gesture from problem-solving activities
- A focus on activities that promote home/setting partnerships and learning from home
- A knowledge box focusing on plant growth and pollution.

Introduction

In Section 1 we looked at children's development in science. Now, in Section 2 we are going to look at the contexts in which that development occurs. In Chapter 3, we used Bronfenbrenner's (1995) Ecological Systems Theory **(see Figure 4.1)** to structure the factors affecting the development of attitudes. In this chapter we will start by looking at the microsystem, the closest system to individual children, involving their immediate surroundings, their immediate family, their immediate carers and the community in which they live and play (see also Johnston & Nahmad-Williams, 2008).

The home is the first and most important context in a child's life and there is compelling evidence indicating the part played by the home and the family in children's development (Carneiro *et al.*, 2007; EPPE, 2002, 2003). Home may look different for different children (Johnston & Nahmad-Williams, 2008). Traditional homes include flats, bungalows, terraced houses, semi-detached and detached houses, but some children live in non-traditional homes such as caravans or boats, or in communes, community hostels and children's homes. Some children remain static in their home throughout their lives while

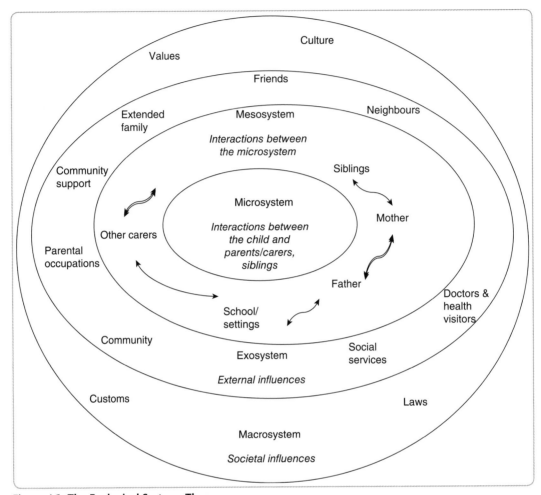

Figure 4.1 The Ecological Systems Theory
Source: Bronfenbrenner (1995)

others move frequently. Home environments are also varied and can be rural, urban, suburban, **monocultural**, **multicultural**, working class, middle class and so on. There are many different types of family group, too, including:

- Nuclear – where the family unit consists of two parents (traditionally a mother and father) and child/ren
- Single-parent families – where there is one parent and child/ren
- Extended – where children, parents, grandparents and other relatives (e.g. aunts, uncles, cousins) live under one roof or nearby (in the same street or town)
- Blended or **reconstituted** – where adults and children from different family groups combine to make a new family (or step-family)
- Adopted – where children are not the biological children of the family.

There are a number of different parenting styles within families (Baumrind, 1971), as follows:

- **Authoritarian** – where the parents control and direct their children, do not consult their children and rarely give praise or celebrate achievements

- **Permissive** – exercising limited control and being inconsistent about discipline, but loving and affectionate, even to the extent of being overindulgent
- **Authoritative** – showing high levels of warmth and achievement demands, with firm control, good levels of communication, clear expectations, and being responsive, attentive and sensitive to the children's needs
- Rejecting-neglecting – disengaged and emotionally detached from the children with low involvement.

There are advantages and disadvantages associated with each family type, location and parenting style as far as children's early scientific development is concerned. Families with more than one parent or with extended families are likely to offer more support for children (Kaplan & Owens, 2004), with more time to devote to them and to provide experiences to support their development. The kinds of experiences that benefit from greater available time include making bathtime a fun learning experience, with children exploring bubbles in a bubble bath, lathering up shampoo for themselves, and playing with bath toys, such as water wheels, funnels, boats and colour-change ducks; children helping with cooking and baking, so they see how materials change when mixed or heated; children digging in the garden and planting seeds; going to the park to feed the ducks or play on the swings or roundabout, thus allowing them to experience different habitats and the forces involved in playground equipment.

An authoritative parenting style can allow children to develop a degree of autonomy, taking responsibility for their own learning and so developing scientific understandings, skills and attitudes from their experiences and from the involvement of their parents. Children who are given responsibility for and ownership of their development and learning are more likely to make progress in all areas of development.

Blended families have the advantage of being economically stable, but there are consequent social (Pryor, 2004) and emotional disadvantages, as the loss of one primary **attachment** and the reconstitution of what is often a larger family require a period of adjustment that can adversely affect the developing child. Multicultural families are likely to provide children with a breadth and depth of experience that a monocultural family may not be able to, and a monocultural family living in a different and perhaps conflicting cultural context may create additional problems for the developing child.

STUDY SKILLS

Observation as a research tool

Observation can help professionals to understand processes, events and development. As a research method, it can develop from reflective practice and support learning and teaching (see Pollard, 2005; Gillham, 2008). Observation is about more than just looking. It involves watching closely, listening critically, discussing or questioning, and analysing work/answers/observations. Observations can be focused, where the observer is looking for something specific, or unfocused, allowing for interesting but unexpected events, and it can support generation of theory. The observer can be inside the observation (participant observation, e.g. the classroom teacher involved in the teaching or learning being observed) or outside it (non-participant observation; e.g. an independent observer).

Participant observation can involve an element of ethnographic (naturalistic) research, but this only really happens if the researcher is part of the research group being studied, perhaps by using pupils as researchers. Non-participant observations are more objective and

Study Skills (*continued*)

less open to problems of external validity, but the observer can sometimes affect the data collected as those being observed may not behave in normal ways.

All observations need to be analysed and discussed with others for verification, to ensure that the observer does not assign meanings to the data that are not valid.

Analysing observations (see Oversby, 2012)

When analysing data from observations, you need to understand what is happening and why individuals react in certain ways and in certain situations. This involves looking beyond the obvious. This type of analysis may be used to resolve problems and clarify purposes and intentions. Through analysis you may be able to identify the main factors/issues/components in actions. Videoed or photographed observations can be analysed using analytical software, or simply viewed and the main actions noticed and categorised. The analytical framework should be decided upon at the research design stage, when decisions about observations or photographs should be made, or when an observational schedule should be prepared. Analysis can be triangulated by comparing observations with another professional or a critical friend, or by asking the children about their version of experiences. Both observations and photographs may be analysed and validated during the course of the data collection process (Prosser & Schwartz, 1998), so that you can make decisions on further data collection. Photographs should be looked at holistically before carrying out microanalysis. In research in which the children are co-researchers (see Haw, 2008; Schratz & Steiner-Löffler, 1998), the choice of photographs used as part of the analysis is made by the children and this will influence the analytical framework.

Birth to 3 years of age

Much of early learning about the world occurs in the home. As discussed earlier in this chapter, the quality of these experiences depends on many factors. Through the home, children can learn about the living, material and physical world. They can learn about the living world by playing in the garden (see the Case study that follows), going to the park, and helping to look after pets or younger siblings; they can learn about the material world by helping with the cooking, making their own cakes, dressing up and making mud pies; and they can learn about the physical world by playing on swings, roundabouts and slides in the park, through ball games, bath play, experiencing the seasons, making noises and experiencing echoes and music. These experiences are rich in science but they are not expensive to provide in monetary terms. They do require time, something that many busy families find difficult to provide (Palmer, 2006). Excursions such as trips to the zoo, to go swimming, to the seaside and to adventure parks can also provide additional experiences to support scientific development, but of course they require more expense.

Research undertaken on behalf of the Department for Children, Families and Schools (DCFS) by the Centre for the Economics of Education has looked at the impact of early cognitive and non-cognitive skills on later outcomes (Carneiro *et al.*, 2007). The key findings indicate that both cognitive and non-cognitive skills are strongly dependent on family background and other characteristics of the home learning environment. This is due to both genetics and the environment. By the time children are 7 years of age, there are gaps in social and cognitive abilities related to socioeconomic status (identified by the father's social class), so that children from both professional and non-manual family backgrounds exhibit significantly greater cognitive and social skills than children from manual backgrounds. Social skills appear to be unaffected by the number of years a parent has spent in education (although this does have an effect on cognitive skills). Other aspects of the home learning environment (amount of reading by parents and the interest shown in their education) were also found to be important.

Since early experiences and the factors associated with the home, families and parenting have an important effect on scientific development, it seems sensible to suggest that early years professionals should liaise more effectively with parents and carers. The case study that follows looks at one early home experience and, through the reflective tasks, considers how professionals can find out about these experiences and the expertise of parents and use them to the advantage of scientific development and learning.

CASE STUDY

Exploring the garden

Gabriel (a 2-year-old boy) was in the garden with his parents, who were gardening. He copied his parents and dug a hole with his small trowel. His father put a bulb in the hole and showed Gabriel how to cover the bulb with some soil. When all the bulbs were planted, his father told him that the bulbs needed to be watered and gave him a small watering can and helped him to fill it up, so he could water the planted bulbs.

He then wandered over to his mother who was clearing weeds out of another bed. She showed him how to use a small rake to smooth over the soil after she had cleared it. He saw a worm in the soil and his mother picked it up and put it carefully in his open hand, telling him not to squash it. She explained that worms are good for the garden and help to dig up the soil, but that they like damp dark places, so Gabriel carefully put the worm back on the ground and watched as it burrowed into the soil.

Later, he picked up some small stones from the gravel pathway and put them in small pile and got

Photograph 4.1 Child exploring the garden at home

Case study (*continued*)

his watering can and watered them and saw that they changed colour and sparkled in the sun. His father explained that they would not grow like the bulbs and suggested that they look at the stones and the bulbs each time they went into the garden to see what had happened to them.

When they had finished gardening, his mother and father showed him where to put the gardening tools in the garden shed and showed him some other garden tools that were kept there (spade, lawn mower, fork).

Reflective tasks

Early career professional

- What experiences do you expect children to have when they start formal education settings?

- How can you find out about the children's early experiences at home and use these as starting points in your planning?

- How can you ensure that early experiences do not hinder later development?

Developing career professional/teacher

- What experiences do children need in the early years to give them a good start in scientific development?

- How can you ensure that your scientific experiences build on those the children already have?

- How can you liaise with the home and carers to support and improve scientific experiences?

Later career professional/leader

- What scientific experiences do you provide that build on early experiences in the home?

- How can you use parental expertise to support scientific development?

- How can you bridge the gap between home and school and support children's scientific development?

Knowledge box

Growth in plants and pollution in the environment

Plants need water, nutrients, energy and air in order to live and grow. Water helps them to keep their structure and allows them to transport nutrients and food around the plant. Nutrients come from the soil or, in the case of insectivorous plants, from insects that land on them and are absorbed by them. Energy from the sun is required for the process of photosynthesis. Air is needed for respiration, during which carbon dioxide is taken in and oxygen is emitted, and also to turn carbon dioxide into carbon which is laid down in the plants cells (resulting in growth) and oxygen (during photosynthesis).

It is a common **misconception** that plants:

- need soil for food – if this were the case, a growing tree would use up all the soil in the area where it is growing;

- need the sun for warmth – if this were so, plants would not grow in cold environments;

- breathe air – breathing is a process seen in animals with lungs; plants respire but do not breathe;

- grow and get larger as a result of the nutrients – if this were the case, plants in conditions with few nutrients (e.g. plants growing in air, in cracks in brickwork or out of chimneys) would not grow.

It is also a common misconception that seeds require the same conditions to germinate as plants need to grow. Seeds (and bulbs) contain the energy needed to begin growth and so mainly require warmth and water to grow and not energy from the sun. This is why we often grow bulbs in dark, warm airing cupboards to start the growing process and seeds will germinate under the soil. Once seeds and bulbs have germinated and green shoots and leaves emerge, they then need the energy from the sun in order to photosynthesize and continue to grow.

Some seeds need a period of cold before they germinate (e.g. acorns) and others need to pass through the gut of an animal (e.g. blackberries and raspberries). These germination requirements are actually supportive of seed dispersal; so that the new plant is not in competition with the mother plant. Seeds utilise a variety of dispersal methods:

- Air (e.g. dandelion, sycamore, lime)
- Mechanical (e.g. poppy, beans and peas – they 'throw' the seeds into the air)
- Water (e.g. coconut, iris, foxglove)
- Animal (e.g. apple, berries, acorns)
- Fire (e.g. banksia and Australasian tree – the seeds drop after a fire and just before the rainy seasons, so there is no competition and good fertiliser from the ashes of other plants).

Teaching growth in plants

When we teach about growth in plants, we need to be very careful that we do not perpetuate misconceptions in the children we teach. We often teach children, and many schemes of work imply, that plants need the sun for warmth, soil for food and never mention the need for air. This could be because photosynthesis is a very complex concept taught to children in secondary school. However, we make conceptual development very difficult for children later in their education if we do not mention that plants need air to grow. A poem by Danielle Sensier called *Experiment* says it all:

at school we're doing growing things
with cress.
sprinkly seeds in plastic pots
of cotton wool.
Kate's cress sits on the sill
she gives it water.
mine is shut inside the cupboard
dark and dry.
now her pot has great big clumps
of green
mine hasn't.
Mrs Martin calls it Science
I call it mean.

Pollution in the environment

Pollution in the environment can affect growth of plants as well as our health. Below are some indicators of pollution that we can see.

Water pollution

The presence of the following in local ponds or rivers can help to identify the level of water pollution:

- Trout, mayfly nymphs, fresh water shrimps → NO POLLUTION
- Caddis fly larvae → SLIGHTY POLLUTED

- Bloodworm, waterlouse → HEAVILY POLLUTED
- Sludge worm, rat-tailed maggot → VERY HEAVILY POLLUTED

Air pollution

Air pollution is caused by acid rain, a solution of weak acids in water caused by domestic and industrial emissions of gases. Lichens can be a natural indicator of air pollution. Lichens are two plants (algae and fungi) which live together for mutual benefit (symbiosis). The algae provide food by photosynthesis while the fungi provide protection, water and minerals. Some lichens are very sensitive to the amounts of sulphur dioxide in the air.

- No lichens, although there may be a powdery alga called → VERY BAD AIR POLLUTION
  Pleurococcus
- Only crusty lichens, which look like crazy paving and are → FAIRLY HEAVILY POLLUTED
  very flat. They can be grey or green and are often found
  on trees, brickwork, paving stones and gravestones
- Leafy lichens look like flat patches of small thin leaves → SLIGHTLY POLLUTED
  which overlap each other. They can be all colours (white,
  grey, green, yellow, orange or black) and are found on
  trees, stones, brickwork, roofs and tombstones
- Shrubby lichens look like little bushes with lots of branches → NO AIR POLLUTION
  which can be quite long. They are usually green or grey
  and can be found on the branches and trunks of trees.
  Most of these lichens only grow where the air is clean

3 to 5 years of age

When children enter formal education settings (e.g. playgroup, nursery, school), they have a variety of different experiences, depending on the home situation and their previous experiences (see earlier). The quality of early settings varies, as does the quality of home experiences. A number of research projects have provided information about the impact of early years settings. The Effective Provision of Pre-school Education (EPPE) project, a 5-year longitudinal study (between 1997 and 2004), looked at the attainment and development of children aged between 3 and 7 years. It generated many technical papers (e.g. EPPE, 2002, 2003) and a final report (Sylva *et al.*, 2004). Five questions were explored:

- What is the impact of **pre-school** on children's intellectual and social/behavioural development?
- Are some pre-schools more effective than others in promoting children's development?
- What are the characteristics of an effective pre-school setting?
- What is the impact of the home and childcare history on children's development?
- Do the effects of pre-school continue through Key Stage 1 (ages 6 and 7 years)?

Evidence for the research was collected from standardised child assessments taken over time, child social/behavioural profiles completed by pre-school and primary staff, parental interviews, interviews with pre-school centre staff and parents, quality rating scales and case study observations and interviews.

The Effective Pedagogy in the Early Years (EPEY) project undertaken by Siraj-Blatchford *et al.* (2002) was also informative about early care and provision. It was conducted alongside the EPPE research and involved some of the same settings as EPPE. The research aimed to identify the early years pedagogical strategies that are most effective in supporting the development of young children's skills, knowledge and attitudes and that enable them to develop in school. The EPEY study involved detailed case studies of a range of early years settings, collecting data through observations of staff pedagogy and children's learning, as well as interviews with parents, staff and managers and telephone interviews with childminders. More recently, early years provision was a strand of the Cambridge Primary Review, which collected evidence between 2004 and 2009 through wide-ranging consultation, formal written submissions, meetings, surveys and evaluations and then published a final report (Alexander, 2010) and a collection of the research surveys (Alexander *et al.*, 2010).

These three pieces of research can help to inform us in three areas (see Johnston, 2011):

- The effect of quality pre-school education on cognition **(see also Chapter 2)**
- The effect of early social development **(see also Chapter 1)**
- The effect of the home on early development.

They can also help us to consider the impact on scientific educational development.

The effect of quality pre-school education on cognition

The research indicates that pre-school attendance (whether part- or full-time) supports children's holistic development, particularly for socially disadvantaged children (Sylva *et al.*, 2004). This is probably due to the importance of quality adult–child verbal instructive interactions, which can advance cognition through 'sustained shared thinking' (Siraj-Blatchford *et al.*, 2002). The EPEY research found that the most effective early years settings encourage this 'sustained shared thinking', although it was not commonly seen in practice. Alexander (2010) also identified the link between the quality of the early years professionals and the quality of the children's development (see also Goswani & Bryant, 2007).

Quality pre-school education has lasting effects on cognitive development into Key Stage 1 (Sylva *et al.*, 2004), so that when children start pre-school between the ages of 2 and 3 years, there is likely to be a positive effect on cognitive development and attainment. Alexander (2010: 99) also identifies the importance of professionals having high expectations of children and recognising the individuality of children's cognitive development: 'The message is clear: expect more, teach better, and all children will respond.'

The effect of early social development

The EPPE research case studies (Sylva *et al.*, 2004) identified that early settings are more effective if they understand the part played by social development on children's holistic development. Dialogic teaching (Alexander, 2010), that is teaching where children discuss their learning with both peers and adults, and also teaching where adults model language (Siraj-Blatchford *et al.*, 2002), is thought to develop 'sustained shared thinking', where children and professionals work together to solve problems or understand a concept (Sylva *et al.*, 2004). This type of social interaction must involve all parties and not be a monologue by the professional with the child passive in the process, and the EPPE research (Sylva *et al.*, 2004) indicates that it is more likely to occur when children are interacting with an individual adult or child or in focused group work.

Recent research evidence (see Johnston, 2010) indicates a common emphasis on social interaction with others and dialogue in emergent scientific development, endorsing what we already know, namely that exploration, or play, and talking with both peers and expert adults, in individual and small group contexts, are vital in supporting children as they develop scientifically.

The effect of the home on early development

There is consensus in the research as to the positive effects of the home and parents on early development; not the home or parents themselves, but the quality of the home environment (Sylva *et al.*, 2004), with 'some parents' pro-active behaviour towards their children's learning in the embedded, cultural context of the home, [providing] a good basis for sustained shared thinking' (Siraj-Blatchford *et al.*, 2002: 11).

Alexander (2010) identified the importance of the home as a language laboratory and the research does indicate the link between parental wealth and improved pre-school language development. EPPE found only a moderate link between wealth and early development, but researchers did identify a range of effective activities that parents undertake, including reading, teaching songs and nursery rhymes, painting, drawing, visiting the library and taking children on visits (Sylva *et al.*, 2004). Indeed, EPPE demonstrated a strong relationship between children's cognitive development and parental interaction. This is especially evident where adults (both family and professionals) model behaviours and professionals have good pedagogical content knowledge (Siraj-Blatchford *et al.*, 2002: 11).

The implications for science education are twofold: children learn best when they can explore the world around them and experience scientific phenomena in everyday life; and support by knowledgeable adults is essential for good scientific development. This indicates the need for curriculum changes that recognise and build upon the social and emotional aspects of children's development (Alexander, 2010) and do not see cognitive development as existing in an educational vacuum, so that the part played by the home and family in that development becomes the foundation of future scientific development. It also has implications for early years professional and initial teacher education courses, which need to focus on the informal as well as formal opportunities for scientific development.

The long-term effect of high-quality early years education has been well documented (e.g. Cambell *et al.*, 2002; Ramey *et al.*, 2000). Secure grounding in reading, other forms of communication, such as speaking, listening and drawing, and numbers provides basic skills for further development in all areas of learning, not least in science. A strong early start in science education sets the foundation for high achievement later, leading to greater opportunities for social mobility. Further research in the area of early years science education would support strong professional development for teachers working with these children, and increase our confidence in making sense of teaching at that level.

Observation as a research tool

A class of 5-year-old children used the story of *Handa's Surprise* (Browne,1997) to initiate some work looking at parts of plants. After reading the story they were given a collection of fruit and vegetables. They sorted all the fruits into one group and this included some that are regarded as vegetables in culinary terms (aubergine, tomato, pepper). The children discussed the term fruit and what it meant and then cut open some fruit to see if they contained seeds. They looked at what was not in the fruit pile (celery, lettuce, cauliflower, carrot, potato, peas and beans) and looked at what part of the plant each came from.

They then took the seeds from the fruits and decided to try to grow them, taking care of them by watering them and checking for signs of growth.[1] Finally they made a fruit salad, an ordinary salad and tasty vegetable soup. This widened their experiences of food, as there were fruit and vegetables some of them had never tasted before.

Practical and reflective tasks

Practical tasks

Give children a collection of fruit and vegetables or seeds and ask them to sort them. Observe them as they observe and sort the collection. Decide the focus of your observation and use an observation schedule (Figure 4.2) to aid observation and analysis.

Reflective tasks

- How did the observation schedule help you to focus on the observation?
- What follow-up activities could support the learning outcomes?
- How could you follow up the activity to support home school liaison?

Photograph 4.2 Children sorting fruit and vegetables

[1]The story of *The Tiny Seed* (Carle, 1987) could be used when looking at seeds.

Case study (*continued*)

EXAMPLE SCHEDULE 1

Setting:	Observer's name:		Date:
Time:	**Focus:**		**Context:**
	Sorting a collection of fruit and vegetables		
10:00	*John puts all the round fruit and vegetables in one pile*		
10:15	*TA asks if there is another way to sort the fruit and vegetables and John does not answer. Sophie suggests they could put all the red ones together and all the green together.*		
10:30	*Sophie and John are sorting the fruit and vegetables according to colour and putting them into sorting hoops. They find an apple that is red and green. John suggests that they put it in the middle.*		
Comments from the observation:			

EXAMPLE SCHEDULE 2

Setting:	Observer's name:		Date:
Time:	**Focus:**		**Context:**
	Sorting a collection of fruit and vegetables		
• **What criteria did the children choose to sort by?**			
• **Did the children recognise the characteristics of a fruit?**			
Comments from the observation:			

Figure 4.2 Examples of observation schedules

5 to 8 years of age

If we look at a class of Year 1 children at the beginning of the academic year, we will have up to 30 individuals who will vary in age (from just 5 years or nearly 6 years of age) and have between them a huge variety of experiences. Some children will have had 5 years of experiences and interaction (through home and the extended family, childminders, playgroups, nurseries, Reception classes and so on) and will enter school with attitudes commensurate with learning, social skills and practical skills that support scientific development and learning and knowledge and understandings of the world around them and everyday scientific phenomena that schools can build upon. Other children will have much more limited experience and start school timid and not fully ready to learn **(see also Chapter 6)**. All the children will have common experiences in school but will vary in the way they access these experiences and in how the experiences and views they are exposed to resonate with their home life, including the values, culture and moral views held by their family group. For some children, the language used in school may differ slightly (e.g. different accents, less colloquial language) and in others the language may be completely different from that used at home or even (in the case of international schools) from the local community or country in which they live.

Professionals working with children in compulsory schooling need to be able to elicit the children's understandings, assess their skills and understand how their development and learning to date is a result of their pre-school experiences. This requires professionals to make effective links and work in partnership with parents and carers. Parents and carers can have three different roles in school (Vincent, 2000; see also Johnston & Nahmad-Williams, 2008). They can be passive consumers, receiving a service for their children from the professionals and schools responsible for their children's care in a relationship where the school is dominant. They can be supporters or learners themselves, part of effective parent partnerships in which parents confirm that they will support their children and the school. This, too, implies more dominance on the part of the school but is less passive than the parent as a consumer, as it does not recognise parental individuality, responsibility, expertise and initiative. Parents and carers can also be participants, or fully active, and therefore full partners in the learning process, along with the school and with rights and responsibilities.

The relationship between the home and school or parents/carers and professionals in school can be difficult and professionals need to have particular skills, especially if they make home visits (Caffrey, 1997). In compulsory schooling, most teachers have limited experience of home–school liaison as part of their initial teacher education and what they have is mainly restricted to school placements, where they can only fit in with the current school provision. There are a number of initiatives that schools can introduce to support effective home–school partnerships and support children's development and learning, including:

- *Book and toy loan schemes* – these can help parents to introduce stories and books, play with their children and develop language (including scientific vocabulary) and science in stories. For example, reading a book like *Mrs Lather's Laundry* (Ahlberg, 1981) can lead to parent and child washing together and looking at the lathers made by different washing powders. Reading *Oliver's Vegetables* (French, 2007) can lead to looking at vegetables whilst shopping or planting vegetables in the garden or in pots on a window sill or balcony.

- *Establishing a two-way communication about individual children*, so that professionals can build up a better picture of the child and their scientific experiences and future needs. Parents and carers have in-depth knowledge of their children which they can share with professionals to the benefit of children. In an effective partnership, both parents and professionals will engage in an honest dialogue about the children's achievements and work together to help them to meet their challenges. For example, a child may have a particular interest in electrical toys, perhaps building a remote-controlled Lego vehicle, which could be brought to school to show others how it works and lead to them building one in class. In another example, a child may have limited experience of animals and be frightened of spiders; the school could arrange for a wildlife expert to bring some animals (including large spiders) into school, taking particular care to address the child's concern and helping to overcome his or her fear.

- *Utilising parents' expertise and sharing it in school*. A parent or relative with medical knowledge (a doctor, nurse or dentist, say) could talk to the children about their job, giving them an insight into their responsibilities and allowing them to experience some of their equipment (stethoscope, heart monitor, thermometer), perhaps letting them play with these items in a role play area. A parent or relative who is an electrician might work with a small group of children on an electrical problem-solving activity, such as how to make a set of traffic lights. A parent or relative who has an allotment and enjoys growing things may be interested and willing to run an after-school club for children to grow their own vegetables.

● *Communicating with parents through parental information sessions,* family learning workshops and newsletters. Traditionally schools will invite parents to summative class assemblies or class sessions that celebrate what the children have achieved. However, parental information sessions may take place before a topic or theme and provide information on how the theme will be delivered and what parents can do to help their child to learn. In this way, parents do not always have to be reactive in responding to children's questions when they come home, but can be proactive in planning discussions and experiences to complement the class theme and so feel more involved in their children's development and learning. Family learning sessions can be provided by the school and involve children, their siblings, parents and extended family in working together on a problem or theme. They could, for example, work as a family unit, undertaking a number of exploratory and problem-solving activities in one or more scientific conceptual areas.

● *Providing some simple challenges for parent and child to undertake together,* such as building a bridge out of one sheet of A4 paper (see the Activities and key questions box at the end of this chapter) or a drinks can dragster **(see Figure 9.2, p. 218)**.

Photograph 4.3 A family learning session

The most important feature of an effective working relationship is two-way communication and consultation. The Education Act 2002 identified that professionals should consult with parents more widely regarding the provision of extended childcare, homework, sport and science clubs. Extended and integrated services enable opportunities for professionals to work together with parents, although this involves challenge as to how to work effectively with a range of partners and the whole school community.

Practical tasks

These tasks are designed to improve current home–school partnership (see the Activities and key questions box at the end of this chapter).

Early career professional

Look at your relationship with parents and consider how you can adapt homework to improve the home–school partnership so that it is equal in nature and supports children's development and learning in science. Identify success criteria that will show you how effective the homework is in improving the partnership and supporting children's learning in science. Implement the idea and evaluate how successful it is by using the success criteria.

- How successful was your homework plan?
- What affected success?
- How could you continue to improve the success of the home–school partnership through homework?

Developing career professional/teacher

Plan a class activity session on a planned theme or scientific objective. Identify success criteria that will show you how effective the activity is in improving the home–school partnership and supporting children's learning in science. Implement the session and evaluate how successful it is by using the success criteria you planned.

- Was the activity session a success? If so, why? If not, why not?
- What affected success?
- How could you continue to improve the success of the home–school partnership through future activity sessions or other initiatives?

Later career professional/leader

Plan a school family activity session. Identify success criteria that will show you how effective the family learning session is in improving the home–school partnership and supporting children's learning in science. After the session, evaluate how successful it was by using the success criteria you planned.

- How was the session successful and why?
- What affected success?
- How could you continue to improve the success of the home–school partnership through future family learning activities and other initiatives?

Research

Understanding children's ideas from a multimodal perspective

Carol Callinan and John Sharp

What do we mean by multimodal?

Constructivism remains one of the most influential and contemporary approaches to understanding how children come to learn science either formally at school or informally elsewhere. The **constructivist** perspective maintains the view that children, like adults, form initial representations of many natural phenomena and that these initial representations can influence what they later come to know about and understand. The body of research investigating children's ideas, which often reveals a range of 'alternative' rather than scientific 'explanatory frameworks', has been successful in helping teachers to work within the science curriculum more creatively and to plan the sorts of tasks and activities considered more effective at helping children move on.

One particularly important research project which contributed greatly to our understanding of the development of children's ideas across the primary years was the Science Processes and Concept Exploration project (SPACE, 1989–1998). However, children's ideas research has conventionally focused on the analysis of children's verbal responses to questions at interview, their scientific writing and their responses to short tasks and problems. Such multi-method approaches do, however, focus on triangulation and methodology and may overlook other important forms of communication. **Multimodal** perspectives, on the other hand, focus on attending to a range of response types, including language, but also incorporate analyses of non-verbal responses such as gesture. They also focus on the child.

Multimodality in early years classrooms

Research in science education from both the US and the UK has shown that children and their teachers display and present conceptual knowledge not only through their spoken and written language but also through their non-verbal gestures. A more recent study involving 51 Year 2 children attending several schools in the East Midlands region of England has already begun to highlight the advantages of both verbal and non-verbal communication analysed from just such a multimodal perspective. Within this study, children's ideas in activi-ties attached to floating and sinking and electricity were explored in detail. These activities, conducted using a dialogic approach, took place with the children working as they would do normally in small groups (four to five in each). In all cases, the activities were video-recorded (with audio) in order to aid later analysis, particularly how the children were using gesture in the discussion of their science ideas.

Focusing only on floating and sinking here, these activities began with a discussion of what children think causes some objects to float and sink. This was followed by grouping and testing materials, a plasticine modelling activity in order to explore children's approaches to making it float, and finally a practical demonstration of the concept of upthrust and water displacement using an inflated balloon. The analyses revealed that the children indeed used gestures, sometimes accompanying and supporting speech and also sometimes in isolation, but in a meaningful and scientific way. The results supported previous research and the view that gestures themselves served a number of functions. One example which illustrates the use of gesture conveying scientific meaning came from 'Amy' (7 years of age):

> Amy stated that 'light things float', and as she said this she also made a cupping motion with her hands. This gesture began with the hands together and the fingers interlaced. As she spoke, she moved her hands apart, paused and held her hands stationary. She then moved her hands apart a little more, paused again, and finally moved her hands even further apart.

Whilst Amy's verbal response appeared to attend only to the 'weight' of the object, the non-verbal gesture also revealed a consideration of 'size'. On the face of it, Amy appears to be telling us that bigger objects are heavier and would therefore sink. However, of course, and while this is not always true, Amy is displaying a relationship between mass and volume which might easily be developed further to challenge this simple notion, a notion that would have been easily overlooked without the gesture. From this seemingly straightforward example, it is clear that gesture is important. It is important to the child and it is important to how they express their

Research (*continued*)

ideas about the natural world and to the development of their scientific knowledge. It also appears that it might help with their scientific reasoning, thinking skills and problem-solving, and this is fundamentally important for teachers. In addition to considering specific gestures from individual children, these were considered as a whole and categorised according to the form that they took and the possible meanings conveyed. The two main categories identified included scientific gesture and social gesture.

Scientific gestures in relation to science activities

Scientific gestures came in four main forms:

- Referential – e.g. pointing to objects, pictures or people in the immediate environment;
- Representative – e.g. re-enacting the behaviour of objects, pictures or people;
- Expressive – e.g. often including repetitive movements or building on representative gestures revealing the values associated with objects, pictures or people;
- Thinking – e.g. finger drumming, waving hands, head holding or face and hair stroking.

In another example drawn from floating and sinking, 'Mary' frequently used representational gestures as she worked through her ideas of floating. In the instance of focus here Mary was discussing what she thought floating was.

> As she spoke, Mary used both hands in a gesture that revealed deeper insight into her ideas. One hand was used to represent an object and one to represent the liquid (water) in which the object is floating. Her hands were positioned one above the other, both palms facing downwards. The lower hand, which represented the water, remained stationary whilst the top hand was gently lowered towards the stationary hand before being brought to a stop on top of it.

This representational gesture was interpreted as Mary's non-verbal way of saying whilst the object is lowered into the water, it is supported by the water and remains above the surface.

Social gestures in relation to working in groups

While scientific gestures appear to play a crucial role in facilitating our understanding of children's scientific ideas, social gestures also have an important role in facilitating our understanding of how young children use input from peers in order to structure their responses to probes of knowledge or seek social support when they are experiencing uncertainty or difficulty in generating a response.

In a final example 'Daniel' used a non-verbal social gesture to check whether there was social support from his peers for the ideas that he was expressing.

> Daniel began to speak about his ideas for floating and sinking. As he was speaking, he paused mid-sentence, moved his head to look in turn to each of his neighbours, and after receiving no response from them, he continued to speak.

This social gesture was interpreted as Daniel's non-verbal way of asking the other members in his group whether they were in agreement with his ideas, and he was looking for confirmation and support. Social gestures such as these are incredibly important for teachers, as they can help us understand what children know, what they are capable of doing and how understanding is negotiated in groups.

Gestures lend a hand to understanding children's ideas

Taken as a whole, the results of this study are beginning to reveal that understanding children's gestures as well as their various responses to tasks is important, particularly if children are unable to clearly or fully discuss what they know. Understanding the use of gestures by younger children in the early years is particularly important, as they may often lack the vocabulary to articulate what they know. Attending to gestures has the potential to reveal not only children's ideas, but also those moments of uncertainty and the way that children try to elicit help from their peers when they are experiencing uncertainty or unable to answer our questions.

As discussed earlier, research has also shown that teachers use non-verbal gestures when teaching, so perhaps it is even more important that we understand the impact that our own responses may have on others. How often do you find yourself 'stuck for words' when explaining things? Do you find yourself using gestures in order to convey your meaning to others? Have you ever seen children who are unable to answer a question start drumming on the table with their fingers? All of these non-verbal responses may contain important clues and cues. Perhaps as adults we need to 'listen' with our eyes as well as our ears if we are to fully understand those around us.

Research (*continued*)

Additional reading

Crowder, E. M., & Newman, D. (1993). Telling what they know: the role of gesture and language in children's scientific explanations. *Pragmatics and Cognition*, 1, 341–376.

Kress, G., Jewitt, C., Ogborn, J., & Tsatsarelis, C. (2001). *Multimodal Teaching and Learning: Rhetorics of the Science Classroom*. London: Continuum.

Primary SPACE Project Reports (1990–1994). Available online at http://www.nuffieldfoundation.org/primary-science-and-space (accessed 25 May 2011).

Practical and reflective tasks

Practical tasks

These tasks are designed to help you observe children and use non-verbal gestures to assess scientific development, as described in the preceding research box.

Early Years Foundation Stage

Set up an exploratory activity such as exploring in the environment, focusing on living things in the environment **(see Chapter 3)**; exploring a range of materials, focusing on understanding of materials and their properties **(see Chapter 3)**; or water play, focusing on floating and sinking **(see also Chapter 8)**. You may wish to set up a video to capture the interaction and non-verbal gestures more clearly.

Observe the children as they explore and interact with each other. You may ask specific questions to elicit their ideas about the scientific phenomena they are exploring.

Key Stage 1

Set up a problem-solving activity such as:

- 'What fabric makes the best waterproof hat/umbrella?', focusing on the material world

- 'Which paper is best for which pen?', focusing on the material world

- 'How can you make a box to protect an egg?', focusing on the material and physical world (see also Chapter 3).

Most problem-solving activities focus on understandings in the materials and physical world or a combination of both; there are few suitable ones that focus on the living world. You may wish to set up a video to capture the interaction and non-verbal gestures more clearly.

Observe the children as they undertake the problem-solving activity and interact with each other. Ask them to explain what they did and what they found out, probing their understandings about the science underpinning the problem.

Key Stage 2

Set up a collaborative investigation for children **(see Chapter 9)**. This may involve investigating their pulse rate before and after exercise, focusing on the living world, investigating the effects of temperature on how sugar dissolves in water, or investigating the distance vehicles travel from a ramp, focusing on the physical world.

Observe the children as they undertake the investigation and interact with each other. Ask them to explain what they did and what they found out, probing their understandings about the science underpinning the investigation.

Reflective tasks

● How did the children use non-verbal gesture in the activity and interactions?

● What did the non-verbal gestures tell you about their scientific development and learning?

● How could you use multimodality in other formative assessments for children?

ACTIVITIES AND KEY QUESTIONS

To promote science in the home

Living world

In the garden or yard, children can look for a variety of living things. Compare when back in school.

Key question: Where can you find animals/plants living/growing?

Give each child a seed or plant to take home. Children can plant the seeds, look after them as they germinate and grow and bring them back to show the school or tell the class about their plant.

Key question: How is your seed/plant changing?

Either go on a class visit to a large pet store and see how the animals are cared for or, alternatively, arrange for some pets to be brought into school by parents. At home children can help to take care of any pets.

Key question: What do the animals need to live and be healthy?

Ask children to bring in a baby photograph and a recent photograph and see if others can match the then and now. At home children can look at family photograph albums and look for family traits or talk about growing up. Be sensitive as some children may not be living with biological parents.

Key question: How has mummy changed as she gets older? How am I different from when I was a baby?

Talk about the things you like to put on a passport **(see Chapter 2)**. Take the passport home and compare with the 'likes' of other family members.

Key question: Is there something we all like?

Material world

Set up a laundry in the class [stimulated by *Mrs Lather's Laundry* (Alhberg, 1981)] and explore different detergents to see the lathers they produce. Try to remove stains from different fabric and see which detergent is best. At home the children can help with the laundry and try to remove a stain from their own clothes.

Key question: Which detergent is best for removing stains?

Make some play-dough with children **(see recipe in Chapter 3)**. Allow them to take a small piece of play-dough home to play with.

Key question: How do the ingredients change as you mix and/or heat them?

Read *Mr Bembleman's Bakery* (Green,1978) and follow up by making bread rolls and butter (by shaking full fat cream until it separates and pour off the liquid, leaving the butter) and jam. Invite parents to join the children for a picnic.

Key question: How do the ingredients change as you mix, heat them?

Activities and key questions (*continued*)

Photograph 4.4 *Mrs Lather's Laundry play area*

Set up the class activity to explore a range of materials such as a collection of solids, e.g. cornflour, salt, sugar, plaster of Paris, jelly powder, artificial snow (powder that, when mixed with water, makes jelly), wallpaper paste (with no fungicide), bicarbonate of soda; a collection of liquids, including, a large jug of water, vinegar, colour-change bubble bath, oil, lemon juice (see Chapter 2).

Key question: What do the materials feel like? How do they change when . . . ?

Give the children some artificial snow powder to take home and surprise their family with. When they are at home, they can ask their family what they think will happen when they add a little water to the snow powder and then try it and see if they were right.

Key question: What do you think will happen if we add water to the powder?

Physical world

Allow children to borrow a water play toy or a syringe for a week.

Key question: What did you find out when you played with the toy?

Give each child a pot of bubbles to take home and share with their family. Bubble mixture can be made in school with the children by mixing two parts detergent with eight parts water and one part of glycerine.

Key question: What can you see in a bubble?

Activities and key questions (*continued*)

Set up a class or school family learning session and give them a simple problem-solving activity such as to make a bridge out of a sheet of A4 paper, or make a tall tower out of newspaper.
  Key question: What makes the best bridge/tower?

Give each child a piece of plasticine to take home and make a boat shape that will float. The children can bring the 'boats' back to school and compare designs.
  Key question: What is the 'best' boat design?

Look at the school trikes and bikes and see how they work. Ask children to look at toys at home or the play equipment in the park and see how they work. Bring the findings back to school to share with others.
  Key question: How does a . . . work?

References

Alexander, R.J. (ed.) (2010). *Children, their World, their Education: Final Report and Recommendations of the Cambridge Primary Review*. London: Routledge.

Alexander, R.J. with Doddington, C., Gray, J., Hargreaves, L. & Kershner, R. (ed.) (2010). *The Cambridge Primary Review Research Surveys*. London: Routledge.

Ahlberg, A. (1981). *Mrs Lather's Laundry*. London: Penguin (Picture Puffin).

Baumrind, D. (1971). Current patterns of parental authority. *Developmental Psychology* Monograph 4(1, Part 2).

Bronfenbrenner, U. (1995). The bioecological model from a life course perspective: reflections of a participant observer. In: Moen, P., Elder, Jnr, G. H. & Lüscher, K. (eds) *Examining Lives in Context*. Washington DC: American Psychological Association, pp. 599–618.

Browne, E. (1997). *Handa's Surprise*. London: Walker Books.

Caffrey, B. (1997). Working with parents in the home. In: Whalley, M., ed. *Working with Parents*. Abingdon: Hodder & Stoughton.

Cambell, F.A., Ramey, C.T., Pungello, E., Sparling, J. & Miller-Johnson, S. (2002). *Early Childhood Education: Young Adult Outcomes from the Abecedarian Project*. Applied Development Science, 6(1), 42–47.

Carle, E. (1987). *The Tiny Seed*. London: Hodder and Stoughton.

Carneiro, P., Crawford, C. & Goodman, A. (2007). *The Impact of Early Cognitive and Non-Cognitive Skills on Later Outcomes*. London: Centre for the Economics of Education.

Effective Provision of Pre-school Education (EPPE) (2002). Measuring the Impact of Pre-School on Children's Cognitive Progress over the Pre-School Period. *The EPPE (Effective Provision of Pre-school Education) Project Technical Paper 8a*. London: Institute of Education.

Effective Provision of Pre-school Education (EPPE) (2002). Measuring the Impact of Pre-School on Children's Cognitive Progress over the Pre-School Period. *The EPPE (Effective Provision of Pre-school Education) Project Technical Paper 8b*. London: Institute of Education.

French, V. (2007). *Oliver's Vegetables*. London: Hodder Children's Books.

Gillham, B. (2008). *Observation Techniques. Structured to Unstructured*. London: Continuum.

Goswami, U. & Bryant, P. (2007). *Children's Cognitive Development and Learning. The Primary Review Research Survey 2 ÷ 1a.* Cambridge: Cambridge University Press.

Green, M. (1978). *Mr Bembleman's Bakery.* New York: Parents Magazine Press.

Haw, K. (2008). Voice and video. Seen, heard and listened to? In: Tomson, P., ed. *Doing Visual Research with Children and Young People.* London: Routledge Falmer.

Johnston, J. (2010). What emergent science is telling us about scientific development. *Primary Science*, 111, 3.

Johnston, J. (2011). Research focus: the impact of home and school on early years scientific development. *Education in Science*, 245, 30–31.

Johnston, J. & Nahmad-Williams, L. (2008). *Early Childhood Studies.* Harlow: Pearson.

Kaplan, C. & Owens, J. (2004). Parental Influences on vulnerability and resilience. In: Sylva, K., Melhuish, E., Sammons, P., Siraj-Blatchford, I. & Taggart, B., eds. *The Effective Provision Of Pre-School Education (Eppe) Project: Final Report. A Longitudinal Study Funded by The DfES.* Annesley, Notts: DfES.

Oversby, J. (ed). (2012). *ASE Guide to Research in Science Education.* Hatfield: ASE.

Palmer, S. (2006). *Toxic Childhood. How the Modern World is Damaging our Children and What we Can Do about It.* London: Orion.

Pollard, A. (2005). *Reflective Teaching: Evidence-informed Professional Practice* 2nd edn. London: Continuum.

Prosser, J. & Schwartz, D. (1998). Photographs within the Sociological Research Process. In: Prosser, J., ed. *Image-Based Research. A Sourcebook for Qualitative Researchers.* London: Routledge Falmer.

Pryor, J. (2004). Parenting in reconstituted and surrogate families. In: Hoghudhi, M. & Long, N., eds. *Handbook of Parenting: Theory and Research For Practice.* London: Sage.

Ramey, C.T., Campbell, F.A., Burchinal, M., Skinner, M.L., Gardner, D.M. & Ramey, S.L. (2000). Persistent effects of early childhood education on high-risk children and their mothers. *Applied Development Science*, 4(1), 2–14.

Schratz, M. & Steiner-Löffler, U. (1998). Pupils using photographs in school self-evaluation. In: Prosser, J., ed. *Image-Based Research. A Sourcebook for Qualitative Researchers.* London: Routledge Falmer.

Siraj-Blatchford, I., Sylva, K., Muttock, S., Gilden, R., & Bell, D. (2002). *Researching Effective Pedagogy in the Early Years.* Nottingham: DfES.

Sylva, K., Melhuish, E., Sammons, P., Siraj-Blatchford, I. & Taggart, B. (2004). *Effective Provision of Pre-School Education: Final Report.* London: Institute of Education.

Vincent, C. (2000). *Including Parents? Education, Citizenship and Parental Agency.* Buckingham: Open University Press.

Chapter 5

Learning science in the curriculum

Overview

In this chapter we look at:

- The history of science in the early years and national curriculum and the effects of curriculum change on scientific achievement
- Research into children's talk by Jane Johnston and the Creative Little Scientists research project
- Listening as a research tool, as part of the study skills theme
- Practical and reflective tasks that explore the analysis of children's talk using different analytical lenses
- Activity and knowledge boxes focusing on forces and sound.

Introduction

This chapter will look at the place of science in the early years and national curricula. It will look at the history of the curriculum and how ideas about what science should look like in the early years (birth to 8 years of age) has changed and how these changes have influenced provision and practice.

Science in the Early Years Foundation Stage

The first formal curriculum for the early years in the UK was introduced in the 1990s (SCAA, 1996). Science was part of knowledge and understanding of the world which also included technology, history, geography and information and communication technology (ICT). Through knowledge and understanding of the world, the young child from 3 years of age should 'explore and recognise features of living things, objects and events in the natural and man made world and look closely at similarities and differences, patterns and change' (SCAA, 1996: 4).

This quote really encompasses all science for young children, even though it was supposed to be relevant to the other subjects within knowledge and understanding of the world. Through their explorations, children could explore the living world, recognising changes with time, season and weather of life and growth and seeing patterns in the changes to living things. They could explore the material world and the changes that occur to materials with time, by heating, cooling, mixing and the like. They could also explore the physical world and the changes that occur to, and patterns within, the world: day and night, seasons, light, sound and so on. The curriculum was skills-based, as opposed to the knowledge-based curriculum of compulsory schooling (DfEE, 1999), and had a profound effect not only on early education, but on science in the national curriculum (see later). The focus on play and exploration as a pedagogical approach was found to have great impact on children's development and learning **(see Chapter 7)**.

In 2000 a new early years curriculum (QCA, 2000) was introduced which identified that:

> . . . learning for young children is a rewarding and enjoyable experience in which they explore, investigate, discover, create, practise, rehearse, repeat, revise and consolidate their developing knowledge, skills, understandings and attitudes. Many of these aspects of learning are brought together effectively through playing and talking. (p. 20)

This also came at a time when creativity was regarded as a missing but important component of education and professionals welcomed the emphasis that creativity was 'fundamental to successful learning' (QCA, 2000: 116). A further change in 2008 (DCSF, 2008a,b) widened the remit of the curriculum from birth to the start of compulsory schooling. Knowledge and understanding of the world involved six strands (see Cooper *et al.*, 2010):

1 Exploration and investigation (science)

2 Designing and making (design technology)

3 ICT

4 Time (history)

5 Place (geography)

6 Communities (citizenship).

In 2012, a revised Early Years Foundation Stage curriculum (DfE, 2012a) was introduced after a review of the curriculum the year before (Tickell, 2011). This identified seven areas of learning, comprising three prime areas and four specific areas:

- Prime areas:
  - Communication and language
  - Physical development
  - Personal, social and emotional development
- Specific areas:
  - Literacy
  - Mathematics
  - Understanding the world
  - Expressive arts and design.

Understanding the world is not dissimilar to the previous version (DfES, 2007), but the learning has three components, which includes aspects of science in each.

People and communities

In this area of learning, children talk about their past and present, describing events and things they have experienced in their immediate environment. This can happen as part of a topic on 'Ourselves' **(see Chapter 2)**. They can prepare personal passports **(see Figure 2.1)**, identify what they like and dislike and so realise that not everyone has the same ideas or preferences as they do. They will begin to recognise similarities and differences between themselves and others, and among families, communities and traditions **(see also Chapter 4)**. Listening to children as a research tool is also the focus of the study skills box in this chapter.

STUDY SKILLS

Listening as a research tool

We can tell a great deal about a child by listening to them. We want to encourage children to talk to us, to ask questions and to be curious about the world around them. We also want to find out how they feel, what worries them, what they enjoy doing and why and how we can support them in stressful situations. In order to assess children's ideas and feelings and provide experiences to support their development, we need to have access to them. This is best done by listening to children in a relaxing, questioning environment which encourages them to express themselves and to ask questions, but not to feel stupid in doing so.

We can listen to children while the children are playing, exploring, investigating and discussing. If they feel free to talk about their ideas and emotions while they are working, their discussions can be very revealing. Taping conversations can be very enlightening and tell us a lot about children's thinking and sometimes reveals some hidden ideas and concerns that have been overlooked in a busy classroom. We can also listen to the way in which children answer our questions. When asking questions of children, we are more successful at finding out about them if the questions are non-threatening and personal. For example, it is better to ask 'What do you think will happen next?' than 'What will happen next?' The first question appears to value the child's opinion, whereas the second question might appear to require a specific 'correct' answer.

As well as personalising questions, it is better to ask open-ended questions, as these are usually more successful than specific questions in eliciting children's ideas and feelings. Open-ended questions are ones which do not have a predetermined or limited choice answer, for example we might ask 'What can you tell me about this?' rather than 'What is this?'

Discussions and interviews or focus groups are useful ways to collect evidence. You can interview a range of adults, such as parents and professionals, ascertain their views on a range of issues and tap into their expertise and ideas. You can instigate discussions with adults and children and listen to their responses and interactions. The discussions can be in the form of focus groups, which can help to collect and analyse data, providing an element of triangulation. Discussions, interviews and focus groups can also help to verify and illuminate data collected in other ways. They may:

- be fluid in nature to allow for unexpected lines of discussion and subsequent unexpected data;
- have a structure or specific activities to ensure that areas of enquiry or research questions are answered;
- be an open forum involving some active participation/negotiation;
- be captured on video or audio tapes or in a notebook.

The use of focus groups (Morgan, 1997) can be helpful in gaining different perspectives about the same issue, but they can also elicit data on relationships, interaction and influence. However, they are not good at eliciting individual responses. The moderator of the group (who is not necessarily you) has a difficult role and requires good interpersonal and leadership skills. The focus group can provide an insight into and data about the interaction between participants and draws out the group's attitudes, feelings, beliefs, experiences and reactions. This is data that cannot be collected using other methods.

Study Skills (*continued*)

A problem with discussions is that the moderator or practitioner researcher can lead the participants and this will affect the validity of results. Focus group discussions can be particularly useful when there are power differences between groups, when the interactions of the group and the language they use are analysed and when opinions on an issue are being elicited (Morgan & Kreuger, 1993).

Discussions can be used at the start of a research project, during it or even at the end. They can help to evaluate or triangulate data collected using different methods. Data can be captured on video or audio tapes or in a notebook, and transcripts of tapes (audio or video) can support self-evaluation and help to identify overlooked interactions/ideas etc. However, taping may affect the quality of the data, as you may find some group members will not be comfortable disclosing data if they are being recorded.

In analysing responses you will have to scratch beneath the surface of what is being said – analyse the words to understand their explicit and implicit meanings. One way to ensure that interview data is rich for analysis is to ask analytical questions (how and why and so what?) as opposed to descriptive questions (when and where and what?). Wysocki and Lynch (2007) identify the difficulty of transcribing taped interviews accurately. The spoken word is often less articulate than the written word, containing many contractions, changes of direction, hesitations and inconsistencies that make sense in dialogue but not in the written form. When these have been removed in the transcript and some sense has been made of the words, the end result is very different from the social encounter of the actual interview (Cohen *et al.*, 2000) and will contain much of the researcher's understanding. This makes it even more important to ask the interviewees to verify meanings. The data from interviews can be collated and categorised, perhaps according to predefined categories relating to the actual questions, or according to themes arising from the analysis. This may include the occurrence of themes or words in the interview, or patterns in the themes. It may include behaviours observed during the interview or relationships between interviewees, their answers and behaviours. Even though the data can be categorised, it is likely that much of the analysis will be interpretative (Cohen *et al.*, 2000) or have an interpretative element and this poses analytical difficulties, but it has the advantage of leading to different levels of interpretation and validity.

The world

In this part of the EYFS curriculum (DfE, 2012a), children will explore similarities and differences in relation to places (geography and science), objects, materials and living things (history and science). Again 'talk' is important and time is needed to ensure children can talk about the world around them, the living, material and physical worlds, making observations of animals and plants and beginning to predict, hypothesise and interpret **(see Chapters 1, 3 and 4).**

ACTIVITIES AND KEY QUESTIONS

To promote understanding of forces

Set up an activity focusing on the concept of forces. Listen to the children as they undertake the activity. If you have another adult who can interact with the children, you can engage in active listening. If you are working alone in the class, it can be a good idea to video or audio tape the children because you may miss important views, as it is very difficult to actively listen and interact with the children. After the activity, set up a small group discussion to discuss their observations and findings. Ask some pre-planned questions to probe their understanding, remembering to make them personal and open-ended.

Some ideas for activities are outlined below.

Activities and key questions (*continued*)

Early Years Foundation Stage

- Play with objects that float or sink. Try to make a ball of plasticine that usually sinks, float, some aluminium foil that usually floats, sink, or a lemon that usually floats, sink.
  Key question: What do you think makes things float/sink?

- Play with gears and explore how they work.
  Key question: What is happening when you turn that wheel?

- Fill a glass with water and place a piece of card on top and then carefully turn it upside down with your hand over the card. Remove your hand and the water should remain in the cup. Try it out first and do it over a bucket or bowl if you are unsure if it will work (see the Knowledge box that follows). You can do this as a magic trick and get the children to explain why it is not magic.
  Key question: Why do you think the water does not fall out?

- Play with trikes and bikes and ask children to explain how they work.
  Key question: How do you get the trike/bike to move?

- Play with some moving toys e.g. a Jack-in-the-box, a wind-up toy, a spinning toy such as a magnetic gyroscope or an electrical spinning top and a toy that uses air to move (it moves when air in a bulb is squeezed into the legs; Johnston, 2009, 2012) **(see also the research box in Chapter 1).**
  Key question: How do you think the toy works?

Key Stage 1

- Observe a Cartesian diver. When you squeeze the bottle, the diver should sink and when you release the pressure it will rise again **(see Photograph 5.1)**.

Photograph 5.1 A Cartesian diver

Activities and key questions (*continued*)

Key question: What do you think is happening? Why do you think the diver is going up and down?

- Explore toy cars rolling down a ramp. Change the height of the ramp and see what happens.
  Key question: How do you think the height of the ramp makes a difference?

- Try removing a tin lid without and with a lever. Find out about Archimedes and his work on levers **(see Introduction, Figure 1.1).**
  Key question: Why do you think it is easier to remove the lid with a lever?

- Take a piece of paper and blow over the top of it. The paper should rise up. Get the children to try this for themselves.
  Key question: Why do you think this happens?

- Make a climbing teddy **(see Figure 5.1).**
  Key question: How does it work?

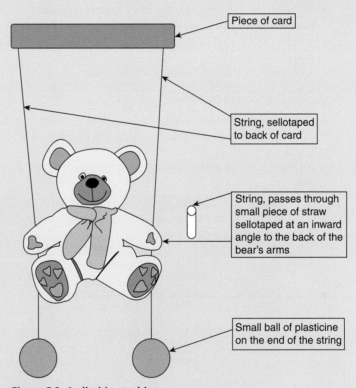

Piece of card

String, sellotaped to back of card

String, passes through small piece of straw sellotaped at an inward angle to the back of the bear's arms

Small ball of plasticine on the end of the string

Figure 5.1 A climbing teddy

Key Stage 2

- Investigate what happens when you roll toy cars of different weights down ramps of different heights.
  Key question: What do you think makes a difference to the speed and distance of the cars?

Activities and key questions (*continued*)

- Put a lemon pip or raisin in a glass of fizzy water or lemonade. Watch closely and try to explain what happens (see the Knowledge box that follows).
  Key question: What do you think is happening?

- Children can investigate what happens when they inflate a balloon attached to the end of a balanced stick **(see Chapter 3)**.
  Key question: What do you think is happening?

- Take two pieces of paper and hold them up in front of your face and blow between them. The two pieces of paper should move together and touch (see the Knowledge box that follows). Get the children to try it for themselves.
  Key question: Why do you think this happens?

- Get the children to make a ball sorter out of junk material. You need some different balls, with different sizes and weights and so on.
  Key question: How did you make the ball sorter?

Books to help motivate and stimulate explorations of forces include *Naughty Bus* by Jan and Jerry Oke (2004) and *Traction Man is Here* by Mini Grey (2005).

Reflective tasks

Early career professional

- How did listening to the children help you understand the children's ideas?
- How did listening to children affect behaviour?
- How could you develop active listening?

Developing career professional/teacher

- How did listening to the children's dialogue help you assess learning?
- How did listening help you evaluate your teaching?
- How can you improve dialogue in future planning?

Later career professional/leader

- How did the approach (problem-solving and dialogue) affect learning and behaviour?
- How can you improve listening skills in professionals in school?
- How can you incorporate the approach in your setting?

Technology

The third area in Understanding the World (DfES, 2007) is technology. It involves children understanding the range of technology in their homes, schools and microsystem (Bronfenbrenner, 1995) and selecting and using technology. The link between science and technology is very strong and the boundaries are hazy. Science (see the Introduction) is about the living (biology), material (chemistry) and physical (physics) world, but in its widest sense it also incorporates social sciences, earth sciences and technologies [design and technology (DT) and ICT]. Technology is about using and applying knowledge and skills (from a range of areas) to solve problems and make products. For the young child in the EYFS and compulsory education, science is about developing scientific understandings, skills and attitudes and sometimes this is done through a technological, problem-solving approach. On other occasions, scientific concepts are applied to solve a technological problem and the synergy between science and technology is recognised (see Activities and key questions to promote understanding of sound later in this chapter; see also Cooper *et al.*, 2010).

The principles underpinning the Early Years Foundation Stage

The learning within the strand understanding of the world (and, indeed, within the whole Early Years Foundation Stage) is set within four themes that embodied the principles of the EYFS (DfE, 2012a).

A unique child identifies the importance of child-centred provision, recognising the rapid development in young children and that each child is capable of significant achievements during these years. It is important not to underestimate young children, who may be capable of action, thinking beyond our expectations. It is easy to think that children are too young or inexperienced to engage in some ideas or activities, but we need to be open-minded as children are very good at exceeding our expectations. Some children may have particular talents, whilst others may be 'all-rounders'. Some children may have particular needs or disabilities. Each child is unique and it is our challenge to ensure that we meet their particular needs, supporting them and challenging them in their development.

Within the EYFS, and science education and throughout compulsory schooling, the best approaches teach and assess science formatively and by outcome. This facilitates individual response to children who may have particular interests and abilities within science but have language and literacy challenges. It does, however, present challenges for teachers in Key Stages 1 and 2 (KS1 and KS2) who are less familiar with individual approaches, despite the focus on personalised learning (DfES, 2004, 2006). Recognising children as individuals is advocated by many theorists (Montessori, 1989; Rousseau, 1911; Steiner, 1996) and most professionals but seems difficult in practice as we have never really perfected it throughout a child's educational life **(see Chapter 6).**

This theme appears to lead to the fourth theme, that *children develop and learn in different ways and at different rates*, which acknowledges the need to accommodate children and differentiate for children with special educational needs, who are gifted and talented and everyone in between (see also Johnston & Halocha, 2010, ch. 16). In the early years, effective differentiation is through open-ended activities and differentiated interaction and support. Open-ended activities allow children to use and develop from previous experiences and to differentiate for themselves. Support through modelling, questioning and direction can come from experienced peers and adults, and will enable the individual child to develop at a rate appropriate for them.

Positive relationships are identified as the second theme (DfE, 2012a). Positive relationships are essential whilst we support and challenge children so that they move from dependence to independence, familiarity to unfamiliarity, and learn how to be secure and confident individuals who begin to understand themselves and others. Positive relationships are key to all areas of children's development. Emotional development requires children to have attachments and positive relationships, initially with close family members, but

Photograph 5.2 An enabling environment in the Early Years Foundation Stage

increasingly with secondary carers, peers and other adults. The link between emotional and social development is very strong and positive relationships will also help children to become independent and develop new relationships and begin to see their position and role in society. Positive relationships also support language development, understandings about the world, a range of skills and, indeed, play a part in all development **(see Section 1).**

The third theme is **enabling environments**, which provide rich experiences that respond to children's individual needs. This involves a strong partnership between home and the setting/school, and the provision of effective contexts for development and learning **(see Chapter 4).** Enabling environments should be ones that make children feel secure and confident, that stimulate and motivate and which support and extend children's development and learning (Johnston, 2011a). The environment needs to be physically and emotionally safe and secure to enable the child to explore his or her world and develop an understanding of it. The indoor environment should provide opportunities for children to interact socially, talk to each other and develop their language and understanding of the world. The outdoor environment should encourage children to develop scientific skills and understandings in a safe and motivating way, so that they develop an interest in the world around them and, with support and care for their safety, the wider world (Johnston, 2011a).

Rich environments for learning in science in the EYFS

In order to support learning in science, the EYFS learning environment needs to be one that:

● stimulates and motivates;

● leads to exploration from children's own observations and curiosity;

- builds on home experiences in a meaningful partnership with the home;
- is rich in language and will encourage development in communication and language.

The classroom can provide motivating resources for children to observe, handle and explore. Some of these can be in 'feely boxes' so that children use and develop their senses. Resources should be used carefully so that children are not over-stimulated or bombarded with too much choice that can lead to demotivation. It is best to provide a mixture of quieter and noisier, familiar and novel activities, with a well-thought-out rationale for what is offered and some resources being put aside for a while and then re-offered.

Play areas can support holistic development as well as science specific development (Compton *et al.*, 2010; Johnston & Halocha, 2010) **(see also Chapter 7)**. A building site play area can develop children in many areas. The play area can have large and small bricks for building, hard hats and high-visibility vests, a balance beam and a frame to climb and clip boards and paper to design structures. Through the play children can develop understandings of structures and forces, design and build structures, work together and develop communication and language skills. They can use and develop their imagination (Compton *et al.*, 2010; Johnston & Nahmad-Williams, 2010). Children can even help to develop the role-play area, suggesting what resources they need and helping to resource and develop it.

Research

Dialogue between children and adults (Johnston, 2011b)

Jane Johnston

Research questions

- What does dialogic teaching in early years science look like?
- How does dialogic teaching support early years scientific development?

Research design

This research focuses on six groups of children, from 15 months to 11 years of age, playing with toys and supported by adult professionals. The youngest children (under 4 years of age) attended a private day nursery in a rural location and the older children (between 4 and 9 years of age) attended a one-form entry primary school. The schools volunteered for the research, and parental permission was obtained. In all cases, the research took place during the school/setting day, as part of normal practice, and all children whose parents had given permission were included in the research.

In the youngest children (under 4 years of age), free play was observed for 10 minutes, whilst the children played independently with adult interaction from the professionals who worked with them and with the

researcher mainly observing. For these children, a collection of toys was placed on the floor, including:

- Moving toys, such as a battery-operated hen that danced while singing, and wind-up toys;
- Aural toys that made sounds, such as a rattle, a battery-operated chick that cheeped and a Jack-in-the-box;
- Operated toys that involved some operation by the child, such as a ball and hammer set, a helicopter (whose propellers moved when pushed) and colour-change ducks (which changed colour when warm);
- Soft toys, such as a large dog, a sheep rug that could be worn);
- Other toys, such as a large multi-faceted mirror, a magnetic elephant with magnetic body parts and a wooden person (with moveable limbs).

In the older children (4 years and older), toys were placed on a table, and an initial period of free play was followed by the researcher questioning about the toys. No other adult was involved in these interactions. The toys included:

Research (*continued*)

- Electrical toys, such as a cheeping chick, an electric car and flashing sound and light balls;

- Magnetic toys, such as a monkey and an elephant with magnetic body parts, magnetic frogs and magnetic marbles;

- A variety of wind-up toys, such as a spinning aeroplane and a jumping dog;

- Spinning toys, such as a magnetic gyroscope and an electrical spinning top;

- Toys that use air to move, such as a jumping frog and a jumping spider (which moved when air in a bulb is squeezed into their legs) and a snake (whose tongue stuck out when squeezed);

- Other toys, such as a 'slinky', a sprung jumping man (who jumped up after being pushed down onto a sucker) and a trapeze artist and monkey (who somersaulted when the wooden sides of the trapeze were squeezed).

The play was videoed and the interactions were transcribed to identify the effect that personal, adult participatory and peer participatory interaction had on scientific development (Rogoff, 1995).

Summary of findings

The findings were presented as a series of (four) case studies that focus on the individual, peer and adult interaction and dialogue, and the effect of each on the children's scientific development is analysed.

Case study 1

This case study focused on 10 minutes of play and interaction with one child under 2 years of age. The play took place in a group of six children aged 15 months to 2 years, with two early years professionals, plus the researcher.

In this case study, play was solitary and often aimless. Interactions, including affective responses, were non-verbal.

> Boy 2 watched other children but mainly interacted with them when encouraged and led by an adult, encouraging the children to put the ducks in the water and asking them 'What colour has yours gone?'

So, adult modelling of play or participation in play, as well as talking about the toys, was needed to encourage any social interaction and to focus on the functional aspects of the toys. In this way, there is some evidence of Rogoff's personal and community/contextual planes (1995).

Case study 2

This case study was part of play and interaction in a group of nine children aged 2–4 years, with four professionals and the researcher. The case study focuses on the play and interaction of one child (Boy 1) and one adult professional/practitioner.

In this case study, with a slightly older child, there was an occasional verbal response, such as when Boy 1 described the dog as a 'sheep dog', although non-verbal responses still predominated; even the negotiation between children for the megaphone was mainly non-verbal with gestures and pointing.

> Boy 1 initiated some social interaction by taking toys to the practitioner and the practitioner responded by focusing attention on how a toy works (demonstrating how the megaphone works and asking questions about the Jack-in-the-box). However, Boy 1 appeared aimlessly to pick up one toy after another, and had almost peripheral engagement with others, or engaged in parallel or companionship play (Bruce, 2004).

Again there was evidence of Rogoff's personal, interpersonal and community/contextual planes (1995). The adult interaction involved questions that focused on the function of the toys, such as 'How do you get that one to work?' and 'Push it in' (when encouraging Boy 1 to work the Jack-in-a-box). Boy 1 did engage in a number of functional responses by looking very intently at different toys and watching how they worked, but self-initiated functional responses were not particularly seen.

Case study 3

The case study involved two separate interactions. The first was with eight Reception children (aged 4 and 5 years) in a one-form entry primary school. The children had only recently started at the school and attended for part of the school day. The play was part of the normal school day. In the initial free play, which preceded this interaction, the children were solitary and static in their play; they did not leave their seats, even to pick up a fallen toy, possibly because they associated table-top play with more formal activities for which they were expected to remain in their seats. In the following interaction, between the children and the researcher, the children were questioned about the toys. The second interaction was with eight Year 1 children (5 years of age) and the focus was on one toy: a trapeze artiste (who somersaults when the wooden sides of the trapeze are squeezed). In both interactions the adult is the researcher.

These interactions were very adult-led. However, all responses were mainly verbal and in response to the adult questioning. In the first interaction, with the younger children, the adult led the interactions

Research (*continued*)

and the children needed prompting from the adult to make responses. The questioning focused on the function of the toys but did not appear to support social interaction and discourse. This is possibly because of their age, their limited scientific experiences and their unfamiliarity with the researcher. In the second interaction, although the adult was leading the discussion, there were more social interactions with peers and the beginnings of children focusing more closely on the function of the toy and using the ideas and answers of other children as starting points for their ideas. These ideas were more sophisticated and the discourse (both adult and peer) appears to be helpful in developing the children's scientific ideas.

Case study 4

This case study involved two interactions. The first was with eight Year 3 children (aged 7 and 8 years) and the second was with eight Year 4 children (aged 8 and 9). In both interactions, the play took part of the normal school day and involved free play with no adult interaction; the adult was the researcher who observed the interactions and later questioned the children about the toys they were playing with.

Interaction 1

Many of the interactions during the free play involved emotions and are characterised by exclamations such as 'Wheee!' Many were also social, in that they were requests for attention: 'Hey, look! Look at that mouse', 'Look! Look! Look!', 'Look at the aeroplane', and focused on the functions of the toys: 'Look! It's jumping up. It's jumping up'. Social interactions were characterised by increasing verbal negotiation with their peers (as compared with younger children):

> 'I want this.'
> 'Can I look at this after you?'
> 'You've got this.' (giving child the frog).
> 'I'm going to have a racing one.' (racing spider and frog).

Some social interactions began to move from the functional to the exploratory, with children asking, 'How do you do that?', 'Look at the legs' (of the frog and pulling them down) and 'I'm going to...'. The functional interaction was later seen in the adult questioning phase of the activity that followed the free play:

Interaction 2

The interactions with these children (aged 8 and 9 years) were also characterised by emotional responses, but with more comments, such as 'Oooh', 'Wicked', 'Ahhh' and 'It's really fit', rather than social exclamations. Their interactions were more functional:

> 'Listen, it cheeps.'
> 'Jumper.'
> 'It spins.'
> 'It flips.'
> 'Oh look, it flips.'
> 'It wobbles.'
> 'It flips.'

They were also social:

> 'Look at this.'
> 'Watch this.'
> 'Look at mine. It's good mine is. Look at mine.'
> 'I'll swap you.'
> 'Watch this, watch this!'
> 'Hey pass that.'

There was only one example of exploratory play, with one girl quietly exploring the working of three separate toys with no interaction with her peers. The adult questioning did not encourage peer interactions, as can be seen by an exchange, when children were being questioned about the electric car.

These interactions appear to indicate that the free play was more supportive of social interaction that leads to scientific exploration and that the adult questioning had limited value, particularly in terms of social dialogue. In both interactions, the social dialogue encouraged the children to explore the toys' functions and to move from superficial, random engagement with the toys to a scientifically more focused, although limited, engagement.

Conclusions

The research indicates the importance of adult support and dialogic interaction to encourage children to observe, make links between ideas and develop further lines of inquiry.

In this research, the need for a balance between adult, peer and contextual support in older children was also evident. In Case study 4, the adult observed during the free play but then tended to lead during questioning. The free play appeared to be more supportive of scientific development, even with limited social interaction, than adult-led questioning. What appeared to be needed with older children was a more 'dynamically changing' (Rogoff, 1995: 151) combination of interaction, which cannot be planned for but is needed to scaffold scientific engagement and learning. In this way, adult-initiated rather than adult-led discourse appears

Research (*continued*)

to be effective, especially where social dialogue between peers is encouraged so that the adult initiates but does not lead or dominate.

The research findings appear to indicate the importance of social interaction in play, encouraging more peer discourse, scientific play and observations. This social interaction enables children to negotiate social boundaries (Broadhead, 2004) and develop conceptual understandings through cultural mediation (Bruner, 1991). This confirms ideas concerning effective pedagogy for young children as including interaction between children, their environment and adults (Vygotsky, 1962). Children should be active participants in their own understanding of the world, exercising some autonomy and developing understanding from experiences that build upon their previous knowledge (Piaget, 1929). They should have opportunities to scaffold their own and others' learning (Bruner, 1977), through talk (Alexander, 2008) with adult support (Stone, 1993). However, it is unclear if this is a conscious pedagogical approach adopted by professionals working with young children. It may be that this needs to be explored more fully with professionals working with very young children, to ensure that the children move seamlessly from solitary and quiet to more socially and orally supported functional and exploratory scientific development.

References

Alexander, R. (2008). *Towards Dialogic Teaching: Rethinking Classroom Talk*, 4th edn. York: Dialogos.

Broadhead, P. (2004). *Early Years Play and Learning: Developing Social Skills and Cooperation.* London: RoutledgeFalmer.

Bruce, T. (2004). *Developing Learning in Early Childhood.* London: Hodder & Stoughton.

Bruner, J.S. (1977). *The Process of Education*, 2nd edn. Cambridge, MA: Harvard University Press.

Bruner, J.S. (1991). 'The narrative construction of reality'. *Critical Inquiry*, 18(1), 1–21.

Piaget, J. (1929). *The Child's Conception of the World.* New York: Harcourt.

Rogoff, B. (1995). Observing sociocultural activity on three planes: Participatory appropriation, guided participation, and apprenticeship. In: Wertsch, J.V., Del Rio, P. & Alvarex, A., eds. *Sociocultural Studies of Mind.* Cambridge, UK: Cambridge University Press, pp. 139–164.

Stone, C.A., (1993). What is Missing in the Metaphor of Scaffolding? In: Forman, E.A., Minick, N., & Stone, C.A, eds. *Contexts for Learning; Sociocultural Dynamics in Children's Development* New York: Oxford University Press, pp. 169–183.

Vygotsky, L. (1962). *Thought and Language.* Cambridge. MA: MIT Press.

Reflective tasks

Rogoff's (1995) three sociocultural planes – personal, interpersonal and community/contextual – have been found to be useful as an analytical lens in early scientific development (Fleer, 2002; Johnston, 2009; Robbins, 2005).

Observe some children interacting and actively look and listen to them. You may wish to video the interaction and work with a colleague and critical friend in analysing the video.

Early career professional

Choose one of Rogoff's (1995) planes as an analytical lens and see how it influenced the interaction. Look for the evidence of children's personal engagement or engagements with others or how the context affected the activity and subsequent learning.

- How did using the plane as an analytical lens help you to focus your analysis?

- How could you improve the effect of the plane on development and learning in your future practice?

Developing career professional/teacher

Use Rogoff's (1995) personal and interpersonal planes as analytical lenses and see how much of the interaction was personal and how much with peers or adults.

● How did using the planes as analytical lenses help you to focus your analysis?

● How could you improve both personal and interpersonal interaction to support development and learning in science?

Later career professional/leader

Use Rogoff's (1995) three planes as analytical lenses and see how the context affects the personal and interpersonal interactions.

● How did using the planes as analytical lenses help you to focus your analysis?

● How could you improve the context to encourage interaction and support development and learning in science?

The outdoor environment for the EYFS should also be one that encourages curiosity, enquiry and exploration. In the early stages of the EYFS, children will be naturally curious and want to explore the world around them; to touch, taste, smell and listen to things they encounter in the world around them (where it is safe to do so). There needs to be space for energetic and loud activities and space for more sedentary and quiet activities. The space for energetic activities could include play areas, such as building sites, garden centres and the seaside. Quiet areas could include sensory gardens where the children can explore:

● Colour in leaves, flowers, stones

● Smells through herbs and flowers

● Tastes through vegetables and fruit grown

● Things to touch and experience, e.g. the different textures of bricks, bark, leaves.

This can particularly appeal to children with sensory disabilities or who learn best in quiet and contemplative environments.

The outside environment can involve messy play and exploratory activities, such as playing with wet sand, mud and puddles [see also the Forest School's initiative (**www.forestschools.com**) for other ideas to develop and use the outdoor environment].

Practical tasks

What scientific understandings, skills and attitudes do you think early years children need to develop in the EYFS? In the boxes below, identify those you think children should develop in the EYFS.

Understandings	Skills	Attitudes

Exploring sounds

A Foundation Stage unit was focusing on sound as a conceptual area. They made sounds using their hands and clapped, banged on the floor and tables and compared the different sounds. Hakim went and found a variety of boxes of different sizes and made of different materials (e.g. plastic, wood, card) and began to compare the sounds they made when hit. The professional asked another child, Paige, what she thought and together they put the boxes in order of whether they made a loud sound or a quiet sound. The children then looked at the different musical instruments they had in the class and compared them.

Jack was outside the class in the outside play area and was making noises by twirling a plastic tube above his head. The professional asked him if he could make a noise with other plastic tubes and he collected ones of different lengths and diameter and tried them out.

Nina and Lachlan drew a map of the classroom and identified noisy areas and quiet areas. The book corner was identified as a quiet area, but they said that they could hear the noise from the more physically active play areas and so the professional suggested they made a pair of ear muffs that children could wear if they wanted to be quiet and concentrate on reading a book. They looked at all the materials they had in the junk material box and the professional suggested that they used two different materials and compared how soundproof each was. Nina chose some furry fabric, whilst Lachlan chose some cotton wool.

At the end of the session, the children showed the others in the class what they had done and found out.

Reflective tasks

Early career professional
- How did the activities help to develop an understanding of sound?
- How could the professional have supported the understandings of sound by extending the activities?
- How could a plenary discussion session facilitate understandings further?

Developing career professional/teacher
- How could the activity use dialogic teaching (Alexander, 2008) to support the development of scientific understandings?
- How could the dialogue and interaction be strengthened at different stages of the activity?
- How could you develop your own teaching to support children's interaction and talk in science?

Later career professional/leader
- How could you use ideas from the case study to develop effective approaches in your setting/school?
- How could dialogic teaching (Alexander, 2008) be used more effectively in your setting/school?
- How could you support professionals in your setting to develop skills in dialogic teaching?

Knowledge box

Sound

Sound is a form of energy that travels from a source in a sequence of waves of pressure. These waves propagate through compressible media such as air or water as a result of vibrations of packets of air (or water) at the macroscopic level. Sound propagates through solids as well, as a result of vibrations of molecules.

Sound travels through a medium from a vibrating source. The medium that the human ear hears best is air (a gas) and when the vibrations in the air reach the ear, this in turn makes the bones in the ear (the hammer, anvil and stirrup) and the eardrum vibrate. Sensory cells in the ear receive the vibrations and send impulses through nerves cells to the brain, which translates them. Some animals have different sensory receptors and use different media to receive vibrations; for example, whales and dolphins have fatty deposits under their jaws and these receive vibrations in the water. Hippopotamuses can actually 'hear' through both air and water. When hippos are in water they can be submerged or have their heads sticking out above the surface. When a hippo gives a warning call to others, those under the water will 'hear' the call before those above the water. This is because sound travels faster through solids (where the molecules are closer together) than through liquids and faster through liquids than gases – sound travels through air at 330 metres/second (m/s), water at 1,500 m/s, brick at 3,700 m/s and steel at 6,000 m/s. Echoes occur when sound waves hit an object and some of the waves are reflected back and some pass through. Bats use echo sounders to detect obstacles and humans use them to measure the depth of the sea or identify obstacles under water.

Sound waves can differ in amplitude (loudness), which is measured in decibels, and frequency. Loudness is determined by the pressure the sound vibration makes on the ear. Normal conversation is at about 50 decibels and a busy street is at about 70 decibels. Sounds over 120 decibels are painful and can cause impaired hearing. The frequency affects the pitch: the higher the frequency (the closer the waves are together), the higher the pitch and the lower the frequency, the lower the pitch. The human ear can only hear a small range of frequencies (between 20 and 20,000 cycles), but some animals (e.g. bats and dogs) can hear higher frequencies than humans and children can hear higher frequencies than adults. Low frequencies produce low-pitched sounds and these can be heard by humans as rumblings or hums of heavy machinery and be quite disruptive as sound pollution.

The timbre of the sound is its quality and we use sound quality to identify different sounds and different human voices in speech. This is because human voices are capable of vibrating at several different frequencies at the same time. The sound boxes of musical instruments also affect the timbre which is why good-quality instruments sound better than poor-quality ones.

Musical instruments make sounds in different ways:

- Stringed instruments make sounds when the strings vibrate after being plucked, hit or bowed. The pitch of the note changes with the length of the string, its thickness and how tightly stretched it is. Musicians use their fingers to change the length and tautness of strings and thus to change notes.

- In woodwind instruments, the air is vibrated by blowing into the mouthpiece. Different notes can be produced by covering and uncovering the holes along the instrument's length.

- Brass players make notes by altering the shapes of their lips and making the air vibrate at different speeds. In many brass instruments, tubes can be lengthened and shortened, while valves also change the length of the column of air inside the instrument. This also changes the note produced.

- Percussion instruments make the air vibrate when hit. Drums and cymbals produce one note, but xylophones and timpani can have a variety of notes of different pitch.

- The human voice makes sounds when air is passed over the vocal chords which vibrate. Different lengths of vocal chords mean that different people can make different sounds; men have longer and thicker vocal chords than women and children. Additionally, humans can use muscles around the vocal chords to alter them and use their tongues, lips and teeth to change sounds.

Science in the curriculum

Before the introduction of the UK National Curriculum in 1989, science was taught in a very ad hoc way and by enthusiasts. This meant that if children were fortunate to have a teacher who was interested in and included science in their teaching, then they had some good experiences of science. However, if their teachers were not confident, competent or interested in science, then they could go through primary school with no real scientific experiences, let alone positive ones. That is not to say that science initiatives and good primary science education were not available. As de Bóo & Randall (2001) have shown through the contributions to their book *Celebrating a Century of Primary Science*, primary science education has a long history, including:

- Peripatetic science demonstrators who travelled from school to school from 1877 with their resources in a handcart;
- Nuffield Primary Science projects of the 1960s (which I took part in as an infant pupil);
- Science 5 ÷ 13 projects in the 1970s;
- Government-funded 35- and 20-day courses in the 1980s and 1990s.

In 1988, science was identified as a core subject in the primary curriculum and became a compulsory and core subject for all primary children when the National Curriculum was introduced in 1989. Since then, the nature of science in the National Curriculum has changed considerably (Figure 5.2).

Science was one of the first subjects to be mapped out in the National Curriculum and provided considerable support for teachers in primary schools who lacked confidence and expertise in teaching science. Upon the introduction of the National Curriculum in 1989, science was used as a theme and other subjects were planned around this. The curriculum identified the percentages of time to be spent on science (about 20%, with equal weighting with English and mathematics) and with each aspect of science (skills and knowledge) having equal weightings so that all science should be taught through practical experiences **(see Section 3)**. The result was that every child had science experiences and science was regarded as the success story of the National Curriculum, as mentioned in many government reports and texts at the time and in the next few years. This contrasts with recent evidence from the 2012 SAT results in Science (DfE, 2012d) that 19% of pupils did not reach Level 4, the standard expected. In many ways this is to be expected from the 1989 high, as the place of science in the curriculum has declined over the years. In 1992, a new science curriculum

119

Figure 5.2 The Nasher Cricklem by Trevor Dunton

was introduced and a discussion paper on teaching (Alexander *et al.*, 1992), both of which started the decline:

- The National Curriculum removed the support for teachers and the links to using science in real life situations, so children were less likely to see the relevance of science or its place in society.

- The discussion paper identified that cross-curricular teaching and learning were ineffective and advocated subject-based science teaching that led to science being seen as a subject rather than permeating the curriculum and life. Curiously, two of the authors of the report went on to review the primary curriculum (DCFS, 2009; Alexander, 2010) and recommended a more thematic approach to teaching and learning subjects.

Further changes to science in the National Curriculum were made in 1995, and in 2000 the whole of the primary curriculum, including science, was changed. These changes further marginalised science in the primary curriculum and made science more about learnt knowledge than application of understandings (scientific literacy). In 2012, a long-awaited draft new curriculum (DfE, 2012b) was introduced, which furthered the decline. It set the scene for primary education to prepare children to 'be equipped to do more advanced work once they start secondary school' (DfE, 2012c). The publication of the draft programmes of study was followed by an 'informal' consultation, with the view that it would be implemented in September 2014. The framework (DfE, 2011) was based on a report by the Expert Panel, who recommended that a key focus was subject knowledge. Professionals having to consider and implement the new framework are confused for a number of reasons: they don't know whether the Expert Panel took soundings from experts in the field; some experts have voiced concern about the resulting curriculum in published correspondence with the Secretary of State; other respected experts appear not to have been consulted. There is also no evidence that the curriculum builds on previous reviews such as the Cambridge Primary Review, which collected evidence between 2004 and 2009 through wide-ranging consultation, formal written submissions, meetings, surveys and evaluations and published a final report (Alexander, 2010) and a collection of the research surveys (Alexander [ed.], 2010).

The resulting programmes of study (DfE, 2012b: 1) identified that:

> … a high quality science education provides the foundations for understanding the world through the specific disciplines of biology, chemistry and physics. Science has changed our lives and is vital to the world's future prosperity, and all pupils should be taught essential aspects of the knowledge, methods and uses of science. Through building up a body of key foundational knowledge and concepts, they should be encouraged to recognise the power of rational explanation and develop a sense of excitement and curiosity about natural phenomena. They should be encouraged to understand how key foundational knowledge and concepts can be used for explanation of what is occurring, prediction of how things will behave, and analysis of causes. This foundational understanding should be consolidated through appreciation of specific applications in society and the economy.

There is nothing controversial here or in the aims of primary science (DfE, 2012b: 1).

The National Curriculum for science aims to ensure all pupils:

- develop scientific knowledge and conceptual understanding through the specific disciplines of biology, chemistry and physics
- develop understanding of the nature, processes and methods of science through practical activity
- are equipped with the scientific knowledge required to understand its uses and implications today and for the future.

There is incongruence between the aims, the programmes of study that are supposed to follow on from the aims and current good practice. For example, the emphasis on scientific understanding and language in the aims is good but does not fully resonate with the programmes of study, which focus on naming and identifying and key terminology and vocabulary, rather than dialogic learning and teaching (Alexander, 2008) that leads to understanding of scientific concepts. Embedding understanding of the nature and the scientific processes in the content of science is also welcome and would appear to advocate a reversal of previous years where scientific enquiry was regarded as a separate entity. However, there is a tension between scientific enquiry as 'performing simple tests' (DfE, 2012b: 3) and demonstrations at Key Stage 1 and evidence of how children develop scientific skills **(see Chapter 1).** Where assessments are likely to remain focused on ephemeral knowledge, rather than on understandings and scientific skills, this tension can only be exacerbated. The programmes of study are mapped out for each year group and this also appears to ignore evidence of the way children develop and personalised learning (see, for example, *Every Child Matters*, 2003). They are also based on the mistaken opinion, unsubstantiated by any evidence, that learning facts and regular testing raise standards.

The move away from levels represents an assessment change from the last 24 years of the National Curriculum and possibly undermines the whole foundation of national curriculum testing. The criterion-referenced levels were an important move away from the norm-referenced assessment prior to the introduction of the National Curriculum (DES, 1988) and recognised that children could achieve because of their ability, rather than because they were in a year group of 'less able' children. However, this is more consistent with SAT results, which measure percentage of achievements in one year group of 30 children against previous cohorts and consider any increase as a rise in standards and a decrease as falling standards.

Practical and reflective tasks

Practical tasks
What scientific understandings, skills and attitudes do you think early years children need to develop in KS1 and KS2? In the boxes below identify those that children at these stages should develop in the National Curriculum.

Key Stage 1

Understandings	Skills	Attitudes

Key Stage 2

Understandings	Skills	Attitudes

Reflective tasks
- How does the National Curriculum match the understandings, skills and attitudes you have identified in the boxes?
- How can you bridge any gaps between the National Curriculum and what you have identified?

Research

Creative Little Scientists

Creative Little Scientists: Enabling Creativity through Science and Mathematics in Pre-school and First Years of Primary Education is a European Commission 7th Framework Programme research project involving academics and teachers across Europe in nine countries: the UK, Finland, Belgium, Germany, Portugal, Romania, France, Malta and Greece.

These nine European countries were chosen because they represent a wide spectrum of educational, economic, social and cultural contexts, as well as a wide spectrum of practices regarding science and mathematics education in general, science and mathematics education in early years, and creativity in education.

The project lasted 2 years beginning in 2011 and produced a Conceptual Framework (CLS, 2012) and four literature reviews:

1 Review of science and mathematics education in pre-school and early years of primary school

2 Review of creativity in education

3 Review of teacher training for early years educators and primary teachers

4 Review of comparative education.

The project also mapped, compared and analysed existing practices in creative early years science and mathematics, through an online survey of teachers and visits to schools. Finally the project provided directions for teacher training and disseminated the research findings.

More information about the project can be found at **http://www.creative-little-scientists.eu/home**.

Knowledge box

Forces

Forces are measured in newtons (N; after Sir Isaac Newton, 1643–1727). A newton is defined as the force necessary to accelerate a 1 kg mass at a rate of 1 m/s^2. Sir Isaac Newton's laws of motion describe forces:

First law: When forces acting on an object are equal and opposite, they cancel each other out.

Second law: If an unbalanced force acts on an object, it accelerates in the direction in which the force acts,

Third law: For every force, there is an equal and opposite force called a reaction force.

Forces act in pairs and when the paired forces are balanced, an object will not move (if stationary), slow or stop or change direction (if moving). So when a glass with water with a piece of card on top is carefully turn upside down and the water remains in the cup, this is because the force acting downwards (gravity) is balanced by the force acting upwards (air resistance). When an object floats, it is because the force acting downwards (gravity) is balanced by the force acting upwards (upthrust resulting from the water pressure).

There are a number of different forces:

- Weight – this is a downward force due to the effect of gravity (it is not a measure of the mass of an object). Weight is affected by gravitational force, which is in turn affected by the mass; so the greater the mass the greater the gravitational force and the weight. The Moon is smaller in mass than the Earth (one-sixth of the mass) and has less gravitational force and so weight of an object on the Moon will be one-sixth of the object's weight on Earth (but the mass remains the same). Weight is measured in newtons.

- Gravitational force **(see Chapter 1)** – the force exerted on an object due to gravity.

- Friction – the force opposing movement.

- Air resistance **(see Chapter 1)** – a type of friction force on objects moving through air.

- Floating/upthrust **(see Chapter 2)** – the force pushing up when the density (= mass/volume) of an object is less than the density of the liquid it is immersed in.

- Centrifugal force is, in some opinions, a type of force resulting from centripetal acceleration which acts towards the centre of the rotation. It pulls the spinning object onwards.

- Centripetal force – the force on a spinning object pulling it inwards as in the gravitational force on planets, which keeps them in orbit **(see Chapter 7).**

Inertia is a property of an object due to its mass and results in large objects needing greater force (and smaller objects needing less force) to move them and/or to stop them moving. Speed measures how fast an object is moving and can be calculated as distance divided by time taken. Velocity involves direction as well as speed, and terminal velocity is the constant speed at which an object moves after initial acceleration; this can be seen when you drop a feather, as it falls faster at first and then slows down to a constant speed. Acceleration is the rate of change of velocity (= change in velocity/time). An accelerating object will have a force exerted upon it. A large force will accelerate a small mass more rapidly than a small force will accelerate a large mass.

When an object moves, slows down, speeds up or changes direction, this is because the forces are not balanced and one force acting on the object is greater than others. When a vehicle rolling along the floor or down a ramp slows down, this is because of friction between the surface of the floor/ramp and the wheels of the vehicle.

When a Cartesian diver dives **(see Photograph 5.1)**, this is because the density of the diver is increased when the bottle is squeezed and there is an imbalance of forces acting upon the diver. Look carefully at the small test tube on the diver's back. When the bottle is squeezed, the air bubble in the tube is squashed (the same number of air molecules but compressed into a smaller space) and more water enters the tube. This increases the mass in the tube and the density of the diver. The raisin diver is similar in that air bubbles attach themselves to the raisin and then pop, so altering the balance of forces and the raisin dives to the bottom of the glass and rises to the surface.

When an inflated balloon alters balance or lifts an object, this is because compressed air has increased 'mass' and exerts greater force on an area. This is why compressed air is used to lift very heavy objects and to inflate tyres on vehicles.

When you blow over a piece of paper and it rises, or you blow between two pieces of paper and they move together, this is because fast-moving air has lower pressure than slower-moving air. This is the basis of flight; that on take off, fast moving air over the curved surface of the wings reduces the air pressure above the wings, as compared with below the wings, and so the plane lifts off the ground.

ACTIVITIES AND KEY QUESTIONS

To promote understanding of sound

Early Years Foundation Stage

- Read *Noisy* by Shirley Hughes (1985) or *Shhh!* by Jeanne Willis and Tony Ross (2004) as a stimulus to explore sound.
  Key question: What is noisy? What is quiet?

- Use a 'story' apron (an apron with many pockets) with each pocket having a different musical instrument in. Explore the instruments and use them to make the sounds to accompany a favourite story.
  Key question: What sound would best make a happy/sad sound?

- Go on a sound hunt and look for a hidden ticking clock by just listening.
  Key question: What can you do to help you to listen?

- Make a percussion instrument using junk material. Explore the different sounds made using different seeds and beads inside the instrument and different containers.
  Key questions: How does your instrument make a sound? How can you change the sound?

- Use a stethoscope to listen to things.
  Key question: What difference does the stethoscope make?

Activities and key questions (*continued*)

Key Stage 1

- Explore sounds with a collection of resources (rulers, tubes, dried beans, tuning fork, musical instruments, funnels and tubing of different sizes, stethoscope). Use the resources available to explore sounds, vibrations, pitch, resonance, e.g. by twanging a ruler, playing a musical instrument, exploring a tuning fork and its effect on a glass of water or beans on a drum or a table tennis ball. Try putting it in a glass of water or next to a table tennis ball or some rice, listening using a funnel or stethoscope, making noises through the tubes.
  Key question: How do you think the noise is made?

- In a group of four or five, make a set of instruments that make sounds in different ways (banging, plucking, blowing, scraping, hitting). Make each instrument so that it can produce a number of different notes or even a scale. Be able to explain how the instrument makes a sound and how the different notes and a scale can be produced. Use bottles and different amounts of water and blow across the top of each bottle or hit the bottle. What is the difference between the scales? Use plastic tubes or straws of different lengths to make pan pipes. Use plant pots of different sizes and hang them upside down from a cane. Use a beater to hit or add a short stick or nail to the end of the string inside the pot (as a clanger for a bell). Stretch rubber bands of different thicknesses (but the same size) or different sizes (but the same thickness) across a stout cardboard box to make a stringed instrument. Which rubber bands make high-pitched notes? Use plastic tubes of different lengths and thicknesses and blow down them. Use the instruments to compose a tune to perform.
  Key question: How can you change the sound the instrument makes?

- Draw a map of the classroom and/or playground and make a note of the noisy and quiet areas in school.
  Key question: Where is the best place to go if you want to be noisy/quiet?

- Make some ear muffs.
  Key question: How do the ear muffs work?

- Play with stethoscopes, funnels and plastic tubes. Listen to objects with them and talk down them and see what happens.
  Key question: What have you found out?

Key Stage 2

- Investigate yoghurt pot telephones. See what makes a difference to the sounds you can hear. You could try length of the string, what the 'string' is made of, the size, shape and material of the pots.
  Key question: What makes the 'best' telephone? Why?

- Explore the effects of a vibrating tuning fork on a drum, seeds on a drum, a glass of water or a table tennis ball.
  Key question: Why do you think this happens?

- Make a hearing aid (a sound trumpet or stethoscope).
  Key question: How does your hearing aid work?

- Investigate which materials are 'best' at soundproofing a ticking clock in a box.
  Key question: Why is this the 'best' soundproofing material?

- Explore sound using datalogging sensors.
  Key question: What have you found out about sound?

References

Alexander, R. (2008). *Towards Dialogic Teaching: Rethinking Classroom Talk*, 4th edn. York: Dialogos.

Alexander, R. (ed.) (2010). *Children, their World, their Education: Final Report and Recommendations of the Cambridge Review.* London: Routledge.

Alexander, R., Rose, J. & Woodhead, C. (1992). *Curriculum Organisation and Classroom Practice in Primary Schools: A discussion paper.* London: DES.

Bronfenbrenner, U. (1995). The bioecological model from a life course perspective: reflections of a participant observer. In: Moen, P., Elder, Jnr, G. H. & Lüscher, K. (eds). *Examining Lives in Context.* Washington DC: American Psychological Association, pp. 599–618.

Creative Little Scientists (CLS) (2012). Conceptual Framework and Literature Reviews as addenda. Online at: http://www.creative-little-scientists.eu/content/deliverables. Accessed 28/5/12.

Cohen, L., Manion, L. & Morrison, K. (2000). *Research Methods in Education,* 5th edn. London: Routledge: Falmer.

Cohen, L., Manion, L. & Morrison, K. (2011). *Research Methods In Education,* 7th edn. London: Routledge: Falmer.

Cooper, L., Johnston, J., Rotchell, E. & Woolley, R. (2010). *Knowledge and Understanding of the World.* London: Continuum.

Compton, A., Johnston, J., Nahmad-Williams, L. & Taylor, K. (2010). *Creative Development.* London: Continuum.

Department for Children, Schools and Families (DCSF) (2008a). *Statutory Framework for the Early Years Foundation Stage; Setting the standard for learning, development and care for children from birth to five.* London: DCSF.

Department for Children, Schools and Families (DCSF) (2008b). *The Early Years Foundation Stage; Setting the standard for learning, development and care for children from birth to five; Practice Guidance.* London: DCSF.

Department for Children, Schools and Families (DCSF) (2009). *Independent Review of the Primary Curriculum: Final Report.* Nottingham: DCFS.

De Bóo, M. & Randall, A.(eds). (2001). *Celebrating a century of Primary Science.* Hatfield: ASE.

Department of Education and Science (DES) (1988). *A Report: National Task Group on Assessment and Testing.* London: DES.

DfES (2003). *Every Child Matters.* London: DfES.

Department for Education (DfE) (2011). *The Framework for the National Curriculum. A Report by the Expert Panel for the National Curriculum review.* London: DfE.

Department for Education (DfE) (2012a). *Statutory Framework for the Early Years Foundation Stage. Setting the Standards for Learning, Development and Care for Children from Birth to Five.* London: DfE.

Department for Education (DfE) (2012b). *National Curriculum for Science. Key Stages 1 and 2 – Draft.* London: DfE.

Department for Education (DfE) (2012c). News and Press Notices. New Primary Curriculum to bring Higher Standards in English, Maths and Science. Online at: www.education.gov.uk/inthenews/inthenews/a00210127/newnatcurric. Accessed 12/6/12.

Department for Education (DfE) (2012d). National Curriculum Assessments at Key Stage 2 in England 2011/2012 (revised) London: DfE http://media.education.gov.uk/assets/files/pdf/m/sfr33-2012v2.pdf

Department for Education and Employment (DfEE) (1999). *The National Curriculum: Handbook for Teachers in England.* London: DfEE/QCA.

Department for Education and Science (DfES) (2004). *Excellence and Enjoyment: Learning and Teaching in the Primary Years: Classroom Community, Collaborative and Personalised Learning.* London: DES.

Department for Education and Science (DfES) (2006). *2020 Vision: Report of the Teaching and Learning in 2020 Review Group.* London: DES.

Department for Education and Science (DfES) (2007). *The Early Years Foundation Stage: Setting the standard for learning, development and care for children from birth to five.* London: DfES.

Grey, M. (2005). *Traction Man is Here.* London: Random House.

Hughes, S. (1985). *Noisy.* London: Walker Books.

Fleer, M. (2002). Sociocultural assessment in early years education: Myth or reality? *International Journal of Early Years Education,* 10(2), 105–120.

Johnston, J.S. (2009). How does the skill of observation develop in young children? *International Journal of Science Education*, 31(18), 2511–2525.

Johnston, J. (2012). The development and support of observational skills in children aged under 4 years of age. *Journal of Emergent Science*, 3, 7–14.

Johnston, J. (2011a). Enabling environments. In: Beckley, P., ed. *Learning in Early Childhood.* London: Sage.

Johnston, J. (2011b). Children talking: teachers supporting science. *Journal of Emergent Science* 1, 14–22.

Johnston, J. & Halocha, J. (2010). *Early Childhood and Primary Education; readings and reflections* Maidenhead: Open University Press.

Johnston, J. & Nahmad-Williams, L. (2010). Developing imagination and imaginative play. In: Compton, A., Johnston, J., Nahmad-Williams, L. & Taylor, K. *Creative Development.* London: Continuum.

Montessori, M. (1989). *The Child, Society and the World. Unpublished speeches and writings. The Clio Montessori Series.* Oxford: Clio Press.

Morgan D.L. (1997). *Focus Groups as Qualitative Research*, 2nd edn. London: Sage.

Morgan, D.L. & Kreuger, R.A. (1993). When to use focus groups and why. In: Morgan, D.L., ed. *Successful Focus Groups*. London: Sage.

Oke, J.& Oke, J. (2004). *Naughty Bus.* Budleigh Salterton: Little Knowall Publishing.

Qualifications and Curriculum Authority (QCA) (2000). *Curriculum Guidance for the Foundation Stage.* London:QCA/DFEE.

Robbins, J. (2005). Brown paper packages? A sociocultural perspective on young children's ideas in science. *Research in Science Education*, 35(2), 151–172.

Rogoff, B. (1995). Observing sociocultural activity on three planes: participatory appropriation, guided participation, and apprenticeship. In: Wertsch, J.V., Del Rio, P. & Alvarex, A., eds. *Sociocultural Studies of Mind.* Cambridge, UK: Cambridge University Press.

Rousseau, J.J. (1911). *Emile.* London: J. M. Dent and Sons.

SCAA (Schools Curriculum Assessment Authority)(1996). *Nursery Education: Desirable Outcomes for Children's Learning on Entering Compulsory Education.* London: DfEE.

Steiner, R. (1996). *The Education of the Child and Early Lectures on Education.* New York: Anthroposophic Press.

The Telegraph (2012). Primary schools 'failing one in five science pupils. *The Telegraph*, 28 May 2012. Online at: http://www.telegraph.co.uk/education/educationnews/7936841/Primary-schools-failing-one-in-five-science-pupils.html. Accessed 28/5/12.

Tickell, C. (2011). *The Early Years: Foundations for Life, Health and Learning. An Independent Report on the Early Years Foundation Stage to Her Majesty's Government.* London: DfE.

Willis, J. & Ross, T. (2004). *Shhh!* London: Anderson Press.

Wysocki, A.F .& Lynch, D. A. (2007). *Compose, Design, Advocate.* Harlow: Pearsons.

Chapter 6

Transitions between stages of development

Overview

In this chapter we look at:

- Children's perspectives as they move through the early years and the effect of the transitions they experience on scientific development
- Research by Beatriz Sena into transitions in the early years and how to ease these transitions
- Narrative as a research tool, as part of the study skills theme
- Practical and reflective tasks that look at analysing narrative and stories
- Activity and knowledge boxes focusing on electricity, magnetism and variation and classification

---

Introduction

This chapter will consider transitions in the early years from the perspective of the child who experiences them. We experience transitions throughout our lives and each transition needs to be handled carefully to ensure our cognitive learning and our emotional, social and physical development are not adversely affected.

The first transition a child will experience is birth. This involves them leaving the comfortable and familiar environment of the womb, where they recognise their mother's heartbeat, sounds and share the emotions of their mother. Birth is a difficult transition physically and emotionally – physically, because it involves foetuses moving from one environment to a very different one, where suddenly they have to breathe on their own, and because the process itself is very physical and not without physical risk (e.g. lack of oxygen can cause brain damage and future physical and cognitive impairments). Emotionally it is taxing because the child will spend long periods away from its mother after birth and any problems with bonding/attachment can affect emotional and subsequently social development.

Other important transitions in the early years include the birth of siblings, moving house, family breakdown, being cared for by childminders, starting compulsory education, moving classes, schools and the key stages.

STUDY SKILLS

Narrative as a research tool (see also Johnston, 2012)

Danto (1985) argued that the basic structure of knowledge is narrative. Narratives use the participants' own voices as data, providing a way of organising the complex forms of experience in ways which can be told, recounted and hence made predictable. It is by being able to tell a story again and again that a sense of stability, identity, recognisability and hence action and learning become possible. Despite the flux and the change that takes place, a story points to recurrent features and essential structures and processes. Narratives can be more than anecdotes and provide powerful insights into situations; they can be in the form of case study exemplars of practice or research or identification of critical incidents in the participant's life. Sometimes the narrative is supported by images, such as photographs or drawings (Leitch, 2008). The story can be told by different participants, triangulating data and getting a more vivid and comprehensive picture of the action, event or situation being described. A story told from different perspectives allows layers of data to be analysed and a more valid (truthful) picture to be revealed.

Analysing narratives

Narratives can enable unexpected data to be collected and help illumination and understanding of data and analysis. Analysis of narrative can help us to understand why something has happened or why an idea is held, provide alternative explanations to events or ideas and help researchers to look at a situation from other perspectives or points of view. Bassey (1999) presented interviews from various sources as a series of letters from a fictional trainee teacher, ensuring the trustworthiness of the interpretation by triangulating the analysis asking the interviewees for comment. Bassey (1999) suggested that the advantages of using fiction as a technique in research writing are that it provides a coherent and readable interpretation of different data sources, and that incidents remain vivid and powerfully expressed, but are not traceable to any one source.

Stronach and MacLure (1997) offered different interpretations of the same interview data to illustrate the 'struggle' between researchers and their subjects. The contrast between the portraits is fascinating in itself.

The meta-analysis of the methods raises important questions about the roles of research and researchers. Handy (1989) used anecdotes as vehicles for conveying considerable amounts of information and also for facilitating understanding, persuading and learning. The anecdotes are not used in any rigorous manner, but are still effective because they can be used in relation to other experiences.

Narrative analyses involve the identification of sequential data (a timeline of events) and contexts (the situation, people involved etc.). Sequences may be of different kinds, such as cause–effect sequences where a particular stimulus or input is associated with a particular response or output. There may also be particular inputs but several possible associated outputs. In addition, the relationship may be merely a correlation with no necessary causal relationship. The context is of two kinds, symbolic and material. A symbolic context involves all the values, norms, beliefs, linguistic and cultural forms of a given society or group. A material context refers to the resources, the nature of the physical environment, and the built environment of housing, roads and so on. The material context can, of course, have symbolic import just as the symbolic context can have a material form. In analysing narrative, the researcher explores the main characters, their beliefs, values and the ways in which the narrative relates experience and relationships. Consideration of narrative from different participants (e.g. children, professionals and parents) can provide valuable insights into the different views held of themselves, their role in the context and the relationships between them. Gender or power relationships may be explored; for example, the relationship between professionals and parents could be analysed or the child's development through the curriculum **(see Chapters 4 and 5).**

The end result of a narrative is essentially a case study (Bassey, 1999), which provides a rich database that can be analysed in a number of different and holistic ways, so that a more valid (truthful) picture begins to be revealed.

Transitions from birth to 3 years of age

In the following case study, we tell the story of Jamie as he moves through the early years and experiences transition, and the effect it has on his scientific development. In this part of the case study, the story is told by Jamie's mother.

CASE STUDY

Transitions from birth to 3 years of age – a mother's perspective

Jamie was born by Caesarean section, as he was a very large breech baby. I was expecting a girl and when told the baby was a boy, I was not sure if he was mine. Despite this I bonded quickly with Jamie, and his father was delighted. I had planned carefully to ensure that his older brother was not jealous of him and we experienced few relationship difficulties, even though Jamie was not the only child in the family and did not have my undivided attention.

Despite being very busy with two young children I tried to give Jamie many positive experiences. He particularly enjoyed baking with me and exploring in the garden. One day we moved a plant pot and a woodlouse ran out onto the patio. I explained to Jamie that woodlice liked dark, damp places and so he was looking for somewhere to go now I had moved the pot. Jamie then went and stood on the woodlouse, saying 'Now it's dark for him' and was surprised when he moved his foot and the woodlouse did not move! Jamie was curious about things, but timid in social interactions, although his size (he was in the top percentile for height and weight) often made people expect more of him, thinking he was older than he was. He was more challenging than his brother as he had little awareness of his own safety, was very active and needed considerable adult interaction.

I worked part-time and Jamie went to a neighbour who was a registered childminder. When he was 2.5 years old he experienced three significant transitions, which had a big effect on him and the whole family. First, we moved home and this unsettled Jamie, so that after a few weeks he said that he had 'enjoyed his holiday' and could he go home now. Secondly, he started at a playgroup and found this very difficult, probably because of his lack of social maturity and timidity. Thirdly, he had to change childminders and did not settle with a succession of different carers so that he became very insecure and clingy and many aspects of his development were impaired. This caused a problem for me as I wanted to 'be there' for Jamie, but also needed to work after moving house and taking on additional debt. We then had a particularly bad year where I struggled to help an increasingly anxious Jamie and meet my work commitments.

Reflective tasks
Analysing the story

Early career professional
- How do you think Jamie's scientific development was affected by these transitions?
- How could Jamie's parents support him through these transitions?

Developing career professional/teacher
- How could the professionals in Jamie's life support him through these transitions?
- How could the settings help him to develop scientifically despite these negative experiences?

Case study (*continued*)

Later career professional/leader

- What messages does this narrative have for settings and their provision?
- How can settings ensure that the child's transition into the setting is as smooth as possible?

As Maslow (1968) identified in his hierarchy of needs **(see Figure 6.1)**, children need to have their physiological and emotional needs met before they can begin to develop in other ways and so these transitions would have had a detrimental effect on Jamie. Maslow's theory does not just resonate with Jamie, but with all children as they move from one setting to another or from one key professional to another. The theory also identifies the link between the physical, emotional, social and cognitive elements of development. If children are unsettled, physically, emotionally or socially, it is likely that their cognitive development will be impaired. The way children react to emotional and social stress can be very different. Some children will become withdrawn, whilst others become hyperactive or irritable. Some children will not want to come to school, whilst others will develop evasion tactics to avoid contexts that make them feel inadequate.

How a setting looks and the way it is run are important to ease transitions. When children enter a setting, it is helpful for their transition that the setting has some basic familiarity with their home, as this will help them settle. Moving from the familiar to the unfamiliar gradually is helpful. Early settings should consider how the physical environment provides opportunities for all individuals – familiar play experiences, soft furnishings, small rooms and quiet spaces can be helpful. The best settings ease transition by catering for all children and by not expecting children to accommodate to the setting (see Rousseau, 1911), but rather easing them into a routine. Some early settings may provide food for those who arrive without breakfast, with the children making healthy snacks and drinks for themselves. They may have bathing facilities, so children can enjoy bathtime and learn about floating and sinking, volume of water and how materials change, and develop skills of pouring and the like while they bathe. They will have plenty of opportunities for activities that support all cognitive understanding, by exploring the world around them, developing vocabulary through talking about

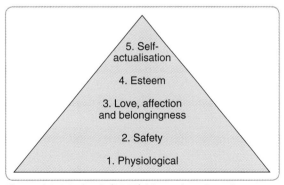

Figure 6.1 Maslow's (1968) hierarchy of needs

what they are exploring. Once children feel secure, they can be more independent in their explorations and encouraged to explore the wider world and take risks in their thinking.

Open-ended activities that take children's interests and experience as starting points can help to ease transitions. In this way, building on the experiences of bathtime, baking, gardening and the park **(see Chapter 4)** can develop into wider and deeper explorations of the way materials change when they are mixed with water, heated or cooled, the way plants grow, what different animals need to live and how we can care for them. This may mean that professionals who care for children need to grasp opportunities when they arise, by, for example, taking advantage of weather conditions. When it rains, children can go out and feel the rain on their faces, splash in puddles and make mud pies. When it snows, children can go out and experience the cold flakes on their faces, build with snow and watch a snowball melt indoors. When it is sunny, the children can feel the sun on their faces and explore shadows and how they change during the day **(see the Activity box on light, p. 189)**. If it hails, the children can feel how hard the hailstones are and collect them up to look at more carefully. Water play can emulate bath play at home, using toy ducks, boats, bubble bath, bath bombs and the like and gradually introducing less familiar water play toys, such as syringes, water wheels and containers of various sizes and shapes. You can even fill the water trough with bubble mixture and explore the bubble liquid; it keeps very well for a long time so making a big batch is not wasteful **(see recipe in Chapter 4, p. 100)**.

In the Activities and key questions box on magnetism that follows, the activities move from the familiar, exploring magnetism in toys, to the unfamiliar, exploring and investigating magnets, but in an open-ended way. When new scientific phenomena are introduced, it is less stressful for children to explore them in an open-ended way so there is no right or wrong. In more formal contexts, older children are often reluctant to explore in this way, as they have learnt by now that education is about 'getting it right'. This emphasis on 'getting it right' is inconsistent both with the nature of scientific enquiry and with good learning. It is also not consistent with smooth transitions, as children who enter a new context and feel they have to learn the rules and 'get it right', even when they are not sure what 'right' is, are more likely to feel stressed and so not be in a position to reach their full developmental potential (see Maslow's hierarchy of needs in Figure 6.1).

We have an opportunity to help children develop and learn about science in an atmosphere of awe and wonder and without the artificial obstacles that we put in their way. These obstacles include:

- Different key stages with very different learning outcomes and emphases from skills-based and child-centred in the Early Years Foundation Stage (EYFS) to knowledge-focused and increasing emphasis on conformity for the individual **(see Chapter 5)**.

- Different professionals who reflect different aspects of development, so the EYFS is likely to have professionals who have detailed knowledge and understanding of child development but less understanding of cognitive development and the science underpinning natural scientific phenomena.

- The increasing emphasis on narrow cognitive outcomes (and 'getting it right') as children move from the EYFS and through Key Stage 1 (KS1) and KS2.

- An apparent lack of understanding on the part of the government about the effect of emotional, social and physical development on children's cognitive development and, even more worryingly, a lack of understanding of the importance of practical engagement in developing scientific understanding **(see Section 1)**. So less is often more and practical exploration can lead to understanding that can be applied in different contexts in the future – as the proverb says, 'I hear and I forget, I see and I remember, I do and I understand.'

Play is a familiar experience for young children and so play contexts can be quite powerful opportunities for children to explore science (see Chapter 7). Play can start from a story or storybook, as we have seen in each chapter of this book. For example, the story of *The Little Red Hen* by Tony Bradman (1990) can be re-enacted and lead to improved understanding of farm animals, life processes and living things. It does not matter that the children are mixing fact and fiction (Johnston, 2005) as this does not appear to adversely affect their development. The story of *The Patchwork Quilt* (Flournoy & Pinkney, 1987) can lead to exploration of different fabrics and making a patchwork quilt for the home corner and help children to develop social skills, such as cooperation. Later, play in the home corner can help mediate in their lives, by imitating behaviour and exploring actions and reactions, through imaginative play (see Compton *et al.*, 2010). The story, *Kassim Goes Fishing*, by Geraldine Kaye (1980) can lead to playing games such as magnetic fishing (see the Activities and key questions box on magnetism) as well as well as understanding of other lives and contexts. Other familiar play areas, such as a focus on the home, can lead to understanding of:

- Plants, mini-beasts, habitats and growth in the garden;
- Life processes and variation between humans by looking at family trees;
- Variation and life processes in other living things by looking at pets in our homes;
- Materials and their properties through focusing on washing in the kitchen;
- Forces through looking at tools in the garage or kitchen.

ACTIVITIES AND KEY QUESTIONS

To promote understanding of magnetism

Early Years Foundation Stage

- Play with magnets and see what they stick to and what they do not.
  Key question: What do the magnets stick to?
- Hide magnetic objects in a sand tray and allow children to try to locate them using a magnet. Add a few non-magnetic objects and try again.
  Key question: Why do you think the magnet does not find the...?
- Play magnetic fishing. You can make your own by tying magnets to a string attached to a stick. You can make fish by using a paper clip or paper fastener on a card fish; some fish can be left without a paper clip or paper fastener. You can also use the games to help develop recognition of colours, letters or numbers by laminating the fish and putting colours, numbers or letters on the back. The child can 'catch' the fish and keep it if they can recognise the colour/number/letter. If they cannot recognise it, they can be told and it is thrown back in the 'pond' until next time.
  Key question: Why does the fish 'stick' to the line?

Activities and key questions (*continued*)

Photograph 6.1 Magnetic fishing game

- Some children's games use magnetism, e.g. Etch-a-sketch or put a moustache on the face. You can make your own games by putting a drawing on A4 paper (e.g. a man's face) and some iron filings in a plastic wallet and sealing very securely. A magnet can be used to put a moustache, beard, hairy ears etc. on the man's face. Be careful, however, not to let children play with iron filings, as they can be breathed in.
  Key question: How do you think the games work?

- Explore the 'push' and 'pull' of magnets in play.
  Key question: What have you found out about the magnets?

Key Stage 1

- Allow children to play with magnets and hypothesise as to why magnets repel and attract.
  Key question: Why do you think magnets push and pull each other?

- See how many paper clips a magnet will pick up. You can make a paper clip 'train' and see how many 'carriages' the engine will pull. Compare with other magnets.
  Key question: Which magnet is the strongest?

- Explore a collection of different objects made with different materials and see which ones are magnetic.
  Key question: What do you notice about the things that are magnetic?

Activities and key questions (*continued*)

- Play with some magnetic toys (e.g. magnetic beans, a magnetic gyroscope) and explore how they work.
  Key question: How do you think the toys work?
- Predict and find out which materials and which thicknesses magnets will attract through.
  Key question: What have you found out about magnets?

Key Stage 2

- Explore a range of different materials, including different types of metal and sort them into those which are magnetic and those which are not.
  Key question: How do you think magnets work?
- Explore a range of magnetic toys and games and see how they work. Make a magnetic toy or game.
  Key question: How does your game work?
- Test drink cans for recycling using a magnet; aluminium cans are not magnetic.
  Key question: How can you use magnets to separate objects?
- Find out which is the strongest part of a magnet.
  Key question: What did you find out about the magnet?
- Read the story of *The Iron Man* by Ted Hughes (1985) and make an iron man with scrap metal held together with magnets.
  Key question: What have you found out about magnets?

Transition has been recognised as an important factor in children's lives and there are many books on the subject, particularly about transition from EYFS to KS1 (Brooker, 2008; Dunlop & Fabian, 2007; Fisher, 2010; Orlandi, 2012). However, the following research box looks at transition from home to nursery at age 2–3 years.

Research

Transition

Beatriz Sena

Research question
What are the features of current effective pre-nursery provision both in the UK and in Brazil that can contribute to effective bilingual pre-nursery education?

Research design
The research was conducted in a large bilingual school in Rio de Janeiro and involved evaluation and action research, collecting parents' and teachers' views through questionnaires and piloting a new pre-school programme collecting data through observation and monitoring.

Summary of findings
Eight out of 12 parents said they believe pre-school is a valuable opportunity to enrich the lives of children and prepare them for formal education and therefore

Research (*continued*)

that they should provide their child with opportunities to achieve this as early as possible; four out of 12 thought that sending their children to early childhood programmes is unnecessary and inappropriate because they are not sure that starting this early (around 2 years old) will have much impact. However, it is important that parents are provided with as much detailed information about the available programmes regarding:

- content
- the type of classroom and out-of-classroom activities
- the qualification of the teachers
- evidence of development from children that have undergone these programmes
- considering their child-preparedness to attend school.

Only then can parents weigh the advantages and disadvantages of pre-school programmes and decide which option is best suited for their family. The school where I work takes that into account and seems to do a good job, since 12 out of 12 parents said they had received enough information about school facilities and methodology. As planning has a great part to play in the success of any programme, informing the parents and starting the parent–school partnership even before the children go to school should be viewed as essential features of the planning step, because in this way parents can obtain a great deal of information about the advantages of starting school early.

What these five features have as their weaving thread is the commitment to the EYFS principle of 'a unique child' (DCSF, 2008). These commitments are all interlaced and affect one another in ways that have to be addressed by curriculum design. If properly addressed and implemented in the classroom, these commitments will become the advantages of pre-schooling that are expressed by the teachers and which will respond to the parents' concerns expressed in their answers to Questionnaire 1.

From both the parents' and the teachers' point of view, there are more advantages than disadvantages in starting school earlier. High-quality early childhood education helps to prepare young children to succeed in school. Every concept that is taught between the ages of 0 to 3 years constitutes first-class raw material to stimulate brain development, and every ability that is developed deeply affects other abilities through the child's neural networks (Fisher, 2002; Karoly et al., 1998). Therefore, pre-schooling constitutes a wonderful chance to enhance children's physical and verbal abilities as well. When viewed from the perspective of the commitments to the EYFS principle of 'A unique child' (National Strategies, 2011), pre-nursery may represent the first intentional and organised action into the child's life that is able to promote the child's wholesome well-being by comprising and interweaving the five domains, provided that the quality of the educational programme has the child's wholesome well-being as its ultimate objective. And within this 'quality', teacher awareness of and preparedness to execute this objective is of the utmost importance.

I personally believe that in addition to the advantages of starting school earlier, as mentioned by the teachers and discussed by Fisher (2002) and Karoly et al. (1998), we should not ignore the innate abilities of some children and also that children's individual cognitive development is processed at a different pace. Quality early education programmes give children the social, language and numeracy skills they need and prepare children, especially at-risk children, for school. They make children more ready to learn, and therefore more likely do better throughout school. Children who get a good start are less likely to fail.

References

Fisher, J. (2002). *The Foundations of learning.* London: Open University Press.

Karoly, L.A., Greenwood, P.W., Everingham, S.S., Hoube, J., Kilburn, M.R., Rydell, C.P., Sanders, M. & Chiesa, J. (1998). *Investing in Our Children: What We Know and Don't Know about the Costs and Benefits of Early Childhood Interventions.* Santa Monica, CA: RAND.

National Strategies (2011). *Themes and principles.* Available at **http://nationalstrategies.standards.dcsf.gov.uk**. Accessed on 29th April 2011.

Transitions from 3 to 5 years of age

Transition is a process rather than an event and should involve a good partnership between professionals and carers **(see Chapter 4)**. Good communication among professionals, children and parents are an essential ingredient in effective transitions (Primary National Strategy, 2006; Sanders et al., 2005). In order to support children in transitions, professionals need to know what the transitions are that affect children and how to support the individual child. Parents identify that within transitions they want their children to be happy, supported by professionals who know them and encourage them, but do not pressurise them (Primary National Strategy, 2006). They also identify the importance of quality relationships with staff who both teach their children and care about them, and sessions where they can be involved in the life of the school or setting and meet other parents.

CASE STUDY

Transitions from 3 to 5 years of age – the professional's perspective

Jamie started in the Reception class at 4.5 years old, coming from a nursery attached to a different school. He therefore had no children that he knew in the school and had to settle socially before he could begin to develop academically. I taught Jamie from Reception through to Year 2, moving with the class each year. Jamie was a clumsy, active child, whose fine motor skills were not very developed and he was likely to knock children over or break things, without meaning to. He also suffered from ear infections that made it difficult to hear when the background noise was high, so whole school assemblies, whole class lessons and the like were difficult for him. I understood this problem, as I have hearing problems myself, but other teachers whom Jamie came into contact with did not understand and thought that he was 'being naughty'.

Jamie loved individual exploration and investigation and developed his motor skills and knowledge of the world through making things, solving problems and exploration. When he had an ear infection, I would often let him do individual problem-solving work, or play with Lego during whole class or school activities. He had a sharp mind and his ideas were often very creative, so he could solve problems in a different way from the expected and so open-ended activities were better for him than direct instructions.

Reflective tasks

Analysing the story

Early career professional

- How did the teacher differentiate to meet Jamie's individual needs?
- How else could the teacher ease transitions between lessons for Jamie?
- How can you meet the individual needs of children in your care?

Developing career professional/teacher

- How could the teacher have eased Jamie's transition into school from nursery?
- How could the teacher improve Jamie's experience through home–school partnership?
- How could you improve transition for children starting school from a variety of different contexts (e.g. other nurseries, home, childminders, playgroups)?

> **Case study (*continued*)**
>
> **Later career professional/leader**
> - How did the class organisation in the school ease transitions for Jamie?
> - What are the problems that children experience in moving from class to class?
> - How could you improve transition by helping colleagues understand the experiences from a child's perspective?

Continuity can aid transitions between classes and professionals. In order for this to occur, professionals need to have shared understandings, values and practices. This does not mean that all settings should be the same or that all professionals should be clones of each other, but it does mean that there should be good and effective professional communication, understanding of the children and their experiences and a shared commitment to adapt practice and procedure to match children's needs.

There are a number of ways that science can ease transitions. One way is to explore a shared science topic from one class or setting to the next, with some shared planning between the classes and transfer of teachers, or even team teaching, if resources allow. For example, within one setting/school, a shared topic could be connected to variation and classification. A story such as *Jim and the Beanstalk* by Raymond Briggs could focus on the differences between individuals, or the story of Noah's Ark could focus on the similarities and differences between different animals. A story sack could be used by the classes, teachers from one class teaching the other class and older children from one class working with younger children from another. Shared play areas can also help to bridge the gap and ease transitions between classes in the same setting.

Bridging units with a shared topic are more common when the transition is from one setting to another, but can still be very effective at easing transitions. Such bridging units are common within many local authorities and are designed to ease transitions from EYFS to KS1, from KS1 to KS2, and from KS2 to KS3. These units can:

- facilitate the adoption of similar routines and good practice across key stages, remembering the importance of a 'bottom-up' approach so that children build on their experiences;
- help children to work with other adults and children and so make the last few weeks of one stage and the first few weeks of the next stage more productive in educational and developmental terms;
- improve liaison between professionals in different settings/schools and provide some joint staff development;
- help teachers to understand transition from a child's perspective.

There are a number of ways that a bridging unit can work. It could focus on a topic/theme or outcome and start in the term before transition (usually the summer term in the UK) and finish in the autumn term once the move to a new class/year group/school has taken place. Variation and classification can be good concepts to focus on and children can look for plant and mini-beast habitats in the school grounds – even

Photograph 6.2 Science across Key Stages

when there is not a single blade of grass, there will be evidence of plants and animals. The children can start by exploring outside their own class/school with their current teachers and later compare a different site outside the new class/year group/school with the new teachers. Children from the different classes/year groups/schools can work together and, in this way, become familiar with the new environment and work across the transition. Older children can help the children moving into the new class to familiarise themselves with what will be their new environment, and guide them in the use of equipment to aid their observations of this environment, e.g. magnifiers, digital microscopes. Professionals in the classes/year group/school can introduce themselves to the children, learn about the practices they are used to, adjust their practices accordingly and help the children to adjust to new practices and new environments.

Another way a bridging unit might work is by starting in the old context, exploring the environment and producing a poster or display of photographs of their explorations and findings, a short video or even dioramas of habitats to take to the new class/year group/ school and share with the professionals and children there. The children could pose questions about the habitats and living things they have found, which would then form the basis of exploration in the new class/year/group/school.

ACTIVITIES AND KEY QUESTIONS

To promote understanding of variation and classification

Early Years Foundation Stage

- Use small world play of a farm and sort the animals into groups. Consider the different noises the animals make, where they live on the farm and what they eat.
  Key question: Why have you put all these animals together?

- Use the story of Noah's Ark and small world play of Noah's Ark to explore the similarities and differences between animals. Sort the animals into pairs and then into groups according to similar features/characteristics (fly, swim, live on land or in trees).
  Key question: Why are these animals different?

- Set up a pet shop in the class and get the children to tell you about each animal: what it needs to live, what it eats, how they should look after it.
- **Key question:** What does the ... need to live? How is this different from the...?

- Set up a garden centre with a variety of plants and look at the similarities between them.
  Key question: What do these two plants have in common?

- Look at a collection of seeds and sort them according to observable features. Try germinating the seeds and seeing if they grow in the same way. You can use the story of *The Tiny Seed* by Eric Carle (1987) as a stimulus.
  Key question: How are the seeds different?

Key Stage 1

- Sort pictures of animals into groups according to their physical features/characteristics.
  Key question: Why have you grouped these together?

- Use the story of *Where the Wild Things Are* by Maurice Sendak (1992) as a stimulus. Create some strange composite animals using the characteristics of existing animals, e.g. head of a rabbit, teeth of a lion, body of a lizard. Group the animals according to their features/characteristics.
  Key question: How did you decide how to group the animals?

- Go on a mini-beast hunt and look at mini-beasts that live below, on top of and above the surface of the ground. Look at the similarities and differences between the mini-beasts.
  Key question: How are these mini-beasts similar?

- Look at a collection of fruit and vegetables and group according to similar physical features. You can use the story of *Handa's Surprise* by Eileen Browne (1997) as a stimulus for this activity.
  Key question: How are the fruit/vegetables similar/different?

- Go on a plant hunt and look for plants that are similar (e.g. shapes of leaves, colour of leaves, size).
  Key question: Why are these plants similar?

Key Stage 2

- Tell the story of Darwin's voyage on *The Beagle* (see Johnston & Gray, 1999). Explore the animals and fossils he found on his journey and look at the similarities and differences between them.
  Key question: What are the similarities/differences between the animals Darwin found?

Activities and key questions (*continued*)

- Go pond-dipping and look at the similarities and differences between the animals you find.
  Key question: How can you group the animals?
- Sort a collection of skulls and look for similar characteristics, such as the shape of skull, the teeth, the eye sockets and the size of brain cavity. Similarly, sort through a collection of fossils and look for features similar to today's animals.
  Key question: What do the teeth/skulls/tell you about the animals?
- Go to a wood and look at the similarities and differences between trees (e.g. leaves, bark patterns). Alternatively, look at a collection of twigs with buds or leaves and sort them according to characteristics.
- **Key question:** What do you think these trees/leaves/twigs have in common?
- Look at a collection of plants and group according to similar physical features.
- **Key question:** How are the plants similar/different?

Transitions from 5 to 8 years of age

Within compulsory education and the curriculum, transitions continue to be problematic, even within one setting or school, for all the reasons discussed earlier and in **Chapter 5.** Changes in the EYFS curriculum (DfE, 2012a) and National Curriculum (DfE, 2012b) have done little to close the gap between the EYFS and KS1; indeed, the gap has probably got bigger.

It is important in transitions at any age, but probably more so in moving from the EYFS to KS1, for professionals to know where children have been, what their experiences are and where they are moving to. It is important to remember that any one stage or year in a child's life is just a part of that child's whole experience, and that professionals working with them during this period are an important, but still relatively small, influence on the whole. In many ways, this is like being asked to write the next chapter of a book that has already been started and that will be finished by others. In order to do this effectively and coherently, you need to know the characters (children), the plot (the children's previous experiences, what comes next and what the overall aims are) and the context (the whole educational environment). In science education, this means professionals should:

- know individual children's strengths and the things they find challenging and not assume that, if they have literacy difficulties, they are less able in science – indeed, many famous scientists were not traditional academics (e.g. Albert Einstein) and many children who are low achievers in literacy can do well in science, as long as we do not focus solely on the written word;
- understand how children develop generally and specifically in science and recognise the part played by physical, social and emotional development in scientific development (see Section 1);
- understand that the narrow, mainly cognitive outcomes of the National Curriculum are only a small part of what we want from a developing child – we should want children to develop as well-rounded individuals, with an interest in the world around them and

Figure 6.2 Ting – to listen

scientific phenomena, with skills that help them learn generally and explore and investigate scientific phenomena specifically, and with creative thinking skills to enable them to solve problems and think laterally;

- have good scientific knowledge and understandings that underpin learning and teaching in the curriculum, i.e. subject knowledge;

- have good pedagogical knowledge, so they know how best children learn and how best to support that learning, and specific scientific pedagogical knowledge to help children learn in science; for example, they should know how to challenge children's alternative conceptions in science **(see Chapter 2)** and how to build on children's natural curiosity **(see Chapter 3)**;

- understand the home context and how good partnership with the home can support learning **(see Chapter 4)**;

- understand the curriculum, how best to support children in achieving in the curriculum and in accessing continuing professional development as needed.

One of the most important skills a professional can have is the skill of listening. Active listening helps to understand children, the home, factors affecting learning and development, and assessment. Interestingly, the Chinese symbol for listening – *ting* **(see Figure 6.2)** – encompasses more than the traditional listening with our ears. *Ting* involves using the ears to detect the sounds and using your 'self' to pick out the pieces of information that are specific or important to you. The eyes watch and build up information from gestures, body language and facial expressions **(see research on multi-modality in Chapter 4)** and searches out truths. Giving undivided attention means that the professional can focus on the child and that the child feels valued and the heart evaluates, sorts and stores the information gained and provides a commitment to the child.

CASE STUDY

Transitions from 5 to 8 years of age – the child's perspective

I always enjoyed science in school but I liked to do science, not write about science. I also remember being very much misunderstood and 'getting into trouble'. On one occasion I remember playing in a sand tray outside the classroom and giving some sand to a baby

Case study (*continued*)

in a pram. I did not understand why the teacher was so cross. On another occasion, I remember telling one teacher why we had an extra day in a leap year and she was cross and called me a 'know-it-all'.

I don't remember much science in school but I do remember in Year 2 making an electrical question and answer board **(see Figure 6.3)**. I was very proud of it but the teacher did not really acknowledge it, although she said to try it out with other children in the class. I used a buzzer that buzzed when the correct questions and answers were connected, but I wanted the teacher's attention so I hid the buzzer in my hand and asked children to shake hands, which set the buzzer off and made them jump. This got the teacher's attention, but not particularly positive attention.

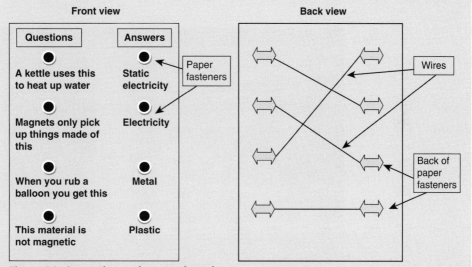

Figure 6.3 A question and answer board

Reflective tasks

Analysing the story

Early career professional

- How could the professionals working with Jamie 'listen' to him and use understandings of him to support his scientific development?
- Are there children in your class that you don't understand? How can you find out more about them?

Developing career professional/teacher

- How could Jamie's interest in practical science be used to help him in literacy, without detracting from the science?
- Are there children in your class who do not like practical science? How could you use their interests to help their scientific development?

Later career professional/leader

- How could smooth transitions help Jamie in his general and scientific development?
- How could you help colleagues to understand children as individuals and build on their strengths and help meet their challenges?

One way to ease transitions, build upon children's interests and support areas they find of less interest and challenging is to use collaborative problem-solving activities **(see also Chapter 3)**. A group of peers within one class or across year groups can work together to solve a simple problem. Working with friends can enable those with more interest or ability to mentor or coach other children with less interest or ability. Care needs to be taken to ensure that children with more interest or experience do not 'take over' and that the ideas of all children are taken into account. Sometimes boys may think that they have an advantage in problem-solving involving technology, whilst the context of the problem may make girls or other groups of children feel that they have an advantage. It is important, however, that all children are empowered by the problem and feel that they have a voice in decisions about how to solve it. There are techniques to help children make fair decisions about how to solve a problem. Each child can

Photograph 6.3 Problem-solving with friends

present his or her solution on which the group then votes, or a teacher or another child mediates, or ideas can be written down or drawn and put in a box and one pulled out. Alternatively, all the ideas can be laid out on the floor or table and the 'best' bits taken from each one, so that each child can see how their ideas have contributed to a final solution.

One example of a problem-solving activity is to make an electrical game or toy that can be used in the next class/year/school. This could involve, for example, making a mousetrap game, with a series of energy transfers, including electrical and magnetic **(see Chapter 9)**.

ACTIVITIES AND KEY QUESTIONS

To promote understanding of electricity

Early Years Foundation Stage

- Explore static electricity by rubbing a blown-up balloon on a woolly jumper and making it stick to a wall or make your hair stand on end.
  Key question: What do you think is happening?

- Play with simple electrical toys (e.g. battery-operated cars, singing and dancing animals, palm pets that cheep when placed in the palm of the hand).
  Key question: How do you think the toys work?

- Find all the electrical appliances in the classroom/home/kitchen.
  Key question: Why do we have to be careful when using electricity?

- Make some electrical appliances for the home corner, out of cardboard boxes (washing machine, oven, fridge, clock) and use a simple circuit to make the appliance light up or buzz.
  Key question: How does the oven/fridge work?

- Look closely at a bulb as it lights up.
  Key question: What happens when it lights up?

Key Stage 1

- Light a bulb using simple components.
  Key question: What do you think makes the bulb light up?

- Make a plastic pen static by rubbing it with a woolly jumper. Play table tennis with charged pens or use to make small pieces of tissue paper move.
  Key question: Why do you think this works?

- Break your circuit in different places and see what happens.
  Key question: What do you think is happening when you break the circuit?

- Make a buzzer buzz using simple components.
  Key question: How do you think the buzzer works?

- Add a switch to a simple circuit with either a buzzer or a bulb.
  Key question: How do you think the switch works?

- Make your own switch using card and aluminium foil.
  Key question: How else can you make a switch?

Activities and key questions (*continued*)

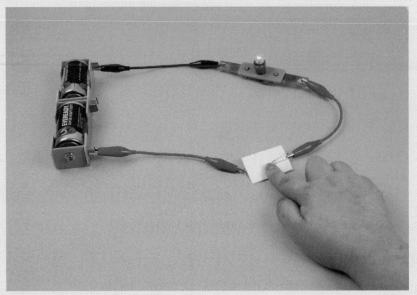

Photograph 6.4 Lighting a bulb

Key Stage 2

- Make up a simple circuit with a bulb, bulb holder, battery and wires. Look closely at the circuit and each of the components (bulb, bulb holder, battery, battery holder and wires).
  Key question: How do you think the electricity moves through the circuit?

- Make a circuit with a motor with a propeller. Turn the battery around and see what happens to the propeller.
  Key question: What do you think is happening in the circuit?

- Make a set of traffic lights.
  Key question: How did you make the traffic lights?

- Make a question and answer board **(see Figure 6.3)**.
  Key question: How does the board work?

- Make a steady-hand game, using a wire coat hanger and a circuit and buzzer **(see Figure 6.4)**.
  Key question: How do you think the game works?

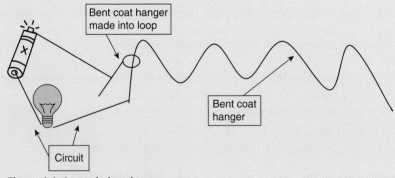

Figure 6.4 A steady hand game

STUDY SKILLS

Evaluating the reliability, validity and ethics of different research methods

In Section 2 of this book we have been looking at collecting and analysing primary data. In Chapter 4, we focused on observation as a research tool and looked at capturing those observations with photographs and videos. In Chapter 5, we focused on listening to children as a research tool and analysing words. In this chapter we have looked at using narrative as a research tool. There are other methods that can be used, such as children's drawings and analysing inter-actions and outcomes, but each method needs to be critiqued to ensure that any issues of reliability, validity and objectivity are taken into account when using and analysing subsequent data. Reliability has to do with whether the data collected using the method would be the same if the collection were repeated. Validity refers to the truthfulness of the data collected. Objectivity refers to how well the researcher is able to analyse the data at face value without taking additional factors, unknown to others, into account. Some methods that are more reliable can be thought to collect data that is less valid, whilst more valid methods can be said to be less reliable. The professional researcher may find it more difficult to be fully objective when using more valid methods and easier when using more reliable methods. This does not mean that some methods are better than others, but more that professional researchers need to ensure that they get the best out of each method used.

Look at Figure 6.5 and consider the following:

- Review each method. Consider whether you have used it and how reliable you think it is.

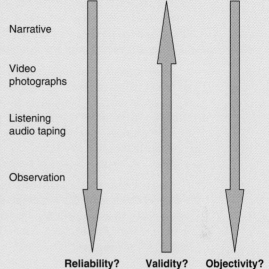

Figure 6.5 Reliability, validity and objectivity of research methods

- Consider the reliability/validity/objectivity arrows. Do you agree that the more valid the method, the more unreliable it is? Or that the more reliable, the less valid it is? Or the greater the validity, the greater the problems with objectivity?
- Which methods could you use in your research? Choose a method with greater validity and consider how you could use it in your research. How would you ensure reliability, validity and objectivity?

Knowledge box

Magnetism and electricity

Magnetism

Magnetism is a form of energy that occurs in some metals, particularly certain forms of iron ore called magnetite or lodestone (iron oxide). Lodestone is an old English word meaning 'way'.

These metals are magnetic because of the special arrangement of the atoms. Magnets attract some metals, e.g. iron, steel, cobalt and nickel, but not others, e.g. aluminium, or non-metals.

The magnetism in a magnet is concentrated at the ends or poles, which are called north (because it points to the magnetic north, as does a compass) and south. Like poles of a magnet repel each other and opposite poles attract. If a magnet is broken in two, the new ends become new poles.

The Earth acts as a huge magnet and magnets are attracted to its poles. The Earth's North Pole obtained its name because it attracts the north pole of a magnet. The South Pole obtained its name because it attracts the south pole of a magnet.

There are four types of energy utilised by magnets:

- kinetic energy – because a magnet makes things move and itself move;
- height (potential) energy – because it can lift things;
- magnetic energy – because it can make soft iron temporarily magnetic and steel permanently magnetic by rearranging their atoms. In metals such as iron, the atoms all point in different ways. You can make iron magnetic by stroking it with a magnet but you must stroke in the same direction.
- electrical energy – by way of kinetic energy in a dynamo or generator.

Magnets exert a force which can be seen by placing a compass near the magnet or putting a magnet under some paper and sprinkling iron filings onto the paper. The lines of force can also be seen when you put two magnets together. You can do this by putting a piece of A4 paper and some iron filings in a sealed plastic wallet and putting it on top of one or two magnets. The iron filings will line up and show the force pattern.

Electricity

Electricity is a form of energy which manifests itself in the flow of electrons from the energy source (e.g. a battery or cell). The first observed form of electricity was static electricity, which the Greek philosopher Thales produced around 600 BC by rubbing amber (a type of resin) with a cloth. The word electricity comes from the Greek word for amber (*electron*).

All matter is made up of small particles called atoms (from the Greek word for uncuttable). Each atom consists of a central nucleus, surrounded by smaller particles called electrons. The whole structure of an atom is held together by electrical charges, with the nucleus being, conventionally, positive and the electrons being negative. Opposite charges attract and so the atom structure is held together.

Static electricity occurs because electrons from the cloth rub off (which becomes positively charged) and onto the amber (which becomes negatively charged). There is then a flow of electrons from negative to positive with accompanied crackles and sparks until the charges equalise. This happens when the rubbed object is a poor conductor. In materials that are good conductors (metals, carbon graphite and salts in solution) some of the electrons are free to move from atom to atom without an unbalanced situation occurring in the atom. In poor conductors (insulators, e.g. non-metals, organic substances in water and oil) there are no free electrons so there will be little or no movement of electrons.

In current electricity there must be a complete circuit for the electricity to flow round and in doing this it may pass through a component such as a bulb or a buzzer. The battery (cell) acts as a pump pushing the electricity around the circuit. The rate of flow of electrons depends upon:

- the electric force making the electrons move; this is the pressure of the battery (the voltage) which is measured in volts;
- the resistance to the movement of the electrons (measured in ohms).

The flow of electricity in a circuit is from the negative side (marked −) of the battery to the positive side (marked +).

- The current that passes through a circuit is measured in amperes (amps) and the power of an appliance is measured in watts (amps × volts). Each component added to a circuit resists the current of electricity, i.e. it acts as a resistor. Tungsten, which is used for the filaments in light bulbs, has a high resistance and so much of the energy is converted into heat and light. Additionally, electricity travels more easily through thick wires and so the thin wire inside a bulb glows as the electricity flows slowly through it.
- Resistance in a circuit (how well it conducts electricity) is measured in ohms and can be calculated by multiplying the voltage of a circuit by its current, i.e. $R = I \times V$.

Knowledge box

Variation and classification

There are similarities and difference between all living things. Plants and animals share seven characteristics – they all:

1 Feed
2 Move
3 Respire
4 Excrete
5 Grow
6 Are sensitive to changes, such as temperature, sound
7 Reproduce.

Animals share common features, e.g. all mammals produce live young at an early stage of development and care for them by feeding from mammary glands. They sometimes look similar, even though they are different species (e.g. zebras, horses and donkeys are all horse-like). Plants, too, can share similar features but be different species.

When Darwin travelled around the world on the *HMS Beagle* as a naturalist, he noticed similarities between fossils of extinct animals and living animals, and between animals in one part of the world and animals in another part of the world. This led him to develop his theory of natural selection and common ancestry, or what we now know as evolution, which is based on the premise that life on Earth is continually evolving, that minor genetic adaptations in animals and plants that support survival are passed on to offspring and that species change over time to adapt to the environment they find themselves in.

Darwin's ideas have been controversial since the day he published them, illustrating the tentative nature of scientific theories, especially when they are in conflict with the more established views and the need to respect evidence, even when it conflicts with one's own viewpoint. Evolution is part of the National Curriculum (DfE, 2012b) but it does not have to conflict with religious education and can be taught in a sensitive way.

Carolus Linnaeus (1707–1778) classified living things according to different categories. The categories we use are:

Kingdom – for a human this would be animal;
Sub Kingdom – for a human this would be metazoa (animals with bodies constructed of cells);
Phylum – for a human this would be chordates (animals with a nervous chord and other features);
Sub Phylum – for a human this would be vertebrates (animals with a vertebral column and well developed brain);

Class – for a human this would be mammals (warm blooded vertebrates);
Sub Class – for a human this would be eutheria (placental mammals);
Order – for a human this would be primates (advanced mammals);
Genus – for a human this would be anthropoid (primates with forward-facing eyes and stereoscopic vision);
Species – For a human this would be homo sapiens (humans).

References

Bassey, M. (1999). *Case Study Research in Educational Settings.* Buckingham: Open University Press.

Bradman, T. (1990). *The Little Red Hen.* London: Methuen Children's Books.

Briggs, R. (1970). *Jim and the Beanstalk.* London: Penguin (Picture Puffin).

Brooker, L. (2008). *Supporting Transitions in the Early Years.* Maidenhead: Open University Press.

Browne, E. (1997). *Handa's Surprise.* London: Walker Books.

Carle, E. (1987). *The Tiny Seed.* London: Hodder and Stoughton.

Compton, A., Johnston, J., Nahmad-Williams, L. & Taylor, K. (2010). *Creative Development.* London: Continuum.

Danto, A.C. (1985). *Narration and Knowledge.* New York: Columbia University Press.

Department for Children, Schools and Families (DCSF) (2008). *The Early Years Foundation Stage: Setting the Standard for Learning, Development and Care for Children from Birth to Five; Practice Guidance.* London: DCSF.

Department for Education (DfE) (2012a). *Statutory Framework for the Early Years Foundation Stage. Setting the Standards for Learning, Development and Care for Children from Birth to Five.* London: DfE.

Department for Education (DfE) (2012b). *National Curriculum for Science. Key Stages 1 and 2 – Draft.* London: DfE.

Dunlop, A.-W. & Fabian, H. (2007). *Informing Transitions in the Early Years: Research, policy, practice.* Maidenhead: Open University Press/McGraw Hill.

Fisher, J. (2010). *Moving on to Key Stage 1: Improving transition from the Early Years Foundation Stage.* Maidenhead: Open University Press/McGraw Hill.

Flournoy, V. & Pinkney, J. (1987). *The Patchwork Quilt.* London: Penguin.

Handy, C. (1989). *The Age of Unreason.* London: Arrow Books.

Hughes, T. (1985). *The Iron Man.* London: Faber and Faber.

Johnston, J. (2005). *Early Explorations in Science,* 2nd edn. Buckingham: Open University Press.

Johnston, J. (2012). Analysing data. In: Oversby, J., ed. *ASE Guide to Research in Science Education.* Hatfield: ASE.

Johnston, J. & Gray, A. (1999). *Enriching Early Scientific Learning.* Buckingham: Open University Press.

Kaye, G. (1980). *Kassim Goes Fishing.* London: Methuen.

Leitch, R. (2008). Creatively researching children's narratives through images and drawings. In Thompson, P. (ed.) *Doing Visual Research with Children and Young People.* Abingdon: Routledge.

Maslow, A. H. (1968). *Towards a Psychology of Being.* New York: D. Van Nostrand Co.

Orlandi, K. (2012). *Onwards and Upwards: Supporting the Transition to Key Stage One.* Abingdon: Routledge.

Primary National Strategy (2006). *Seamless Transitions – Supporting Continuity in Young Children's Learning.* Norwich: Sure Start/DfES.

Rousseau, J.J. (1911). *Emile.* London: J. M. Dent and Sons.

Sanders, D., White, G., Burge, B., Sharp, C., Eames, A., McEune, R. & Grayson, H., National Foundation for Educational Research NFER (2005). *A Study of the Transition from the Foundation Stage to Key Stage 1.* London: Surestart.

Sendak, M. B. (1992). *Where the Wild Things Are.* London: Picture Lions.

Stronach, I. & MacLure, B. (1997). *Educational Research Undone: the Postmodern Embrace.* Buckingham: Open University Press.

Pedagogy

Chapter 7

Scientific play

Overview

In this chapter we look at:

- The importance of play as a **pedagogy**
- Examples of how role-play, imaginative play and **exploratory play** can aid scientific development
- Research into student teachers' views on pedagogical approaches
- Synthesis and discussion of findings as part of the study skills theme
- Practical and reflective tasks that look at synthesising information from play approaches
- Activity and knowledge boxes focusing on life processes, living things and space (astronomy).

Introduction

Play has a strong influence on practice and provision in the early years, in accordance with the writings of many theorists, such as:

- Rousseau (1911), who in his work *Emile* identified his belief that children should be allowed to develop through play free from the restrictions imposed by society and that early pedagogies should provide a balance between individual freedom and happiness and control from society. Rousseau's influence has stretched over the centuries and it is not surprising that he is regarded as the 'father of education'. Child-centred and experiential learning, central to both play and scientific development are legacies of Rousseau's theories.

- Froebel (1826: 53) felt that 'play is the purest, most spiritual activity of man'. He put his ideas about play into practice by creating the first schools for pre-school children, which he called 'kindergarten' (children's garden). These kindergartens stressed the natural growth of children through action or play, with the emphasis on pedagogies that encouraged and guided. Froebel also developed a range of practical resources to support children's play, which he called 'gifts', and educational activities, which he called 'occupations'. Many of the practical educational science resources used today originated or were developed from Froebel's ideas.

- Piaget (1976) looked at the development of play and began to identify different types of play, e.g. symbolic play, which involves children using objects in their pretend play in ways that they were not designed for. Piaget's (1976) ideas on symbolic play emphasise the idea of play as a creative activity that promotes cognition, whereas Vygotsky's (1962) ideas that connect language and thought emphasise the importance of social interaction during play.

Play is also an inherent part of the Early Years Foundation Stage curriculum (DfE, 2012a), although it does appear to have been lost from the National Curriculum (DfE, 2012b), making it difficult for the individual child to develop and learn in any coherent way **(see Chapter 6)**. Although play is fundamental to children's development, it is often not valued by adults, even professionals (Moylett, 2010), as contributing to children's development. There is also a misapprehension in some adults that structured teacher-led activities are play, or that we can direct or control play (Russell, 2010).

STUDY SKILLS

What is synthesis? (Johnston, 2012a)

Synthesis is a very important skill that enables the professional researcher to take a wide range of primary and secondary analysis, and synthesise it; that is, put it back together in order to make sense of it and critically discuss research findings. Synthesis may involve drawing together analysis from different studies, although it should not be mistaken for meta-analysis, described in the previous chapter, where research findings from a range of studies are analysed to answer new questions or provide new insights into the area; nor should it be mistaken for the synthesis that occurs in a literature review **(see Chapter 3)**. When you synthesise data, you combine the analysis of literature (maybe from a literature review) and the analysis of primary data and make sense of it, drawing inferences from the findings. You also generate critical discussion of the implications arising out of the analysis and synthesis. In synthesising data from small-scale research, you may produce new ideas or models and make tentative (fuzzy) generalisations (Bassey, 1998, 1999).

Gardner (2007) identifies that the ability to synthesise is an intellectual skill of increasing importance in modern society. He argues that in modern society, where sources of information are rapidly increasing, it is important to be able to:

- survey a wide range of sources or experiences;
- make decisions about what is important or not;
- combine information in a meaningful way;
- communicate that in an understandable way.

This is because many professions, including teaching, science and communicators, need to be able to synthesise huge amounts of information. A synthesising mind will have an area of expertise (a discipline), know the trusted sources of information within the discipline, have an overview of the area being considered (the big picture), and be able to consider the details. A synthesising mind can be both like a searchlight – having a broad overview, seeing and making use of the links between disciplines/areas, and monitoring changes in the area – and like a laser beam, having in-depth knowledge within the area.

According to Gardner (2007) there are different types of synthesis:

- Fictional and non-fictional narratives, where information from different sources is combined into a coherent whole. The types of narratives that synthesise analysis of evidence from different participants into a fictional narrative (see also Bassey, 1998) are examples of this type of synthesis
- Taxonomies, where information is sorted and ordered
- Complex concepts, where new ideas are synthesised from a range of evidence
- Rules and aphorisms, such as common phrases and folklore
- Powerful metaphors, images and themes
- Embodiments without words, such as can be encompassed within a piece of art, or a model
- Theories, developed from a synthesis of ideas
- Meta-theories, or overarching theories or paradigms that replace previous theories or encompass a number of different theories.

Study Skills (*continued*)

Synthesising involves breadth and depth of understanding, making links between different analyses and engaging in a deep and critical discussion of the ideas, implication or models of thinking that have emerged from the analysis. Most importantly, it does not repeat the analysis, but moves forward from it to greater clarity, sophistication of ideas and understanding. It is sometimes tempting to repeat analysis or deviate into discussions that are very important to the researcher, but not grounded in the research evidence. In order to do this effectively, it may be sensible to identify clearly what will be achieved through the synthesis and how it builds on the research analysis (Gardner, 2007). The 'discussion of findings' section of a research report may start with a brief summary of the findings and then identify the main implications for further discussion. It is important to limit the discussion to the main implications, so that it can be deep and critical, rather than superficial. Each issue should be grounded in the research findings and have an implication for the researcher's practice and provision and perhaps some tentative implications for wider practice and provision. In the discussion of findings, you can identify the impact on you personally and professionally, on the children you teach and the context in which you work.

Educational research should have some applications, i.e. should:

- be accessible to a wide range of professional practitioners and be written in an accessible way;
- have an impact on practice and provision in the researcher's own context;
- have some tentative applications to wider educational practice.

The discussion of each issue should consider the analyses (but not repeat it) from both the literature review and the primary data analysis and then discuss them critically. Care needs to be taken to ensure that relationships between data are not over- or under-emphasised, leading to incorrect results. Cooper (2010) believes in a systematic research synthesis using scientific guidelines, arguing that this does not necessarily inhibit innovative thinking, but poses challenges in collecting, evaluating and analysing data that is an original contribution to the area of research. Roberts (2007: 72) identifies that 'the process of interpretation is not a simple 'mechanical' exercise, but involves 'imagination – connections, choices, insights'. Presenting and analysing data are not enough and the researcher needs to engage in a deep discussion, making the connection between ideas, identifying relationships and extrapolating from the evidence in an innovative, creative, but not fictitious way. In this way the skill of argumentation (Toulmin, 1958) should be exercised.

Critical discussion will involve making links between policy, practice and research, recognising the tensions that exist between them, the ambiguities and inconsistencies between the theory and the evidence from the research. The discussion will use reading from the literature review but also, where appropriate, new reading to reflect the issues being discussed. This is because the issues may be extensions of ideas raised earlier in the research, or be new avenues that start in the data but extend beyond the original ideas or deviate from them. The discussion will explore the conceptual understanding in the area and extend this, showing that the researcher has extended his or her understanding and the contribution to the shared knowledge in the area. Roberts (2007) identified that it is important to remember that the researcher interprets and theorises and does not merely collect and state evidence. Rather, they compare and contrast ideas, juxtapose issues and think deeply about consequences. In this way, while this discussion is challenging and can be arduous, it is also 'exciting, stimulating and rewarding' (Roberts, 2007: 75).

Gardner (2007) identified components to synthesis: to have a goal, a starting point, a strategy and to draft and redraft. He believes that a goal should identify what the researcher hopes the synthesis will achieve and that the starting point is the initial building block for the synthesis, so that the research can develop from this. The strategy can involve decisions about the type of synthesis to be employed (see earlier) and include the scientific guidelines as identified by Cooper (2010).

Types of play

There are several different types of play, all of which can support children's scientific development, but to different extents. The very earliest play is solitary play, as very young children are less likely to be able to play with others. They can, however, spend long periods of time on one task, such as observing an ant or a spider, putting stones in a pile, or playing with a one toy. It is very easy when children are playing quietly on their own to intervene and play with them or rush them onto the next stimulus, but this is a mistake, as children need time to play on their own and can have too much stimulation (Elkind, 2001). Knowing when to intervene is an important pedagogical skill and involves understanding the child's developmental needs and balancing the need to encourage perseverance and cognitive development with social development.

At the start of the book we discussed observation as an important skill in the early years and science and one that initiates children's interest in the world around them, encouraging them to explore **(see Chapter 1)**. We also identified that observation is influenced by theory, so that the observer (whether a child observing a scientific phenomenon, or a professional observing a child) will observe through their own theory laden lens. However, observation tends not to be used to initiate activities and motivate children to want to make inquiries (National Research Council of the National Academies, 2007), or to form a major part of classroom activities (Kallery & Psillos, 2002). Indeed Kallery and Psillos (2002) identified that only 5 per cent of classroom activities involved observations and that these tended to be passive observations made by the teacher, rather than active observations.

Solitary play can lead to parallel play where children play alongside each other, with little or no social interaction. Parallel play may start with children observing another child at play and imitating them. For example, in the water or sand tray, children may watch another child pouring water/sand into containers and then try it out for themselves. They may watch a child observing a puddle drying up in the sunshine and stop to watch the puddle too. Children sometimes imitate a teacher or a parent. Two-year-olds, who are only just developing language, will imitate an adult's action and words and so a curious, vocal adult will encourage children to be curious for themselves.

For one publication (de Bóo, 2004) I set up a garden centre role-play in the classroom for children of 4 years of age. Even at this age the children played alongside, rather than with, each other, although they had very limited school experience as they had only just started school on a part-time basis. At the end of the day, I asked the children to clean up the role-play area and they used brooms and dustpans which were part of the play area. One child told me where there was a class dustpan and brush and I thanked him, but carried on with what I was doing. A short time later he put one hand on his hip and one on the broom he was using and in role said, 'I gave you a job to do', much to the embarrassment of his teacher whom he was imitating!

As children develop and become less egocentric and more social, they may engage in cooperative play, which involves an element of social interaction. Many educational settings, especially at Key Stages 1 and 2 (KS1, KS2), group children to encourage cooperation and this may extend into their scientific play. A small group of children may explore an ice balloon, observing it and exploring what happens to it when they put it in water, sprinkle salt over it or drop it **(see Chapter 3)**. They may play together in an optician's shop and cooperate in role-play as the optician or the customer having an eye test and then choosing and buying a pair of glasses. Again children will often imitate adults in this type of social play – I have seen a 2-year-old child putting a doll to bed in the home corner and telling them that they 'are in big trouble' if they get out of bed.

Towards the end of the early years, children may be able to participate in collaborative play, which is more developed cooperative play. Collaborative play demands even more social interaction and involves children in working towards one aim. This may involve a group problem-solving task, such as making a marble run, a sunhat for teddy, or finding out what gloves keep the ice hand cold **(see Chapters 3 and 9)**. In role-play, collaborative play will involve the different roles interacting more and working together – so, for example, in a spaceship the 'astronauts' will need to work together to launch the rocket. The more developed social play, involving cooperation and collaboration, can help children to develop:

- Social skills, such as the skill of negotiation (Johnston & Nahmad-Williams, 2008);
- Scientific skills, such as observation (Johnston, 2011), through peer dialogue and interaction (see also Rogoff, 1995; Robbins, 2005);
- Important social attitudes such as responsibility for their actions and responsibility towards the world they live in (see Chapter 3).

The role of the professional is crucial in supporting social play, by providing a role model for children to imitate, encouraging cooperation and collaboration, standing back and observing when children are playing well and interacting to scaffold behaviours and encourage further observation and exploration when necessary and, importantly, 'profiling learner agency'(Cremin et al., 2006; CLS, 2012).

As well as developing skills and attitudes, play can also develop children's thinking (cognitive development). In many play contexts, children will bring to the play their previous experiences and knowledge and this can lead to **epistemic play** that starts from existing knowledge and continues towards a deeper conceptual understanding and language development (Johnston, 2011).

Practical and reflective tasks

Practical tasks
Look at Figure 7.1 and decide how the play activities could be used to develop scientific skills, knowledge and understandings and attitudes for your key stage by filling in the relevant boxes. You could try to do the task for each of the key stages and compare the different outcomes possible.

- Look at your current and past planning and consider what type of play is characteristic of your practice. How can you balance the type of play you use in your setting?
- Plan play opportunities that encourage different types of play to support balanced scientific learning and development. Collect evidence on how the children respond to and develop from the play.

Reflective tasks
- How did the children respond to the play opportunities?
- How did the play contribute to the children's scientific development?
- How can you continue to support and extend scientific development and learning through play?

	Scientific skills	Scientific knowledge and understandings	Scientific attitudes
Sand play			
Pet shop			
Building site			
Water play			
Opticians			
The seaside			
Garden centre			
Blowing bubbles			

Figure 7.1 How does play develop children scientifically?

Use reading about play approaches and produce an argument that synthesises your reflective analyses above and analysis from reading.

● How does the reading support your argument?

● Is there a counter-argument that would enhance your discussion of the issues?

Exploratory play is the type of play most often associated with scientific development; indeed, exploration is synonymous with play (Johnston, 2005). Exploration is the focus of the next chapter **(Chapter 8)**. In exploratory play, there is no agenda or structure and children use all their senses to explore scientific phenomena in the world around them. There may be some predetermined learning outcomes and the achievement of these will be supported by the resources, which will lead the children to look at the science underpinning the play, and by adult interaction with the children, which will prompt, probe or question the children. Exploratory play may start from observation of scientific phenomena and can lead to general cognitive, social, emotional and physical development as well as specific scientific development. For example, water play can lead to:

- Mathematical understandings of volume and mass;
- Scientific understanding of floating and sinking;
- Social development in playing with others;
- Language development as children play with others;
- Physical development in pouring and filling containers;
- Emotional development through enthusiasm and curiosity.

If you add bath bombs and colour-change bubble bath, then scientific understandings of materials and their properties can also be added. If you use boat shapes, make sails for the boats and test them out on the water trough or in guttering filled with water, then the learning outcomes might also include:

- Mathematical development in looking at shapes of boats and sails;
- Scientific development of movement on water;
- Social development by taking turns, cooperation.

Where play is socio-dramatic and imaginative role-play, it can involve the children in development in other key areas (**see Figure 7.2** and Johnston & Nahmad-Williams, 2010) as well as science (see Johnston, 2012b). Imaginative play can not only encourage imaginative engagement, it can also enhance thinking, reasoning and conceptual understanding (Goswami & Bryant, 2007; CLS, 2012) although Goswami and Bryant, (2007) argue that adult scaffolding makes this more effective.

Photograph 7.1 Social water play

Area	Key areas of development	Resources
On the road Role-play on the 'road' with ride-on vehicles and small-world play	**Scientific development** Forces (movement, speed, friction) **Physical development** Gross motor development Fine motor development **Personal, social and emotional development:** Social interaction, taking turns	Outside play vehicles Ramp Small toy cars
Tanzania Role-play of planning for and going on a holiday to Africa	**Communication, language and literacy** Reading holiday brochures **Understanding of the world** Places in the world **Scientific development** Packing teddy's bags for weather Animals of Tanzania **Personal, social and emotional development** Social interaction Enthusiasm Exploring feelings and culture **Physical development** Dressing teddy and doll Dressing in African clothes Gross motor skills – following animal footprints	Tanzania display or PowerPoint African holiday brochures Story and factual books (animals/Africa/Tanzania) Clothes, etc. Teddy, clothes and suitcase Animal masks Animal footprints
The band Role-play of being in a band	**Communication, language and literacy** Language for communication Story books **Scientific development** How the instruments make a sound How sound travels How to change the sound **Physical development** Fine motor skills **Creative development** Making instruments with junk material	Story books Musical instruments Junk material for making an instrument Paint, brushes, glue, etc.

Figure 7.2 Role-play areas and development

Area	Key areas of development	Resources
Garden centre Role-play of working in a garden centre and buying plants at the garden centre	**Communication, language and literacy** Eric Carle, *The Tiny Seed* Writing labels for plants Vocabulary (plant, seed, soil, grow, root, shoot, leaf, flower) **Mathematical development** Counting, sorting and buying/selling seeds and plants **Scientific development** Parts of plants, variety of seeds and plants, growth of plants **Personal, social and emotional development** Social interaction, taking turns Care for living things Awareness of the needs of others including plants	Book, Eric Carle, *The Tiny Seed* Collection of seeds, seed packets, plants and flowers Plastic lolly stick labels (some blank and some with vocabulary on) Laminated white labels Dry-wipe pens Sorting hoops Shop front Till and money Trowel, wheelbarrow, rake, etc. Compost and pots
Building site Role-play of working on a building site	**Communication, language and literacy** Communication Vocabulary (describing materials in their own words, introduction of new words where appropriate, e.g. sand, brick, build, stable, safe, climb) **Mathematical development** Counting and sorting building materials **Scientific development** Forces and structures **Physical development** Building structures Climbing and balancing **Personal, social and emotional development** Social interaction, taking turns	Large bricks, blocks, etc. Small building materials PE mats Two A-frames Beam
Seaside Role-play of being at the seaside	**Communication, language and literacy** Seaside books Vocabulary (shell, fish, swim, sand, sea) Writing postcards home **Mathematical development** Sorting seaside objects	Story and information books Collection of seaside objects Sorting hoops Brine shrimps Sand on plastic sheets on floor or in sand tray, water trays and play equipment

Figure 7.2 (*continued*)

Area	Key areas of development	Resources
	Scientific development Variety of life in and around the seaside Materials and their properties – sand and water play **Creative development** Printing with fish and seaside objects Shell pictures	Flat fish, whole prawns Shells, sponges and other seaside objects for printing Printing inks, trays and sponges Pasta shells (different colours) Paper and glue
Space rocket Role-play of a space rocket going to an alien planet	**Communication, language and literacy** Space books Language for Communication **Scientific development** Understanding of the Earth as a planet and the solar system **Physical development** Dressing up Crawling **Creative development** Making space rocket with junk material	Space rocket with computer console, telephones, levers, etc. Tunnel Astronauts' and aliens' clothes Junk material Paint, brushes, glue, etc.

Figure 7.2 (*continued*)

According to Goswami and Bryant (2007) pretend play contexts which prompt children's imagination, help cognitive development in a number of ways. So farm play, as in the case study that follows, would develop:

- understanding of the world by learning about farming and the animals;
- social and language development by interacting with each other;
- physical development by setting up the small-world play;
- imagination by putting themselves in role.

CASE STUDY

Small-world farm play

In a nursery, a farm and farm shop were set up. The farm consisted of small-world farm animals but the farm shop was life-size and had real fruits and vegetables for 'sale'. The science learning outcomes were connected to life and living processes (both animal and plant). The play was initiated using a story sack of *Old MacDonald*, which was also left out for the children to play with.

When the children played with the farm and in the 'farm shop', they used knowledge about caring for animals in their play: what the animals ate, what care they needed, how

Case study (*continued*)

long they lived and so on. In the role-play Bobbie was in the farm shop. She sold some plants and some vegetables to a customer, explaining how the plants should be looked after and how the vegetables could be cooked.

Meanwhile, on the floor, Alex and Harry were pretending to be farmers and taking the cows to be milked. They discussed how the cows needed to be looked after; that they needed grass and fresh water and, when they were indoors in winter, they needed fresh straw every day. As they were telling each other this, they spoke with deep voices, as they were in role. In this way the epistemic play that used their prior knowledge of how cows lived and what they needed to produce milk moved into **ludic play** (Piaget, 1976), or fantasy role-play, as they 'became' farmers. They continued in this play by taking the farm dog and rounding up the sheep and then putting the sheep in its kennel, all the while in role as farmers.

Reflective tasks

For each set of tasks below, use reading to turn your answers into cogent arguments that synthesise reflection and reading.

Early career professional
- How could interaction by an adult further develop understandings of life processes and living things in the play?
- How could you use role-play in your context to develop scientific understandings, skills and attitudes in a holistic way?

Developing career professional/teacher
- How could the role-play be extended to support understandings of life processes and living things?
- What other role-play could develop understandings of life processes and living things?

Later career professional/leader
- How could the adults encourage greater peer interaction to aid understandings of life processes and living things?
- How could you use role-play across your setting or key stage to develop understandings of life processes and living things?

Imaginative play is well recognised as suitable for very young children, but once children enter compulsory education, the need for play appears to be less well recognised. However, play is a powerful pedagogical tool for all early years children and is recognised in the review of literature for the Creative Little Scientist project (CLS, 2012) **(see also Chapter 5)**. When older children in Key Stage 2 are allowed to play, their learning can be enriched and enhanced, but teachers of older children are pressurised by assessments to show that they are achieving high cognitive standards, which are measured by tests of knowledge, and play is thought to interfere with that goal. Indeed, children can achieve greater understanding by doing less and by playing and exploring more, but it takes a brave teacher to do less in the expectation of achieving more.

ACTIVITIES AND KEY QUESTIONS

To promote understanding of life processes and living things

Early Years Foundation Stage

- Put some plastic play mini-beasts into a shoe box along with some straw, leaves, stones, moss and bark and the like. Allow the children to play with the box and make some mini-beast habitat dioramas.
  Key question: Why does the spider/ant/woodlouse like to live there?

- Allow children to play with a small-world farm. Ask them to sort the animals out into areas of the farm that they like to live.
  Key questions: Why do you think the cow/sheep/pig/hen lives here? What do the animals eat?

- Set up a pet shop in the classroom. Allow the children to help you set up the area; they can bring stuffed animals in from home to have in the shop. Encourage them to look after the animals and cater for their needs and to tell customers how to look after the animals.
  Key question: How do I look after the rabbit/mouse/cat/dog?

- Use a story sack of *The Very Hungry Caterpillar* (Carle, 1970) and allow children to re-enact the story, focusing on the life cycle of a caterpillar/butterfly.
  Key question: How does the caterpillar change as it grows?

- Use the book *Outside In* (Smallman & Riddell, 1986) to explore what is inside the human body. Use some cut-out life-size shapes of the brain, the stomach, the lungs and the bladder and ask the children to fit into a body outline (this can be drawn on paper or on the floor with chalk or a dry wipe pen). For older children, more organs can be used and the systems of the body (respiratory, nervous, digestion, renal) can be explored and researched.
  Key questions: Where does the brain/stomach/lung go in the body? What do we use our brain/stomach/lung for?

Key Stage 1

- Use the book *Animals Aboard* (Peters & Coplestone, 2007) as a stimulus to discuss animals and how they live/what they need to live and grow.
  Key questions: Where does a ... live? What does a ... need to live and grow?

- Use the book *See How You Grow* (Pearse & Riddell, 1989) to discuss human reproduction and growth. Use some photographs of people at different stages of their lives and ask the children to put into order. Children can also bring in photographs of themselves and family members at different ages **(see also Chapter 2)**.
  Key question: How has the person changed over time?

- Growing seeds, or hatching chicks in the classroom can also help children to see how plants and animals grow and change **(see also Chapter 4)**. If you hatch chicks, you must arrange for them to go to a good home once they have hatched.
  Key questions: How do the plants/chicks change as they grow? What do the plants/chicks need to grow and be healthy?

Activities and key questions (*continued*)

- Set up a teddy first aid scenario, e.g. a cut head, broken arm, a grazed knee, and allow children to play with caring for teddy and undertaking simple first aid **(see research box in Chapter 2, p. 34).**
  Key question: What should you do if teddy cuts his head/breaks his arm/grazes his knee?

- Have a class pet day or keep a class pet. Arrange a rota to look after the pet and care for it. I have kept and bred rabbits in a school quad and arranged for them to go to good homes when they are weaned.
  Key question: What do we need to do to look after the pet each day/week?

Key Stage 2

- Make some life cycle pictures by cutting and pasting pictures from the internet or clip art and laminating them so they can be used on other occasions. Your pictures could include the life cycle of a frog (spawn, tadpole, tadpole with legs, frog), a plant (seed, seeds with root, seed with root and shoot, growing plant, mature plant), a chicken (egg, newly hatched chick, developing chick, adult chicken), a dog (newly born puppy, growing dog, adult dog) or a butterfly (egg, caterpillar, pupa, butterfly). Ask the children to put the pictures into a sequence or a cycle.
  Key question: What do you notice about the different life cycles?

- Ask children to make a mobile of animal food chains. They can draw their own pictures or print some out from the internet.
  Key questions: How does this food chain work? Which plant/animal is at the beginning/ end of the food chain?

- Go pond-dipping and look for larval/nymph stages of different animals (e.g. mayfly, dragon fly, stonefly) and different stages of life cycles (e.g. frog spawn, tadpoles). Research the life cycle of one of the animals found.
  Key question: How does the animal change as it grows?

- Laminate pictures of the embryos, newborn and adult stages of different common mammals; you can get these pictures from magazines or from the internet. Ask children to match the pictures and put them in sequence.
  Key questions: What are the similarities/differences between the animals at different stages? How do the animals change as they grow?

- Set up a doctor's surgery role-play in the classroom and allow children to play at undertaking simple first aid in different situations (e.g. cuts, grazes, blisters, head injuries, broken bones, sprains). Add some X-ray pictures and consider which parts of the body the bones shown come from.
  Key question: What should you do if someone has a ...?

Organising play

Play can be organised and structured in a number of ways. As already mentioned in this chapter, the resources used in play can help to structure the learning that occurs as a result. So if the learning outcomes are connected to life processes and living things, a play area such as a doctor's surgery should have resources that encourage children to look at their bodies, such as a sight chart, a stethoscope, teddies with injuries and a body-mapping poster (so they can put the organs in the correct place). If the role-play is connected to the Earth and the universe (see the following case study), then star maps, photographs and books of the solar system, a sun dial and so on can help to focus on the planned learning outcomes. Children can help to set up the play area, making resources where possible (e.g. space helmets out of papier-mâché covered in foil and oxygen tanks out of empty plastic bottles covered in foil) and choosing how to set up the area for their play.

The play can be structured by being teacher-led, with the teacher working alongside the children to achieve a specific outcome. The teacher could provide the resources and set the task and then explore with the children, modelling behaviours and suggesting ideas for new avenues of inquiry. However, structured play does not have to mean that the children make no decisions for themselves – the teacher can make professional decisions about how much structure is needed and ease up on support and guidance so that children can be supported and challenged appropriately (see Hohmann & Weikart, 2002).

Even in free play that is partly or fully child-initiated, the teacher can get involved, pose questions or suggest what may come next. For example, in one school, children in Year 1 set up a pirate ship, and the teacher hoped to develop their understanding of magnetism by hiding treasure in the sand (to be found using a magnet) and also to encourage the boys to write by producing treasure maps to locate the buried treasure. The play area and resources encouraged both the learning outcomes and the teacher made suggestions and posed problems to solve. When she suggested that Josh finish his treasure map, he replied in role: 'Ah-ha me hearties, my ship's stuck and the map is soggy.'

Some early years settings set up exploratory and imaginative play in the curriculum to allow the children to move freely from one play area to another and to decide how long they spend at each activity. They may set up the classroom so that children can move from indoor to outdoor play and so that each area of the early years curriculum can be developed. In order for this to be effective, children and adults need to share agreed rules, such as the maximum number of children who should be at each activity, what resources are available/unavailable, and basic precepts of health and safety in play. However, the rules should not adversely affect the quality of the play or subsequent development.

I have set up play days for children from the Early Years Foundation Stage, Key Stage 1 and Key Stage 2. The same play areas and resources have been used for each key stage, although the ways in which the play is approached by the children are different, as are the ways in which the professionals interact with them (see Figure 7.2). This has caused some consternation among the student professionals who are setting up the areas and even some Key Stage 2 professionals whose children come to the play days. This is because they are unable to see, prior to the event, how older children will benefit from free play and suggest structuring the play in various ways. However, after the event, the value of the free play is well recognised, as children take responsibility for their learning and behaviour, make decisions about what to do, and how and when to do it, for themselves. The professionals also generally comment on the purposeful play that they see.

Space rocket role-play

In a group of 7-year-olds, the topic of space was introduced using the story *Aliens Love Underpants* (Freedman & Cort, 2007). After the story, the children began to create a rocket around the class computer in the corner of the room. They used a large roll of corrugated paper for the outside of the rocket, which they painted to look like a rocket. They set up the inside of the rocket with the computer as the control panel and drew or painted pictures of planets to put into the portholes (as viewed from inside the rocket). They made astronauts' outfits by using old boiler suits, helmets from papier-mâché over balloons and sprayed with silver paint (they can also be covered in aluminium foil) and oxygen tanks from empty plastic bottles and tubing also sprayed with silver paint. To get into the rocket a crawl-through tunnel was used, which one child had brought from home.

They children were split into nine groups to play in the rocket and they chose to work in friendship groups. Each group had to decide which planet (including Pluto) in the solar system they were going to fly to and then, once inside the rocket, they had to use the computer to find out about that planet, in particular:

- Its gravity relative to Earth, so they would know what it was like when they landed;
- Its atmosphere relative to Earth, for the same reason;
- What the landscape was like;
- How long each day and year was relative to Earth;
- What aliens living there would look like.

They then had to make a list of what other things would be useful for when they landed on the planet and draw a picture of their planet to add to a mobile of the solar system in the classroom.

Aasim, Fergus and Darren chose to work together and to go to Mars. As they went into the rocket through the tunnel, Fergus started to sing, changing the words of the children's song 'Zoom, zoom, zoom, we're flying to the Moon' to 'Zoom, zoom, zoom, we're flying past the Moon, zoom, zoom, zoom, we'll get there very soon. 5, 4, 3, 2, 1 BLAST OFF!

In the rocket they used books and the internet and found out that Mars was called the Red Planet, because the it was covered in 'rust'. They also found out that the atmosphere is very thin and there are big craters from extinct volcanoes and decided that they would need a beach buggy to drive over the terrain and lots of water to drink, as the water on Mars is thought only to occur as ice. Day and night are very similar to those on Earth and so they did not anticipate any problems in sleeping and working on Mars.

When all the groups had worked in the rocket, one astronaut from each group was put in the hot seat and

Photograph 7.2 Space rocket role-play

questioned by the other children about the planet they had visited. The class as a whole then had to decide which planet was most suitable for a group of humans to colonise.

Reflective tasks

For each set of tasks below, use reading to turn your answers into cogent arguments that synthesise reflection and reading.

Early career professional

- What other learning outcomes associated with space could be developed through rocket play?
- How should the teacher interact with the children during the play?
- How would the scientific development be curtailed/enhanced by proscribing/not proscribing the time spent in the play area?

Developing career professional/teacher

- How could the play area be extended to incorporate other science learning outcomes?
- How can group discussion extend the learning after the hot-seating?
- How much should the teacher intervene or interact in the play?

Later career professional/leader

- What advantages/disadvantages are there to more unstructured play?
- How could you overcome the disadvantages of unstructured play and build upon the advantages?
- How else could you support scientific development in role-play?

The role of the professional in play

In order to effectively incorporate play into the classroom and maximise learning, professionals need to have an understanding of both early years and science and how young children develop and also of the pedagogies that support early scientific learning (BERA, 2003; Fleer, 2007; Johnston, 2005; National Research Council of the National Academies, 2007). One of the main roles of the professional is in **scaffolding**, as this can encourage independent enquiry and problem-solving (Metz, 2004; Rittle-Johnson & Koedinger, 2005), as well as conceptual knowledge (Coltman *et al.*, 2002). Scaffolding will also facilitate social and language development, alongside scientific conceptual understanding through questioning (Vygotsky, 1978) and co-construction of understandings (Siraj-Blatchford *et al.*, 2002). Social interaction, especially where it involves practical exploration that builds upon previous knowledge (Piaget, 1929; Vygotsky, 1962), appears to be most effective with children learning alongside peers and teachers (Bruner, 1991; Stone, 1993). This is likely to be a complex social interaction, with children learning through social interaction on three planes – personal, interpersonal and community/contextual (Rogoff, 1995) – that have been found to be useful in analysing early scientific development (Fleer, 2002; Robbins, 2005; **see also Chapter 5**).

Professionals also need to provide children with sufficient time and space to learn through play and develop thinking skills. Cremin *et al.* (2006) identified that professionals need to provide 'stretchy' time to encourage extended playful activities with enriched and mutually owned space to motivate and involve thinkers (CLS, 2012). Glauert (2009) endorsed this and further suggested that, given time, children will develop observational and questioning skills (see also Chapter 1). If children are given sufficient time to observe, explore and discuss their emerging ideas with others, conceptual understanding can be developed through the creation of conceptual conflicts (Hand, 1988), debate and argument (Alexander, 2008; Naylor *et al.*, 2004) and 'sustained shared thinking' (Siraj-Blatchford, 2009). The amount of time cannot really be allotted and professionals need to be sensitive to children's needs and provide sufficient time to enable quality learning while not enforcing the length of time and risk the children becoming bored.

Children need encouragement and motivation in order to effectively develop and learn. This can be achieved through motivating play contexts and motivating resources. As we have seen in our case studies and activity boxes in this and other chapters, a story can stimulate the play **(see also Figure I.3)**. A story sack or story apron can provide an added dimension. For example, the pockets of a story apron could contain items from *The Three Little Pigs* (see Cooper *et al.*, 2010), such as straw, twigs and bricks, thus encouraging children to re-enact the story, explore the properties of different materials and make a 'safe' house for the pigs. The story of Noah's Ark could have pairs of animals in each pocket, and playing with these and re-enacting the story could lead to an understanding of the variety of life. Samples of material in combination with the story *Aliens Love Underpants* (Freedman & Cort, 2007) could stimulate learning about materials and their properties – the children could be asked to decide, for example, which materials make the best underpants for the aliens. In a similar way, nursery rhymes can act as a stimulus for play with a scientific purpose **(see Figure I.2)**. For example, Jack and Jill could initiate play involving health and first aid **(see also Chapter 2)**, Old King Cole could inititate play about music, and Twinkle, Twinkle Little Star could initiate play about space.

Children should be encouraged to use their imaginations in their play to follow their own pedagogical pathway by utilising their natural interests (Bary *et al.*, 2008), as this will enhance learning, providing an element of self-differentiation that motivates and supports them. This independence in learning is also a feature of many play theories (e.g. Froebel, 1826; Rousseau, 1911; Steiner, 1996).

Research

Are student teachers' espoused views on the nature of science teaching seen in practice?

Research questions

- What do science specialist student teachers feel is the nature of science teaching and learning?
- Is there a difference between their espoused beliefs, planning and practice?

Research design

The research compares student teachers' espoused philosophical views of primary science teaching with their planning and practice. The student group involved 10 science specialist initial teacher training students at the beginning of their second year of undergraduate work. At the start of a module on the science curriculum, the students were introduced to the different types of pedagogical approaches and asked to identify their pedagogical views on science education by identifying where they feel science education fits into two continua – constructivist/positivist and traditionalist/post-modernist (Longbottom, 1999) – as in Figure 7.3, but without the annotations regarding pedagogical practices.

There followed some teaching on good practice in science teaching and learning and individual planning of science teaching. Finally, students' interaction

Research (*continued*)

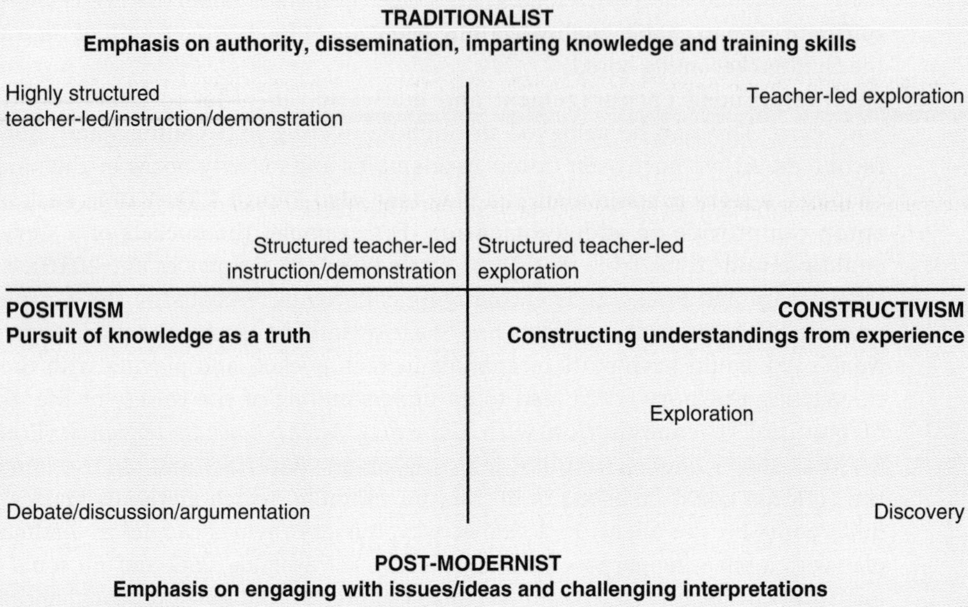

TRADITIONALIST
Emphasis on authority, dissemination, imparting knowledge and training skills

Highly structured
teacher-led/instruction/demonstration

Teacher-led exploration

Structured teacher-led
instruction/demonstration

Structured teacher-led
exploration

POSITIVISM
Pursuit of knowledge as a truth

CONSTRUCTIVISM
Constructing understandings from experience

Exploration

Debate/discussion/argumentation

Discovery

POST-MODERNIST
Emphasis on engaging with issues/ideas and challenging interpretations

Figure 7.3 How pedagogical approaches fit into the constructivist/positivist and traditionalist/post-modernist continua
Source: Longbottom (1999).

with 7-year-old children while engaged in the 'discovery learning approach' was observed. The plans and observed teaching were analysed for evidence of the pedagogical approaches used and mapped onto Figure 7.3. Analysis and triangulation of data occurred with a group of teachers on a research degree.

Research question	Method
What do science specialist student teachers feel is the nature of science teaching and learning?	Questionnaire – identification of pedagogical views by identifying where they feel science education fits into two continua: constructivist/positivist and traditionalist/post-modernist
Is there a difference between their espoused beliefs, planning and practice?	Analysis of planning to identify planned pedagogical approach
	Observation of teaching episode for evidence of pedagogical approach
	Comparison of questionnaire, planning and teaching
	Triangulation of analysis with teachers on a research degree

Summary of findings
Pedagogical views
Of the 10 students involved, five placed science teaching and learning at the centre of the continua, four felt that science teaching and learning were firmly in the constructivist/post-modernist sector and one student felt it was very slightly in the positivist/traditionalist sector.

Analysis and triangulation of data highlighted a number of issues concerning validity and reliability of data in answer to this question. It may be that respondents

Research (*continued*)

will espouse views other than those they hold, that is, identify views on the nature of science teaching and learning they think they should hold rather than those they actually do hold. They may also have been influenced by the language or body language of the tutor when explaining the task, espousing beliefs similar to those believed to be advocated. It is also possible that, despite them all being introduced to the different ideas embedded in the continua, they may have incomplete or alternative understandings that affect their response. However, the influencing factors were the same for all student teachers and so, although we should treat these responses with care, we can be fairly assured that they represented their beliefs at this time.

Analysis of planning

In their planning, nine of the 10 students focused on knowledge objectives and the remaining student did not identify any objectives. The objectives were rooted in three main conceptual areas: sound, senses and materials. Three of the students identified language and literacy objectives:

● To begin to use scientific descriptive language to describe the objects;

● To increase vocabulary for describing of materials;

● To describe observations.

One student identified a skill objective – to be able to plan and carry out a fair test – although this was not fully reflected in the pedagogical approach, with one planned question asking: Do they know a fair way to test a magnet to find out how strong it is? This particular piece of planning was indicative of many others, as there was a lack of coherence among the objectives, science focus and pedagogical approach.

Six out of 10 students identified a pedagogical approach that was predominantly structured, with five of these also being teacher-led and one being exploratory. Five out of 10 students identified an approach that was more exploratory/investigative in nature, although two of these were quite structured, one using cue cards to explain the activity. Two out of the 10 students planned to record the results in the form of a table or word bubbles. In most cases (six out of 10), planning was unclear in terms of the organisation of the activity, but three of these appeared to be more whole class-orientated. Only four students identified organisation, two out of 10 working in groups (one with cue cards), one out of 10 identifying whole class work (discuss the different senses with the class), and one out of 10 working in pairs (work in pairs in

order to help each other and discuss their findings). Two students included aspects of recording, one using a table for results and the other using word bubbles.

There was no correlation between the students' espoused views and the pedagogical approach described in their planning, although four of the five who had initially placed science teaching and learning at the centre of all sectors had moved very slightly into one sector, indicating that their planned approach was very similar to their espoused beliefs. It is possible that these student teachers are espousing the beliefs shown in their planning and that slight differences are due to understanding of the different philosophical stances, evidenced by the fact that these four students placed the nature of science teaching and learning at the centre of all sectors. Discrepancies may occur if respondents identify their ideal approach in answer to the first task, which may differ from the reality of their approach in planning.

Observation of teaching

After further teaching on pedagogical approaches, the student teachers were asked to plan an interactive science discovery table for 7-year-old children on a chosen theme/concept. Their planning was discussed with them and an attempt was made to develop their understanding of more exploratory/discovery approaches.

These activities were used with a class of 30 children, who worked in small groups and moved between the activities. All the activities were knowledge-focused and observations of practice identified the approaches as falling into four out of five categories, from teacher-led exploration to highly structured teacher-led imposition of knowledge:

1 Guided discovery and exploration (0 students) – children are allowed to explore independently, with guidance from the teacher, by way of appropriate interaction, such as incidental questions (DES, 1967: DfES 2003);

2 Teacher-led exploration (four students) – children are led through an exploration, with almost complete teacher involvement;

3 Structured teacher-led exploration (three students) – children are led through an exploration, with teacher instructions and complete teacher involvement;

4 Structured teacher-led imposition (one student) – children are directly taught knowledge through instruction, questioning and practical activity;

Research (*continued*)

5 Highly structured teacher-led imposition (two students) – children are directly taught knowledge through instruction, questioning and teacher demonstration.

There appears to be very little correlation between students' and teachers' espoused views, planning and practice. This is not a new phenomenon, as research has found (Fensham, 2001; Taber, 2002) that the wealth of knowledge on constructivist science teaching has not had a significant effect on the content of science education. Three of the students whose espoused beliefs were central to the sectors, and who had moved slightly in their planning into one sec-

tor, remained in that sector in their practice. This appeared to indicate some consistency between their views, planning and practice. Another student appeared to show a match between their espoused beliefs and their pedagogical practice, whilst the rest showed some differences. There was more correlation between planning and practice, with six out of the 10 students using pedagogical approaches in practice that matched those in their planning. Since the planning was undertaken some time before and in a different area of science, this seemed to indicate that these students had confirmed rather than developed their pedagogical approaches during the intervening period.

Student	Philosophy	Planning	Practice
1	Central	Exploratory (C/PM)	Structured teacher-led exploration with a focus on knowledge (T/C)
2	Central	Structured teacher-led (T/P)	Highly structured, teacher-led with a focus on knowledge (T/P)
3	T/P	Exploratory (C/PM)	Structured teacher-led exploration with a focus on knowledge (T/C)
4	Central	Structured teacher-led exploratory (T/C)	Teacher-led exploration with a focus on knowledge (T/C)
5	C/PM	Structured exploratory (T/C)	Teacher-led exploration with a focus on knowledge (T/C)
6	Central	Structured teacher-led (T/P)	Highly structured, teacher-led with a focus on knowledge (T/P)
7	C/PM	Exploratory group work with teacher cue cards (T/C)	Teacher-led exploration with a focus on knowledge (T/C)
8	C/PM	Structured teacher-led with some problem-solving (T/P)	Teacher-led exploration with a focus on knowledge (T/C)
9	C/PM	Structured teacher-led (T/P)	Structured teacher-led with a focus on knowledge (T/P)
10	Central	Teacher-led experiment (T/P)	Structured teacher-led exploration with a focus on knowledge (T/C)

T/C, traditionalist/constructivist; C/PM, constructivist/post-modernist; PM/P, post-modernist/positivist; T/P, traditionalist/positivist.

Conclusions and implications

Effective teaching requires that all concerned in the teaching process have a clear, shared vision and beliefs about what good science teaching and learning involve. However, it also requires exploration of different perspectives on the nature of science and science teaching and the tension that exists between the science curriculum (static empirical knowledge) and education (constantly evolving understanding in a social context). The process of sharing and developing philosophies involves discourse so that teaching in the curriculum can reflect the shared

understandings of the nature of science and the teaching methodologies that will support holistic pupil development. Such discourse is felt (Duschl, 2000) to be important in making the nature of science more explicit and in developing understanding of the relevance of science.

As well as engagement with ideas about the nature of teaching and learning, student teachers need good role models of planning and practice and opportunities to develop their own teaching style rather than following imposed teaching structures in the form of ready-made lesson plans and schemes of work. They need to

Research (*continued*)

develop skills so that they can choose and use peda-gogical approaches that respond to children as individuals, motivating and challenging them and enabling them to construct scientific knowledge through experience and engagement with scientific ideas. These approaches are not evident in practice, because student teachers are concerned about issues of coverage, control, safety and learning. Where the curriculum contains an enormous amount of material, both teachers and student teachers are understandably concerned with covering the content and resort to imparting knowledge, as this takes less time than exploration and discovery learning. This solution also appears to solve the problem of reaching targets and is compounded by the teaching approach as advocated by national curricula, thus providing control over the children's learning and ensuring safety. It is, however, a deceptive solution, especially in science education, as quality learning occurs through teaching approaches that engage and interest children. This interest is greater in practical experiences, which develop skills alongside understandings and pay attention to detail rather than coverage.

References

DES (1967). *Children and their Primary School: A report of the Central Advisory Council for Education (England), Vol. 1: Report.* London: HMSO.

DfES (2003). *Excellence and Enjoyment: A strategy for primary schools.* London: DfES.

Duschl, R. (2000). Making the nature of science explicit. In: Millar, R., Leach, J. & Osborne, J., eds. *Improving Science Education: The Contribution of Research.* Buckingham: Open University Press, pp. 187–206.

Fensham, P.J. (2001). Science content as problematic – issues for research. In: Behrendt, H., Dahncke, H., Duit, R., Gräber, W., Komorek, M., Kross, A. & Reiska, P., eds. *Research in Science Education – Past, Present and Future.* Dordrecht, the Netherlands: Kluwer Academic.

Taber, K.S. (2002). The constructivist view of learning: how can it inform assessment? Invited presentation to the University of Cambridge Local Examinations Syndicate (UCLES) Research and Evaluation Division (RED). 27 May 2002.

Practical and reflective tasks

Practical tasks

Plan some role-play activities that have a scientific learning outcome. Particularly plan your involvement in the learning, as follows:

- How you will introduce the play;
- How you will interact/support/guide/model during the play;
- What questions you will ask to encourage scientific exploration;
- How you will evaluate your part in the learning.

Reflective tasks

After the play activity, read about teaching approaches and use your reading to help you consider the following reflective questions.

Early career professional

- How successful was the play at meeting your learning outcomes?
- How successful was your interaction/support during the play?
- What do you need now to improve your part in children's play?

Developing career professional/teacher

- How could you adapt the play to better support the learning outcomes?
- How can you develop your role in the play to ensure you are providing support but not being too structured?
- How else can you use role-play to support achievement of scientific development?

Later career professional/leader
- What was the impact of the teachers' role on the children's scientific development?
- How did having less teacher control over the activity affect scientific learning and behaviour?
- How can you support staff in your context to support and extend scientific learning through play?

STUDY SKILLS

Reflective tasks

Look at some synthesis/discussion of findings sections of your writing. Review the quality of your discussion and check for coherence, continuity and compelling arguments. Be ruthlessly honest about your writing style: you are aiming for a style that is consistent, fluent and vivid, yet not over-stated. As you do this consider the following:
- Are research questions explicitly addressed?
- Is evidence from personal research used thoroughly?
- Is new evidence introduced without justification?
- Is evidence from reading integrated within the argument?
- Is the argument cogent and compelling or is it overstated, simplistic or over-generalised at times?

Review the quality of your conclusions by asking yourself the following questions:
- Is there an actual conclusion, rather than a summary?
- Is the conclusion convincing, yet duly tentative?
- Does the research have an apparent or potential impact on the educational setting?
- Does the conclusion justly claim to enhance our knowledge and understanding in some specific area?
- Do you reflect on your personal and professional learning through undertaking this research?

ACTIVITIES AND KEY QUESTIONS

To promote understanding of space

Early Years Foundation Stage
- Observe shadows in the outside play area/garden and how they change during the day.
  Key question: How have the shadows changed?
- Observe the Moon in the sky in the day time and when it gets dark.
  Key question: Why do you think you can see the Moon better at night?
- Make a space rocket (see the preceding case study) and allow children to play at being astronauts and going to the Moon.
  Key question: How do you think the Moon is different from the Earth?

Activities and key questions (*continued*)

- Tell some star stories, such as the story of Orion the Hunter and the Great and Little Bears. Allow children to re-enact the stories.
  Key question: Why do you think people made up stories about the stars?

- Make up stories about the man in the Moon.
  Key question: Why do you think people thought there was a man in the Moon?

Key Stage 1

- Make a human sundial by standing on the same spot at different times of the day and drawing round a child's shadow with chalk.
  Key question: How has the shadow changed during the day?

- Look at the Moon over a period of time and see how it changes shape. (It does not matter at this age that they do not know why the Moon appears to change shape.)
  Key question: Why do you think the Moon changes shape?

- Make a space rocket (see the preceding case study) and allow children to play at being astronauts and going to the Moon.
  Key question: How do you think the Moon is different from the Earth?

- Put a toy rocket, astronauts, rocks, sand etc. into a shoe box. Allow the children to play with the box and make a Moon diorama.
  Key question: What do you think the surface of the Moon is like?

- Tell some star stories, such as the story of Orion the Hunter and the Great and Little Bears. Allow children to re-enact the stories.
  Key question: Why do you think people made up stories about the stars?

Key Stage 2

- Take a photograph with the sun in it from the playground at different times of the day. Compare the photographs.
  Key question: Why do you think the sun appears to move across the sky during the day?

- Set up a space rocket play session in which each group researches a different planet and decides which one is most suitable for human habitation (see the preceding case study).
  Key question: How is Mars/Venus/Mercury different from the Earth?

- In a large space (outside or in the school hall) and as a whole class, get the children to hold hands in a circle (and pretend that the circle is the Earth). The teacher can represent the Sun by holding a torch. Get the circle to turn clockwise slowly whilst the teacher holds the torch and in this way represent day and night in different places on the Earth. Then get the circle to turn clockwise and move around the teacher (so turning in a circle but also moving around the teacher) to represent the year it takes to orbit the Moon.
  Key question: Why do you think it is daytime on one side of the Earth and night-time on the other?

- Observe star maps and try to find the constellations in the night sky. Find out about the star stories and make up your own stories about the constellations.
  Key question: What are the stories behind the constellations?

- Look at a lunar map and try to match to what you can see at night. Make up stories about the Moon that you can retell.
  Key question: Why do you think people thought the Moon was made of cheese?

Knowledge box

Life processes

There are 11 systems of the body:

1 **The circulatory system** pumps blood to and from the body and lungs using the heart as a pump. Oxygenated blood travels through arteries from the lungs and deoxygenated blood travels to the lungs through major veins. Blood consists of white blood cells (made mainly in the bone marrow – 75%), whose function is to kill germs and fight disease, and red blood cells (made in the liver and bone marrow), whose function is to carry oxygen and carbon dioxide. Red blood cells are rich in iron and contain anticoagulants to prevent blood clotting. The liver is the chemical factory of the body and its function is the formation and destruction of blood cells and the formation of blood clotting factors. It also stores carbohydrates, manufactured from proteins and fats, converts liver glycogen to blood glucose and deals with poisons and toxins in the body. The spleen is involved in blood cell formation and destruction of blood cells and acts as a blood filter as well as being a store of blood.

2 **The digestive system** processes food with salivary glands. The organs of the digestive system include the oesophagus, stomach, liver, gallbladder, pancreas, intestines, rectum and anus. Food is mixed with digestive fluids at different stages in the system (mouth, stomach, small intestine) and fluids with nutrients are absorbed into the blood and waste is excreted.

3 **The endocrine system** is the communication system within the body using hormones made by endocrine glands such as the hypothalamus, pituitary or pituitary gland, pineal body or pineal gland, thyroid, parathyroids, and adrenals or adrenal glands. The adrenal glands (just above the kidneys) release hormones, particularly adrenaline and noradrenaline, which affect the nervous system (dilating pupils, making hair stand on end, relaxing bronchioles and increasing the size of airways, affecting blood pressure). The thyroid gland (in the neck) produces hormones, which control calcium levels in the blood, the metabolic rate and blood cholesterol. The pituitary gland (at the base of the brain) produces hormones that regulate the kidneys (reabsorption of water), growth and sexual impulses.

4 **The immune system** protects the body against disease by identifying and killing pathogens and tumour cells (see liver and white blood cell function above).

5 **The skin, hair and nails** form an integumentary system.

6 **The lymphatic system** is involved in the transfer of lymph between tissues and the bloodstream and defends against disease-causing agents with leukocytes, tonsils, adenoids, thymus and spleen. Lymph (tissue fluid) takes oxygen from the blood to cells using lymphatic capillaries and tissue spaces which join to the lymphatic vessels. Lymph nodes act as filters.

7 **The muscular system** involves movement with muscles.

8 **The nervous system** collects, transfers and processes information to and from the brain, spinal cord and nerves. Electrical impulses are sent to the brain via the nerves and the brain makes connections and interprets the signal.

9 **The reproductive system** is the system that enables reproduction.

10 **The respiratory system** includes the organs used for breathing – the pharynx, larynx, trachea, bronchi, lungs, and diaphragm – and is the way in which oxygen enters and carbon dioxide is emitted from the body. Inspiration (breathing in) involves the diaphragm descending and the chest wall moving outwards. Expiration (breathing out) involves the recoil of the lungs and chest wall.

11 **The skeletal system** structures, supports and protects the internal organs with bones, cartilage, ligaments, and tendons.

Knowledge box

Astronomy

The Big Bang theory explains the birth of the universe as dense matter spinning down a black hole, which exploded sending all the matter outwards, forming the solar systems, stars, planets and so on. The universe is thought to be continuing to expand, like an inflating balloon. Our solar system consists of:

- the Sun (a middle-aged, middle-sized star);
- four terrestrial planets close to the Sun (i.e. planets that are made up of rock and metal) – in order of closeness to the Sun these are Mercury, Venus, Earth, Mars;
- four outer gas planets: Jupiter, Saturn, Uranus, Neptune;
- some dwarf planets, one of which is Pluto which used to be thought of as the ninth planet.

Stars are spheres of gas, mainly hydrogen and helium, which shine because of their very high temperatures. Stars are formed from huge clouds of gas and dust known as nebulae that float in the universe. They begin to grow when part of the cloud clumps together. When the hydrogen gas at the centre of the star is burnt up, it begins to 'die', firstly becoming a giant red star and later collapsing into a white dwarf (whose gravitational force is so strong, a cupful would weigh 500 tonnes). It collapses further into a neutron star (some of which spin fast, sending out radio waves and are called pulsars). Eventually the dying star has such a strong gravitational force that it pulls everything in its orbit and becomes a black hole.

Star stories were made up to explain the star patterns in the sky. In the story of Orion and the Hunter, Orion wanted to impress the goddess Diana and so boasted that he could hunt and kill any animal on earth. He challenged Diana to a hunting competition in the forest. Orion came across a deadly scorpion in the forest (possibly arranged by Diana) and it stung him in the heel and he lay dying. Zeus, the King of the gods, took pity on Orion and placed him among the stars for ever. He also put the scorpion in the sky but as far away from Orion as possible. In the story of the Great and Little Bears, the Great Bear was once a lovely maiden called Callisto (a huntress) who loved Zeus. Zeus's wife was jealous of the attention Zeus lavished on Callisto and so changed her into a bear, where she roamed the forest, striking fear in hunters. One day, Callisto's son, Arcos, came across the bear. She was overjoyed to see her son and went to embrace him, but he raised his spear to kill her. Zeus saw this and changed Arcos into a smaller bear and picked both of them up by their tails and swung them into the sky. The pattern of the Great Bear is made up of the stars of the Plough, and the Little Bear's tail ends in the Pole Star.

Each planet is kept in orbit around the Sun by centripetal force as a result of the Sun's gravitational attraction – it acts on the spinning planets, pulling them inwards and stopping them moving away and out of orbit. Each planet rotates on its axis, producing days (on the side of the planet facing the Sun) and nights (on the side of the planet facing away from the Sun). Each planet also orbits the Sun, and on Earth the time taken to complete an orbit is, of course, called a year.

Mercury is the smallest and closest planet to the Sun and it orbits the Sun once in about 88 Earth days, completing three rotations about its axis for every two orbits – so it has three 'days' for each year! We can sometimes see Mercury as a morning or evening star in the sky.

Venus, the second planet from the Sun, is close in size and gravity to Earth, although its atmospheric pressure is 92 times that on Earth. It orbits the Sun every 224.7 Earth days and has a very dry landscape, with an atmosphere mainly of carbon dioxide, sulphuric acid clouds and extremely hot surface temperatures of 460°C. Venus can often be seen as a bright star in the morning and evening from Earth and is called the Morning or Evening Star.

Earth is the next planet from the Sun. It takes 24 hours to turn on its axis and 365.24 days to orbit the Sun. As the Earth rotates on its axis, the shadows on the earth change, being long and thin in the mornings and evenings and fatter and shorter around midday; they also change direction during the day. The Earth's axis is such that the poles sometimes receive less direct energy and light from the Sun (winter) and sometimes more (summer). Its atmosphere, containing oxygen and carbon dioxide, and the presence of water over three-quarters of the planet are conducive to life. The amount of water makes it look blue from space and it is sometimes called the Blue Planet. The Earth has one moon orbiting it and rotating on its axis at the same time so that it always shows the same face towards the Earth; the orbit takes approximately 28 days (a lunar month or 'moonth'). The phases of the Moon follow a predictable pattern:

1 New Moon – the part of the Moon facing the Earth is dark. This occurs on average every 29.5 days.
2 A small crescent of light appears.
3 The amount of light gradually gets bigger until half the surface facing the Earth is lit (first quarter).
4 The Moon waxes until we see first a gibbous Moon (between half and full) and then a full Moon.
5 The Moon wanes so that the visible part gets smaller until we see a gibbous Moon.
6 The final phase before the New Moon is a small crescent Moon.

The Moon exerts a gravitational pull on the Earth that causes tides (high tide being when the Moon is closer to the Earth and low tide when it is further away). The Moon shines because it reflects the light of the Sun.

Mars is the fourth planet from the Sun. It is called the Red Planet because its surface is covered with iron oxide (rust). It has a thin atmosphere and is covered by large impact craters (like our Moon) and volcanoes. Its rotation and orbit are similar to those of the Earth. Mars has two moons, Phobos and Deimos, which are small and irregularly shaped.

Jupiter is the fifth planet from the Sun. It is a large (two and half times the size of Earth) gas planet, composed of hydrogen and helium. It is very hot and this is seen as cloud bands; it also has a great red spot, which is thought to be a big storm. It also has 66 known satellites.

Saturn is smaller than Jupiter (but still a big planet) but has a similar atmosphere. It is recognisable by its rings, which are made up of small ice and rock particles. It has 62 known satellites which are mainly made up of ice, but two (Titan and Enceladus) show signs of geological activity.

Uranus is the seventh planet from the Sun and has the third largest planetary radius and fourth largest planetary mass in the solar system. It is the lightest of the outer gas planets. It orbits the Sun on its side and has a much colder core than the other gas giants. It has 22 known satellites. It takes over 84 Earth years to orbit the Sun because of its distance from the Sun.

Neptune is slightly smaller than Uranus but is more dense; it is the fourth largest planet by diameter and the third largest by mass. Its orbit around the Sun is about 30 times greater than that of the Earth and takes over 164 Earth years to complete. It has very active weather, as opposed to Uranus which is quiet by comparison but it is the coldest planet in the solar system, with temperatures at its cloud tops of −218°C.

Pluto was discovered in 1930 and was considered to be the ninth planet until it was downgraded in 2006 to a dwarf planet. Pluto orbits twice around the Sun for every three Neptunian orbits.

References

Alexander, R. (2008). *Towards Dialogic Teaching: Rethinking Classroom Talk*, 4th edn. York: Dialogos.

Bary, R., Deans, C., Charlton, M., Hullet, H., Martin, F., Martin, L., Moana, P., Waugh, O., Jordan, B. & Scrivens. C. (2008). *Ako Ngatahi Teaching and Learning Together as One. From Leadership to Enquiry. Teachers' work in an Infants' and Toddlers' Centre*. Massey University: Massey Childcare Centre Inc.

Bassey, M. (1998). Fuzzy generalisation: an approach to building educational theory. Paper presented at the British Educational Research Association Annual Conference, The Queen's University of Belfast, Northern Ireland, 27–30 August 1998 www.leeds.ac.uk/educol/documents/000000801.htm.

Bassey, M. (1999). *Case Study Research in Educational Settings*. Buckingham: Open University Press.

British Educational Research Association (BERA), Early Years Special Interest Group (2003). *Early Years Research: Pedagogy, Curriculum and adult Roles, Training and Professionalism*. Southwell: BERA.

Bruner, J. S. (1991). The narrative construction of reality. *Critical Inquiry*, 18(1), 1–21.

Carle, E. (1970). *The Very Hungry Caterpillar*. Harmondsworth: Penguin.

Cooper, H. (2010). *Research Synthesis and Meta-Analysis: A step by step approach, 4th edition*. Thousand Oaks, CA: Sage.

Cooper, L., Johnston, J., Rotchell, E. & Woolley, R. (2010). *Knowledge and Understanding of the World*. London: Continuum.

Coltman, P, Petyaeva, D. & Anghileri, J. (2002). Scaffolding learning through meaningful tasks and adult interaction. *Early Years: An International Journal of Research and Development*, 22(1), 39–49.

Creative Little Scientists (CLS) (2012). Conceptual Framework and Literature Reviews as addenda. Online at: http://www.creative-little-scientists.eu/content/deliverables. Accessed 28/5/12.

Cremin, T., Burnard, P. & Craft, A. (2006). Pedagogy and possibility thinking in the early years. *Journal of Thinking Skills and Creativity*, 1(2), 108–119.

de Bóo, M. (ed) (2004). *Early Years Handbook. Support for Practitioners in the Foundation Stage*. Sheffield: The Curriculum Partnership/Geography Association.

Department for Education (DfE) (2012a). *Statutory Framework for the Early Years Foundation Stage. Setting the Standards for Learning, Development and Care for Children from Birth to Five*. London: DfE.

Department for Education (DfE) (2012b). *National Curriculum for Science. Key Stages 1 and 2 – Draft*. London: DfE.

Elkind, D. (2001). The *Hurried Child. Growing Up Too Fast Too Soon*, 3rd edn. Cambridge, MA: Da Capio Press.

Fleer, M. (2002). Sociocultural assessment in early years education: Myth or reality? *International Journal of Early Years Education*, 10(2), 105–120.

Fleer, M. (2007). *Young children: Thinking about the scientific world*. Watson, ACT; Early Childhood Australia.

Freedman, C. & Cort, B. (2007). *Aliens Love Underpants*. London: Simon & Schuster.

Froebel, F. (1826). *On the Education of Man*. Keilhau, Leipzig: Wienbrach.

Gardner, H. (2007). *Five Minds for the Future*. Harvard: Harvard Business School.

Glauert, E. (2009). Research in early childhood science education: Issues for early childhood curriculum design and implications for primary science education. In: R. Lauterbach, H. Giest and B. Marquardt-Mau, eds. *Lernen und Kindliche Entwicklung*. Bad Heilbrunn: Klinkhardt.

Goswami, U. & Bryant, P. (2007). *Children's Cognitive Development and Learning. The Primary Review Research Survey 2/1a*. Cambridge: Cambridge University Press.

Hand, B. (1988). Is conceptual conflict a viable teaching strategy?: the students' viewpoint. *Australian Science Teachers Journal*, 34(4), 22–26.

Hohmann, M. & Weikart, D. P. (2002). *Educating Young Children*, 2nd edn. Ypsilanti, Michigan: High/Scope Press.

Johnston, J. (2005). *Early Explorations in Science*, 2nd edn. Buckingham: Open University Press.

Johnston, J. S. (2009). How does the skill of observation develop in young children. *International Journal of Science Education*, 31(18), 2511–2525.

Johnston, J. (2011). Children talking: teachers supporting science. *Journal of Emergent Science*, 1, 14–22.

Johnston, J. (2012a). Synthesis of ideas. In: Oversby, J., ed. *ASE Guide to Research in Science Education*. Hatfield: ASE.

Johnston, J. (2012b). Using play pedagogy in the early years of primary school. In: Campbell, C. & Jobling, W., eds. *Science in Early Childhood Education*. Melbourne: Cambridge University Press.

Johnston, J. & Nahmad-Williams, L. (2008). *Early Childhood Studies*. Harlow: Pearson.

Johnston, J. & Nahmad-Williams, L. (2010). Developing imagination and imaginative play. In: Compton, A., Johnston, J., Nahmad-Williams, L. & Taylor, K. *Creative Development*. London: Continuum.

Kallery, M. & Psillos, D. (2002). What happens in the early years science classroom? The reality of teachers' curriculum implementation activities. *European Early Childhood Education Research Journal*, 10(2), 49–61.

Longbottom, J. (1999). Science education for democracy: dilemmas, decisions, autonomy and anarchy. *Paper presented to the European Science Education Research Association Second International Conference, Kiel, Germany*.

Metz, K. E. (1998). Scientific inquiry within reach of young children. In: Biddle, B.J., Godd, T.L. & Goodson, I.F., eds. *International Handbook of Science Education*. London: Springer, pp. 81–96.

Metz, K. E. (2004). Children's understanding of scientific inquiry: Their conceptualization of uncertainty in investigations of their own design. *Cognition and Instruction*, 222, 219–290.

Montessori, M. (1912). *The Montessori Method*. London: Heinemann.

Moylett, H. (2010). Supporting children's development and learning. In: Bruce, T., ed. *Early Childhood*, 2nd edn. London: Sage.

National Research Council of the National Academies (2007). *Taking Science to School. Learning and Teaching Science in Grades K to 8*. Washington, DC: The National Academies Press.

Naylor, S., Keogh, B. & Goldsworthy, A. (2004). *Active Assessment: Thinking, Learning and Assessment in Science*. Sandbach, Cheshire: Millgate House.

Pearse, P. & Riddell, E, (1989). *See How You Grow*. New York: Barrons Educational Series.

Peters, A. F. & Coplestone, J. (2007). *Animals Aboard*. London: Frances Lincoln.

Piaget, J. (1929). *The Child's Conception of the World*. New York: Harcourt.

Piaget, J. (1976). 'Mastery play' and 'symbolic play'. In: Bruner, J., Jolly, A., & Sylva, K., eds. *Play – Its role in Development and Evolution*. Middlesex: Penguin.

Rittle-Johnson, B. & Koedinger, K. R. (2005). Designing knowledge scaffolds to support mathematical problem solving. *Cognition and Instruction*, 23(3), 313–349.

Robbins, J. (2005). 'Brown paper packages'? A sociocultural perspective on young children's ideas in science. *Research in Science Education*, 35(2), 151–172.

Roberts, B. (2007). *Getting the Most out of the Research Experience. What Every Researcher Needs to Know*. London: Sage.

Rogoff, B. (1995). Observing sociocultural activity on three planes: participatory appropriation, guided participation, and apprenticeship. In: Wertsch, J.V., Del Rio, P. & Alvarex, A., eds. *Sociocultural Studies of Mind*. Cambridge, UK: Cambridge University Press, pp. 139–164.

Rousseau, J.J. (1911). *Emile*. London: J. M. Dent and Sons.

Russell, W. (2010). Playwork. In: Bruce, T., ed. *Early Childhood*, 2nd edn. London: Sage.

Siraj-Blatchford, I., (2009). Conceptualising progression in the pedagogy of play and sustained shared thinking in early childhood education: a Vygotskian perspective. *Educational & Child Psychology*, 26 (2), 77–89.

Siraj-Blatchford, I., Sylva, K., Muttock, S., Gilden, R., & Bell, D. (2002). *Researching Effective Pedagogy in the Early Years*. Nottingham: DFES.

Smallman, C. & Riddell, E. (1986). *Outside In*. Abingdon: Frances Lincoln Children's Books.

Steiner, R. (1996). *The Education of the Child and Early Lectures on Education*. New York: Anthroposophic Press.

Stone, C.A., (1993). What is Missing in the metaphor of scaffolding? In: Forman, E.A., Minick, N., & Stone, C.A., eds. *Contexts for Learning; Sociocultural Dynamics in Children's Development*. New York: Oxford University Press, pp. 169–183.

Toulmin, S. (1958). *The Uses of Argument*. Cambridge: Cambridge University Press.

Vygotsky, L. (1962). *Thought and Language*. Cambridge, MA: MIT Press.

Vygotsky, L. & Cole, M. (ed) (1978). *Mind in Society, The Development of Higher Psychological Processes*. Cambridge, MA: Harvard University Press.

Chapter 8

Scientific explorations and discovery

Overview

In this chapter we look at:

- What scientific explorations are
- How exploration and discovery learning can support and enhance scientific development and learning
- Research into pedagogical approaches by Coral Campbell
- How to write up research
- Practical and reflective tasks that look at the effect of exploration and discovery on behaviour and learning
- Activity boxes on discovering light and materials
- Knowledge boxes focusing on light and weather.

Introduction

Exploration is an important element in teaching and learning. I have used the word exploration (Johnston, 2005) when I mean play, as play, exploration or simply messing about is an important part of the scientific process **(see Figure 1.1)**. The history of science is one that emphasises the importance of exploration for discovery, invention and creative thinking (Johnston, 2004, 2009). Many of the scientists identified in the introduction, such as Isaac Newton, Archimedes, Marie Curie, Charles Darwin and Galileo Galilei illustrate this **(see Figure I.1)**. They took time to consider their ideas, explored the concepts abstractly and practically, displayed creative, critical thinking and took great risks in communicating their ideas to a world that was sometimes unwilling and unready to accept them. It is easy to underestimate the important role that exploration plays in the scientific process but if we do this, we seriously disadvantage children's scientific development.

Exploration has been recognised as an important part of science from the science projects of the 1960s and 1970s (e.g. the Nuffield Foundation Junior Science Project, 1964–6 and

Photograph 8.1 Exploration in the nursery

the Schools Council Science 5 ÷ 13 Project, 1967–74) and early versions of the National Curriculum in Science **(see Chapter 5)**. It seems a wasted opportunity for the exploratory focus of the Early Years Foundation Stage (DfE, 2012a) not to be built upon in the National Curriculum (DfE, 2012b), a situation acknowledged by many submissions to the Cambridge Primary Review (Alexander, 2010). This is odd as exploration features in many learning models in science; for example Cosgrove and Osborne's (1985) generative learning as well as early years science (CLS, 2012). Exploration is probably the most common and suitable pedagogical approach for children in the early years. Exploration involves children in observing the world around them, asking questions, formulating hypotheses and developing some basic scientific skills. Explorations can be included in structured play or be part of more structured approaches **(see Chapter 9)**.

Discovery learning was very popular in the 1960s and 1970s (see the Plowden report; DES, 1967). In 2004, I advocated the reintroduction of discovery learning in science (Johnston, 2004) and had some very interesting discussions about discovery both before and after publication. Those professionals of my generation who had been introduced to Plowden at an early stage in their career understood discovery to mean scaffolded, but open-ended learning with clear learning outcomes identified. Professionals of an older generation (and there are a few still around!) considered discovery to be an ad hoc approach where anything could occur and with no identified learning outcomes. Early career professionals who I was working with (see research box in Chapter 7) felt that if a child learned anything, even in a highly structured pedagogical context, such as a demonstration, then they had discovered. I revisited Plowden (DES, 1967; see also Johnston & Halocha, 2010) and realised that, with time, the ideas of Plowden had become distorted in the pre-National Curriculum primary school, where learning was incidental and children played without purpose or learning objectives and made scientific discoveries for themselves. After the introduction of the National Curriculum, primary practice developed into a more exploratory, experiential approach. However, in recent years, pedagogical practice has become more structured, with the role of the professional changing dramatically as a result, so that early career professionals are likely to have little experience of creative planning and being a facilitator in the children's learning and are more likely to adopt didactic pedagogical approaches. My views in the last decade have not changed regarding discovery as an approach and I advocate bringing back more discovery into early years science, but with clear learning outcomes, structured and supported by knowledgeable adults and reintroducing the awe and wonder into learning (CLS, 2012).

STUDY SKILLS

Writing up

In this chapter we look at writing up research and development for different audiences. Written formats can include a short report for professional accreditation, a research report for a thesis and an article for a professional or research journal.

Writing is an iterative process and should begin at the earliest stages of professional enquiry or research, e.g. a proposal for the enquiry or research, a reflective journal, drafts of sections or, in longer pieces of work, chapters. It is important not to leave it until the end of the professional enquiry or research, as this can lead to a lack of coherence between the enquiry/research design, analysis and synthesis. Writing is also an essential tool for professional researchers who are being assessed through the presentation of ideas in short written assignments, longer dissertations or peer-reviewed journals. Excellent professional enquiry and research can fall down at this last hurdle if the written word does not convey the excellence of the work undertaken, and this emphasises the importance of the writing process. The structure for these final reports is often dictated by the guidelines given to you by the awarding body (in the case of a thesis) or by the journal. However, decisions about structure need to be taken with the research methodology or approach in mind as well as the audience. Different types of research or study may need to be written up in different ways, so a report of a piece of action research which tells the story of actions and the analysis of those actions (Elliott, 1991) will look very different from the case study research which synthesises ideas into a piece of narrative (Bassey, 1999; Clough, 2002), and different again from a piece of empirical research. All professional researchers need to provide their own structure for their written work, which best shows their understanding of both research and the subject being researched and reflects the type of research they are doing.

Writing for the professional audience involves a different writing technique (Henn *et al.*, 2006) and the challenge here is to make the research accessible without 'dumbing down'. Articles are likely to be very short and should engage the reader, make the enquiry/research understandable and focus on the implications of the research for practice and provision. In this way, the relevance of the research for practice and provision is much clearer. The audience for professional texts is not just different, it is also potentially larger and so this can be a way of communicating the research to a larger group of academics and professionals. Research can also be written into chapters of edited books or longer professional books. Edited books contain chapters written by different authors collated by a book editor and will involve a commissioning and publishing editor as well. Editors come in a variety of forms and it is useful for the researcher to find out who they are writing for, as this will make the process easier. Most editors are sympathetic to the academic and professional context and are very aware of the publication issues. It is important to ensure that the integrity of the research is not impaired by a desire for consistency of style or content, and researchers may have to negotiate the content with an editor to ensure that what they want to communicate remains intact. The longer professional book can also spend considerable time considering the practical implications for teachers and look more explicitly at research into practice. In this type of publication, authors have more freedom to present their research in a way that they feel best conveys the messages.

Sections

Any writing is best divided into sections with subheadings, which help to structure the piece and help the reader to navigate it.

Study Skills (*continued*)

Introduction

This section is important in any writing you do. It is helpful if it addresses questions such as:

- Why is the study relevant?
- How does it add to understanding of the area?
- What is the expected professional value of the findings?
- What are the exact questions that you seek to answer?

The introduction should identify and describe the focus of the professional enquiry or research and the rationale for the research. It should identify the context in which the enquiry/research takes place and the participants involved and should situate the researcher in the research. It should arrest and engage the reader and ensure both empathy and interest in the research quest.

Review of the literature/background

This can be a short piece of writing on the conceptual framework/background to the enquiry or a longer section of a journal article or a chapter of a dissertation **(see the study skills box in Chapter 3)**. In this section/chapter you show your awareness of the ideas, issues and research that have preceded your work so that an informed argument can be developed.

How the enquiry was carried out/methodology and research methods

In a short piece of professional enquiry, this section should convey to the reader what you did and how you did it. In a journal article or chapter of a dissertation, this should provide a clear rationale for the research methodology, identify detail of the context in which the work was undertaken and provide a description, development and justification of the research methods used to acquire and analyse information. Ethical considerations should be clear and embedded in all aspects of the section/chapter so that you convince the reader of your awareness of the strengths and limitations of the design, including the reliability and validity of both the data collection and the strategies to be used for analysis of data.

Analysis and outcomes

The structure of this section is crucial to enable the reader to understand the data collected and share in the understanding of the analysis **(see the chapters in Section 2)**. It can be structured in different ways depending on the type of enquiry/research and the audience for the intended writing. The evidence on which the discussion is based should be incorporated in the text (graphs, interviews, photographs) so that there is coherence and the reader does not have to constantly look to the appendices. Indeed, stating 'as you can see from the appendix' can be very frustrating for readers, who are being expected to undertake the analysis for themselves, rather than have the analysis explained for them by the researcher. Longer extracts from which the data is taken, e.g. transcripts, detailed numerical data, may be included as an appendix and quoted in the text and this helps the reader see the full context of the data. Other data, such as questionnaires and video footage, do not need to be in the appendix, but can be kept in a separate archive. This section simply presents relevant outcomes clearly and succinctly. It is essential that the researcher analyses the findings and does not simply describe them.

Discussion of the findings

In this section, you need to discuss the findings. This involves synthesising the data (see Chapter 7). The synthesis considers what the research contributes to each of the research questions, reflects on the literature review and how to further develop the arguments begun in that section. You should also consider alternative interpretations and state the findings tentatively.

Conclusions and issues for further research

Like an effective plenary, the conclusion should not simply repeat material already stated but should drive the implications forward. It is important not to overstate the generalisability of the research results; on the other hand, implications for both the site of the research and the wider educational community should be considered. The conclusion should also reflect on the impact of the enquiry/research process on the personal and professional development of the author.

Appendices

The appendices follow the main text and include supporting material (e.g. transcripts of discussion, pupils' work, teachers' plans, tapes and tables of results) or any other evidence which, if included in the main text, would interrupt the flow. However, only material that is directly referred to in the text should be included. The rest of the evidence you simply store in an archive and may be of further use in subsequent writing and research activities.

Study Skills (*continued*)

References

A bibliographical list of references is always the last item in the written report. It must include every published work referred to in the text in such a way that the reader could easily locate the full text. There may be an additional list of further background reading that is not directly referred to in the text.

Reflective questions

1 Who are your audience for the writing?
2 Are there any guidelines/criteria for the writing?
3 What structure would best suit the writing and engage the audience?

Exploration as a pedagogical approach

Exploration is an open-ended exploratory approach that will provide children with opportunities to pursue avenues of enquiry that are of interest to them and allow them to formulate simple hypotheses about their experiences. As a pedagogical approach, it has a number of educational advantages:

● It motivates children by allowing them to start from their natural interests and encourages curiosity **(see Chapter 3)**.

● It helps children to learn through relevant engagement in the scientific process **(see Figure 1.1 and Chapter 1)**. In an exploratory activity, children engage in observations and raise questions from their observations which can be explored further or which may involve more systematic investigation.

● It aids differentiation as children choose differentiated pathways to follow in their exploration. These differentiated pathways are consistent with their needs and abilities. There will be a number of learning outcomes, but in each case the outcome is likely to be relevant to the children's learning needs. A more prescriptive activity will involve all children undertaking an identical or slightly differentiated activity, leading to one learning outcome. This learning outcome may not be consistent with every child's needs and abilities and, as a result, some children may not develop their knowledge or skills further; moreover, there may be an element of disillusionment or frustration.

● It can encourage positive behaviour by motivating children and being relevant to their learning needs. Since exploration is less likely to lead to frustration (because the work is too hard) or boredom (because the work is too easy) and stems from natural curiosity, behavioural problems are less likely.

Exploration that starts from children's natural interests is much more common in pre-school children, who are developing skills in the Early Years Foundation Stage (EYFS; DfE, 2012a), than in Key Stage 1 and 2 children working within the National Curriculum (DfE, 2012b). This is partly because teachers in the EYFS are under less pressure to meet narrow knowledge outcomes and because the EYFS is less structured and overcrowded than the National Curriculum (see Chapter 5). It may be that a less dense National Curriculum will provide professionals with the time necessary to build on children's curiosity and encourage exploration in a more effective way, but in order to do this, teachers will have to hold on to appropriate pedagogical approaches and not succumb to the more didactic approach that the new National Curriculum appears to advocate (DfE, 2012b).

CASE STUDY

Exploring shadows

Year 1 children were exploring shadows in the playground on a sunny morning. They danced about making their shadows move when Carrie cried out: 'My shadow's doing what I'm doing.' Polly said, 'Let's make them dance!' Rupert noticed that the shadow 'didn't turn' when the girls did and Amed pointed to the shadows from the buildings and bushes and said that they 'were all on the same side'. The teacher asked the children why they thought this was and Ahmed said, 'They come from the Sun and it is always there' (pointing to the Sun in the sky). The teacher suggested they watch their shadows during the day and see what happens to them and later they noticed that the shadows moved during the day, so that they got shorter and fatter at lunchtime and 'on the other side' in the afternoon.

The next day the teacher set up an overhead projector on a blank wall and left a range of objects for the children to explore shadows with. He asked them to see which object made the 'best' shadow and later asked them what they thought a 'good/best' shadow was. The children decided that a dark, non-fuzzy shadow was best and so he asked them to show here what the different shadows were like. Other questions he asked were:

- Why do you think some shadows are darker than others?
- How can you make a dark shadow?
- Why are some shadows not dark?
- How can you make a fuzzy shadow?
- Do all objects make shadows?

Reflective tasks

Early career professional

- How did the questioning support the children's understandings of shadows?
- How could the teacher's interaction extend the children's understandings of shadows?
- How could you develop your own questioning during explorations to support learning?

Developing career professional/teacher

- How did the teacher focus learning on shadows?
- How else could the teacher interact with the children during the exploration?
- How can you interact with the children to further support learning?

Later career professional/leader

- How did the teacher build on the children's natural interests in their exploration?
- How did the teacher make use of space and time and allow children independence and not direct exploration?
- How can you support teachers in your phase/school to use children's natural interests in exploration and balance interaction/intervention and questioning as pedagogical tools?

Practical task

Try writing up your reflections on the case study for a particular audience.

Exploratory activities

Explorations can be initiated by the children from their observations and play, as in the preceding case study, and so focus on any natural phenomena. Children may notice their voices echo whilst playing in a tent and this can lead to seeing where else their voices sound distorted. They may notice puddles drying in the sun or when they paint water on the bricks of the nursery or school during outside play as 'painters and decorators' and this can lead to further exploration of evaporation. They may explore the way the sand in the sand tray changes when wet or as it dries and this can lead to them exploring and comparing what happens when other materials are wet or drying (e.g. cornflour, flour, jelly powder, soap flakes).

Professionals can set up explorations for children, either building on their initial interests, as in the preceding case study, or to initiate a topic. This might use a collection of objects **(see Chapter 1)**, as follows:

- A collection of seeds can lead to exploration with a focus on growth.
- A collection of solids (e.g. play-dough, plasticine, cornflour, sand, salt, jelly) can lead to exploration with a focus on materials and their properties.
- A collection of objects by the water trough can lead to exploration with a focus on floating and sinking.

Professionals can also set up specific explorations, such as ice balloons, where an ice balloon is placed on a table and explored so that children can choose which exploratory direction to go in **(see Chapter 3)**. For example, some children may choose to look closely at the balloon, explore how the ice balloon changes when they sprinkle salt on it or put it in water, or what happens if they drop it. In this way the children decide which way their exploration should go and other resources can be introduced by the professional when the children appear to need them. Other specific explorations initiated by an adult could involve:

- Exploring the outside environment for signs of animal life.
- Exploring what happens when bath bombs, bubble bath or salt is added to a water trough (or bath).
- Exploring what happens when we mix the ingredients to make play-dough **(see the recipe in Chapter 3)**.
- Exploring what happens when you drop balls or marbles into the sand trough.

Stories, story books and nursery rhymes can be a stimulus to explore other scientific phenomena. Explorations from different story books are considered in the activity boxes in each chapter **(see also Figure I.3)**. Figure I.1 identifies some key scientists which could initiate some exploration, such as following up the story of Darwin by exploring a collection of animal pictures or bones, or following up the story of Archimedes by exploring the upthrust when objects are pushed down in water. The nursery rhyme *Pat-a-Cake, Pat-a-Cake Baker's Man* could lead to exploration of changes when ingredients are mixed together or heated or cooled and *Humpty Dumpty* could lead to an exploration of forces **(see Figure I.2)**.

ACTIVITIES AND KEY QUESTIONS

To promote understanding of light

Early Years Foundation Stage

- Explore bubbles. You can fill a water trough with bubble mixture (mix two parts detergent with eight parts water and one part of glycerine). It can be stored in big containers for a long period of time; the best bubbles are made when the mixture is rested and not agitated/lathered. Ask children to describe what they can see. Make a note of the words a child would use to describe the bubbles and the more scientific words you can introduce.
  Key question: What can you see in a bubble?

Activities and key questions (*continued*)

- Explore shadows. Use a projector or torch and a screen and a collection of shadow puppets made out of card, paper, greaseproof paper, acetate, coloured acetate etc.
  Key question: How can you make a big/small/dark shadow/fuzzy shadow?

- Explore colour. Look at the colours swirling in a bubble of washing-up liquid or an oily puddle. Explore what you see when looking through glasses made with coloured acetate (or use coloured sweet wrappers) at different coloured pictures.
  Key questions: What colours do you notice in a bubble? What do you notice when you have green/red/blue glasses?

Photograph 8.2 **Exploring shadows**

- Explore coloured spinners (spinning tops with colours, homemade spinners with colours of the spectrum or two colours that mix; **see Figure 8.1**). If red and yellow are used, the spinner (when spun) looks orange; blue and red make purple; and the colours of the spectrum look greyish.
  Key questions: What happens when you spin the spinner?

- Explore three-dimensional glasses and three-dimensional pictures.
  Key question: What can you see?

Activities and key questions (*continued*)

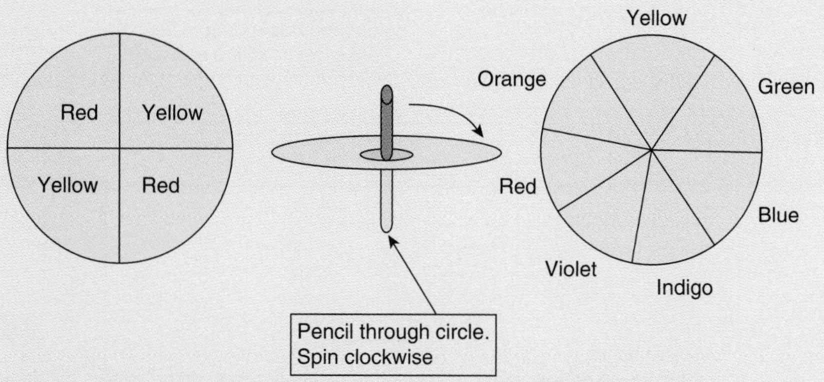

Figure 8.1 Coloured spinners

Key Stage 1

- Explore shadows. Explore shadows and colour by making shadow puppets and by seeing how coloured acetates change the colour of shadows.
  Key question: How can you make a large shadow?

- Explore reflection. Explore different mirrors (plane, concave, convex) and shiny spoons or shiny cylindrical tubes to see how images change when you look into them.
  Key question: Why do you think you are bigger/upside down/smaller in this mirror?

- Make a periscope using plane mirrors, so you can see round corners.
  Key question: How do you think your periscope works?

- Explore mirror puzzles (*The Mirror Puzzle Book* by Marion Walter, 1996)
  Key question: How do you think the puzzles work?

- Try copying a simple shape (a circle, square, triangle or star) by looking only in a mirror.
  Key question: Why do you think it is difficult to do?

Key Stage 2

- Explore lenses. Explore a range of lenses (concave, convex). Add a prism and explore this too.
  Key questions: How does the lens change things when you look through it? How does a prism change the light?

- Explore how light travels by looking at a camera obscura. These can easily be made using a shoe box, with the lid turned into a greaseproof paper screen and a magnifying lens used in the bottom of the box to focus the image **(see Figure 8.2)**. Make sure the depth of the box is the same as the focal distance of the lens, otherwise the image will be out of focus. Look at objects by pointing the lens at them and looking at the greaseproof paper screen.
  Key question: How does the camera obscura work?

- Explore moving pictures and vision by making spinning illusions, flick books or zoetropes. Spinning illusions can be made by drawing a picture of a bird on one side of a circle and a cage on the other, or a horse on one side and a rider on the other. The circle can be attached

Activities and key questions (*continued*)

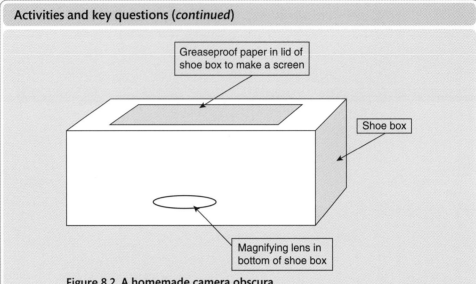

Figure 8.2 A homemade camera obscura

to a stick and, when spun around, the bird appears in the cage or the rider on the horse. Flick books can be made by having a simple image/drawn picture that is slightly changed on each page, so when flicked the image appears to move. With a zoetrope images are drawn in sequence on a crenulated strip of paper with each image slightly different. Join up the paper to make a circle, with the images inside, and put it on a turntable. When spun, look at the images from outside the circle through one of the gaps/crenulations: the image appears to move.

Key question: How do you think the spinner or flick book/zoetrope works?

Photograph 8.3 Exploring a zoetrope

Activities and key questions (*continued***)**

- Explore anamorphosic pictures (pictures that can only be seen in a cylindrical mirror (see *The Magic Cylinder Book* by Ivan Moscovitch, 1988).
  Key question: Why do you think the magic cylinder works?

- Try some mirror writing (writing by only looking in a mirror).
  Key question: Why do you think it is difficult to do?
  See also the Activities and key questions on space in Chapter 7.

The role of the professional in exploration

Professionals need certain professional attitudes in order to support effective exploration. They need to be confident in their ability to follow children's lines of exploration, confident in their own scientific knowledge (subject knowledge) and have the confidence and willingness to develop that knowledge as needed. They need to be flexible in their planning to allow deviations to support new explorations, but they also need to be very well organised to allow for every eventuality. For example, children playing in a tent in the outside play area might stop to listen to the rain on the tent, or children using a stethoscope to listen to the sound that salt makes on an ice balloon might well become more interested in the stethoscope and listen instead to their hearts or the sound of water inside a water trough (by putting the stethoscope on the outside of the trough).

The professional should also act as a good role model during explorations, encouraging children according to their interest and exploratory behaviour to explore and extend their explorations. This may mean exploring alongside the children. It may mean that professionals occasionally interact, or ask passing questions that encourage the children to think more deeply and thus further their exploration, e.g. 'What do you think will happen if…?', 'How can you…?' or 'Why do you think…?' The professional should also know when to stand back and allow children to explore and when to interact with, or even intervene in, explorations. This has been identified as a core pedagogic strategy, nurturing possibility thinking (Cremin *et al.*, 2006) in both science and creativity (CLS, 2012). Professionals who adopt this strategy will prioritise stopping, observing and listening and will notice any unusual or unexpected actions, behaviours or ideas (CLS, 2012).

Research

Science in the Early Years Foundation Stage

Dr Coral Campbell
Deakin University, Australia

Research question

- How do practitioners and others involved in the EYFS interpret and implement the EYFS framework?

Research design

In late 2009, a small pilot study was undertaken around one location in England to investigate the implementation

Research (*continued*)

of the EYFS. The project had wide-ranging aims but primarily it researched how practitioners and others involved in the EYFS were interpreting and implementing the frameworks. One aspect of particular interest to the researcher was the area of emergent science.

The research design involved approaching a number of early childhood providers with an invitation to participate in an interview about the Early Years National Strategy Foundation Stage. The centres chosen were:

- Centre E – an early years children's centre catering for birth to 5-year-olds, including a daycare centre for 3- to 4-year-olds. It is situated in a small rural town about 50 kilometres from the nearest regional city. The centre provides early years support to children from a diverse range of socioeconomic backgrounds. One part is a local authority nursery, which was the site visited. An informal discussion was held with the manager of the centre and the interview was conducted with one of the practitioners (who is also the assistant head teacher).

- Centre I – an urban nursery school for 3- to 5-year-olds, located in the middle of a large regional city. Attending children tended to be from a low socio-economic background. The centre is run by a head teacher and employs a further five staff who provided a focus group interview of 45 minutes.

- Centre F – a reception class for 4- to 5-year-olds within a school on the outskirts of a regional city. It is one of two reception classes catering for a total of 50 children in the school which provides education for about 400 children. The school is in a semi-industrial area. The interview was conducted with one of the reception teachers.

- Centre J – a Montessori-accredited early childhood centre catering for children in the 2–5 year age group. It is located in an old farm residence in a rural area about 50 kilometres from the nearest regional city and about 5 kilometres from the nearest small hamlet of about 20 houses. The Montessori nursery school caters for about 70 children and has about 10 staff, who deal with the daily education and care of the children. The interview was held with the head teacher.

Across these centres, interviews were conducted with three staff individually and a focus group of six staff from one centre. In addition to interviews with providers of early childhood care and education, additional interviews were conducted with two senior regional advisors for the EYFS from two different regions of England, two

early years educators working with pre-service early years teachers, and a local authority officer working with the Early Years Support Service birth–5.

If you view young children at play, you quickly realise how interested they are in the world around them. They are curious about the phenomena they observe and often interact with objects and situations in an effort to gain more information. They are trying to make sense of what they see, what they touch, what they taste and what they smell. In this way, young children are natural scientists. Many of these observations occur through play and it is the role of the early childhood practitioner to enhance these learning experiences by providing opportunities for children to explore the world around them. Within the framework of the EYFS, the researcher asked practitioners how and where science fitted into the frameworks, whether they were comfortable 'teaching' science and how it fitted into their programmes.

Summary of findings

The research identified several interesting aspects of how science was being implemented by EYFS practitioners:

1   All practitioners claimed that they were providing science experiences for the children. However, they also claimed that they had always done so and that, in general, there was little difference now in their practice from what it had been before the implementation of the EYFS. Most were using a 'discovery table' as a way for children to explore interesting science things. As one said, 'I think it [referring to science] has always been there, but it's taught in a broader way basically in the early years because there is so much learning and investigating going on all the time.'

2   Another practitioner indicated, 'I think they were all doing it but weren't calling it "knowledge and understanding" – that was all just part of the discovery bit. The curriculum for that is actually really quite general, there's nothing specific at all, it's all very general so you can do exactly what you were going to do and fit it in.' Yet another practitioner commented, 'I don't think it's a scary prospect for us having this new curriculum because it's probably what most good practitioners were doing anyway.'

3   Apart from the 'knowledge and understanding' component of the frameworks, no practitioner identified where science fitted in other aspects of the framework.

4   One practitioner said that science was an area in which practitioners required more training. He said, 'I think the emphasis tends to be, in early years, on

Research (*continued*)

creativity, but not – I mean science can be creativity... So I think science-type activities and experiments and so on, I think it's sort of qualifications of the staff... I think it is an issue.' He continued, 'I think our staff tend to be more sort of arts creativity. It's the maths and science that I know that we've got an agenda to make sure we deliver.' Another practitioner commented, 'I think it's very much, and especially amongst the women, it's very much a confidence that, that people feel that they can't do science, don't know science, don't know a word, don't know this, not going to do it. So, with the additional training they've had, they're more confident ...'

The interviews with the two regional advisors, the two early childhood educators and the person from the local authority office also attempted to find out how they perceived science to be practised and incorporated into the EYFS.

1 The opinions of the two early childhood educators differed from that of the practitioners. One early years childhood educator lamented the 'everyday science' language of the practitioners who used words like investigate when they were referring to the way children explore. She said that 'investigation is a very particular process that children rarely get involved in until they're at the top of key stage two'. The other early years educator believed that science wasn't seen as core to children's learning. She said, 'I don't think it's quite given the prominence.'

2 The advisor working with the local authority office believed that the focus had moved away from science to language development in addition to personal, social and emotional development. She talked about external assessment which indicated that there had been a drop in children's achievement in 'knowledge and understanding'. She said, 'We've taken our eye off it [science] and we're not encouraging children to ask further questions and take that step forward.'

3 The two regional advisors spoke about their understanding of science in the EYFS. One discussed the ability of early years' practitioners to scaffold children's learning in science, stating, 'I think that we probably know that's a big area for development really. I am very interested in the philosophy of work at pre-schools in science and the opportunities that affords for children to identify their own lines of inquiry and then for practitioners to support and scaffold and extend their thinking.' The other advisor

indicated that the area of 'knowledge and understanding' was broader than science. He commented that all children's learning is 'exploratory, it's investigative, it's practical, it's hand-on. So it doesn't sit within a title, a science. It won't be called science.'

Overall, the research found that science in early childhood had not undergone any revolution or evolution due to the implementation of the EYFS. Practitioners did what they had always done with science, believing quite sincerely that this was sufficient. However, others involved in early childhood education were less positive about the science education children were gaining from their early childhood setting. Science education in early childhood is much more than just discovery: the practitioner needs to be able to scaffold at the time of need, to be able to support new learning, to be able to recognise the 'teachable' moments which occur through play and to become an 'intentional' teacher.

Reflective tasks

Early career professional

- What is the implication for you as an early career professional and for early years science education in the response that 'there is little difference now in their practices'?

- What do you think the practitioner meant when she said, 'You can do exactly what you were going to do and fit it in'?

Developing career professional/teacher

- What is the implication for you as a developing career professional and for early years science education in the response that 'there is little difference now in their practices'?

- What can you infer from the statement that 'no practitioner identified where science fitted in other aspects of the framework'?

Later career professional/leader

- What is the implication for you as a leader and for early years science education in the response that 'there is little difference now in their practices'?

- In terms of staff capabilities and comfort with science teaching, how would you suggest that practitioners gain greater knowledge or ability to scaffold young children's science explorations?

Research (continued)

- What is the relevance of the contextual situation of the early childhood centre in terms of children's learning of science?

Practical task
Write up your answers to create a critical discussion that uses both reading and reflection.

Discovery as a pedagogical approach

As a pedagogical approach, discovery has certain advantages:

- The child is central to the learning and so it is very motivating.
- Children explore and discover things about the world around them, which stem from their own initial curiosity.
- Children construct their own understandings through exploration and from the experience of discovery, as well as developing important skills and attitudes.
- Professionals support and encourage children to ensure that their explorations and discoveries are meaningful to them.
- Teachers utilise knowledge about the children as learners and pedagogical theory and practice to provide an excellent learning environment.

A discovery approach is felt to develop creative thinking (CLS, 2012; Siraj-Blatchford, 2009) and can be structured and supported by teacher scaffolding (Bruner, 1991; Vygotsky and Cole, 1978), questioning and shared talk (Alexander, 2008; Vygotsky, 1962), in a similar way to explorations (as discussed earlier in this chapter). Discovery can stem from explorations initiated by the child or professional as described in the following case study.

CASE STUDY

Discovering snow

Children in Foundation 1 (2- and 3-year-olds) were playing indoors when it started to snow. It was the first snow that most of the children had seen or could remember and they were very excited. The adults working with them helped them to put their boots, coats, hats, gloves and scarves on and they all went outside. They raised their faces to the sky and felt the snow on their faces, exclaiming that it was 'cold' and 'wet'. They stamped in the snow and saw their footprints and how the snow filled up the footprints afterwards. They made snowballs by compacting the snow in their hands and one professional suggested they counted how many they had. Then another professional showed them how they could take a snowball and roll it to make a bigger snowball, which they turned into a body for a snowman. Josh used a spade from the sand pit and collected snow in a bucket. He brought it into the classroom and saw how it melted quickly in the warm air.

Reflective tasks
Early career professional

- What were the children learning during this experience?

Case study (*continued*)

- How meaningful was the learning for the children?
- How often do you 'capture the moment' to enhance learning?

Developing career professional/teacher
- How did the professional support the learning?
- How could the professional extend the learning?
- How could you incorporate more 'discovery exploration' in your context?

Later career professional/leader
- What are the problems for professionals in 'capturing the moment' or discovery exploration?
- How could these problems be overcome?
- How could you support your colleagues to support this approach to learning?

Practical task
Write up your reflections on the case study for a staff development meeting.

ACTIVITIES AND KEY QUESTIONS

To promote understanding of the weather

Early Years Foundation Stage
- Whether the weather be hot, whether the weather be not, we'll explore the weather, whatever the weather, whether we like it or not.
  Key question: What have you found out about snow/rain/sunshine/wind?

- Exploring puddles. After rainfall, allow children to go into the outside area and splash in the puddles, observe the puddles drying up and explore wet soil, sand (in the sand tray) and so on. It is wise to keep a collection of wellies and waterproof coats in different sizes; ask parents for any that their children have grown out of and ask local charity shops for any they cannot sell (or offer then a donation for some). The book *Little Cloud* by Eric Carle (1996) can be used as a stimulus for looking at rainy weather.
  Key question: Why do you think puddles dry up?

- Exploring wind. On a windy day, listen to the wind from inside the setting, but then put on appropriate clothes and go outside. Allow the children to experience the wind on their faces and in their hair. Encourage them to listen to the wind rustling the leaves of trees or whistling through buildings. Hold hands or link arms and face the wind and feel its force. Collect some leaves or small twigs and let the wind blow them.
  Key questions: What have you found out about the wind?

- Explore a collection of rocks with fossils.
  Key question: What do you think the fossils look like?

- Explore the effects of the weather on old buildings or gravestones.
  Key question: Why are some buildings wearing away?

Key Stage 1
- Monitoring/exploring weather conditions – snow. Whilst exploring the snow measure how deep it is in different places. Fill a bucket with snow and see what happens when it melts.

Activities and key questions (*continued*)

Photograph 8.4 Exploring puddles

Key questions: Why do you think the snow is deeper in some places? Why does snow take up more room in the bucket than water?

● Monitoring/exploring weather conditions – Sun. On a sunny day, make a sundial to measure the progress of the Sun in the sky and measure the lengths of the shadows at different times of the day **(see also Chapter 7).** You can also take a thermometer outside to see what the temperature is; it is even better if you can situate a large outside thermometer in the outside area/playground.
Key questions: What happens to the shadows during the day? How does the temperature change during the day?

● Monitoring/exploring weather conditions – thunder and lightning. During a thunderstorm, watch for the lightning and listen to the thunder. Count how long it is between seeing a lightning flash and hearing the thunder; as a rough guide a 1-second gap means the storm is 1 mile away.
Key question: What have you found out about thunder and lightning?

● Explore the effects of the weather on old buildings or gravestones and notice that one side is more weathered than the other.
Key question: Why is one side of a building or gravestone more worn than the other?

Activities and key questions (*continued*)

Photograph 8.5 Exploring snow

- Explore a collection of soils.
  Key question: Why do you think some soils are different from others?

Key Stage 2

Making weather monitoring equipment or a weather station. Simple weather monitoring equipment can be made by:*

- Putting a large empty yoghurt pot in some soil or sand (it can be in a sand trough or garden or a pot) to capture rainfall. The volume of rainfall can be monitored.
  Key questions: How can you measure the rain collected in the pot? What have you found out about rainfall?

- Putting a flag on a pole/stick and watching which way it blows and how hard it blows to measure wind direction and wind speed.
  Key questions: What have you found out about the wind? What does measuring the wind tell you about the weather?

- Measuring the outside temperature. A large outside thermometer or minimum/maximum thermometer is helpful as this can log the lowest and highest temperature over a period of time.
  Key questions: When is the temperature the lowest during the day? Why do you think this is?

*Data-logging equipment can log temperature, wind speed etc over time, but you need to remember that children need to collect measurements themselves before they can understand what the measurements collected using data logging means (see Chapter 1 The development of emergent skills).

> **Activities and key questions (*continued*)**
>
> - Using a sundial to measure the Sun's movement during the day. Children can take a metre stick to a spot outside at each hour of the school day and mark the shadow and the time with chalk. They should then be able to use the sundial to tell the time when outside the classroom (if it is sunny).
>   **Key questions:** When is the shadow from the Sun longest/shortest? Why do you think this is?
>
> - An extension of monitoring and measuring weather can be to compare the weather in your setting with weather in different locations. This can be done by sharing measurements for any one day or week with children in a different school in the country or in another country.
>   **Key question:** How is the weather different? Why do you think this is?
>
> - Explore a collection of rocks and compare how hard or soft they are, what they weigh, their texture, colour or lustre and if the collection has any fossils in it.
>   **Key questions:** What have you found out about rocks?
>
> Use Oscar Wilde's book *The Selfish Giant* (1978) or *Mandy's Umbrella* (Cloke, 1989) to promote discussion of the weather.

The most important feature of discovery learning is that it is child-initiated and therefore self-differentiated, which encourages independence and **metacognition** – understanding of your own learning and your own learning needs (Shayer & Adey, 2002). More directed/structured learning does not allow children to explore and make new discoveries and implies that all the children need the same experiences and that professionals know what individual learning needs are. Imagine what the world would be like if we did not encourage and support the next generation of discoverers. Imagine what would happen if we did not encourage creativity in learning?

When children decide what they want to explore and discover, the learning that takes place is of relevance to them as it stems from their interests. They take control over their own learning and are more likely to develop understandings, skills and attitudes that are appropriate to their needs and experiences and in ways that 'engage, motivate and inspire them' (DfES 2003: 39) because 'excellent teaching gives children the life chances they deserve…. Enjoyment is the birthright of every child. But the most powerful mix is the one that brings the two together' (DfES 2003: Foreword).

The role of the teacher in a discovery approach

The Plowden report (DES 1967: 242) identified the important role of the teacher in discovery by deciding the correct way to support individuals, assessing their level of need and ability, not letting them 'flounder too long or too helplessly' and supporting them by thoughtful questioning. In this way, the role of the teacher is not dissimilar to that of explorations. However, professionals often feel uncomfortable standing back (Cremin *et al.*, 2006) and not directing learning. This is sometimes because they are concerned about issues of time, coverage, control, safety and learning. It is counterintuitive that spending more time discovering and less time focusing on specific outcomes can result in greater achievement in all areas of scientific development. The National Curriculum, even the new slimmed-down version (DfE, 2012b), contains an enormous amount of material and professionals have always been concerned with covering the content. One solution is to impart knowledge, as this takes less time than exploration and this may be a particular danger in the new National Curriculum. It is, however, a deceptive solution, especially in science education, as quality learning occurs through teaching approaches that engage and interest children (Hidi & Harackiewicz, 2000). This interest is greater in practical experiences, which develop skills alongside understandings and pay attention to detail rather than coverage.

STUDY SKILLS

Writing tips

Every writer will have their own ideal environment or time of day for writing (Henn *et al.*, 2006). Some will require quiet and comfortable environments and others will listen to music or the radio while writing. Most will write directly onto a computer but a few will prefer to write by hand and type it up later. There is not one way of writing or one environment suitable for all.

Henn *et al.* (2006) and Trafford and Lesham (2008) recognise the importance of writing for an audience and being very clear on what type of written work they are engaged in. Indeed, Trafford and Lesham (2008) consider that the writer should bear in mind from the outset the final outputs of the writing. This will enable the writer to improve the quality of the output.

Thody (2006) identified that beginnings and endings of written work are important. The beginning captures the readers and the end leaves them with a sense of the worth of the professional enquiry/research. Thody (2006: 162) provided some objectives for abstracts, executive summaries, key points and prefaces in published work. These include 'outlines that guide', 'invitations that attract' and 'summaries that grab'. Continuing to write in an engaging style will help the reader to remain with the text, rather than drift off.

The accuracy of the text is also important. Being literate is essential for all publications of written work and this means that the work should be proof read to ensure that all spelling and typographical errors are removed, grammatical errors are reduced or removed, there is no misuse of words and no 'academic obscurantism' (Atherton, 2005). Accuracy of referencing helps to avoid plagiarism. Neville (2007: 7) identifies five principles of referencing:

1 The principle of intellectual property, thus avoiding plagiarism;

2 The principle of access, providing references that can be easily accessed and checked by the reader;

3 The principle of economy, summarising evidence from referencing in a succinct way;

4 The principle of standardisation, using a standard system of referencing (usually the name, date or Harvard system);

5 The principle of transparency, i.e. there are no ambiguities and all meanings are clear.

Criticality is an important feature of good academic writing. This does not mean being critical or criticising (Atherton, 2005) but comparing and contrasting, seeking out and exploring ambiguities and challenging assumptions and assertions. Criticality involves the use of evidence to support arguments and exploring the values implicit in the work and making them explicit. Criticality also involves recognition and deep discussion of tensions between policy and practice and research, persuasive arguments and the use of evidence strategically as part of a deep analysis or discussion.

One problem that adversely affects criticality is the presence of irrelevant data in the final report. This can occur when the professional has collected a great deal of data, much of it relevant to the area of enquiry and informing their conceptual understanding, but some of it not directly relevant to the study and not answering the research/developmental questions. It is advisable for the professional to sift through the data carefully and take out irrelevant material. This material is not

Study Skills (*continued*)

wasted, as it will have informed ideas and can be used on another occasion. The urge to 'sneak it in' by adding it to the discussion of findings or putting it in the appendix may be strong, but it will just detract, not enhance.

Researchers should also avoid assigning meanings to the findings without evidence and avoid, too, over-inflating the application of the research findings; the researcher who is desperately seeking significance can only be disappointed. If the data is not as conclusive as the writer would like, it can be tempting to try to persuade the reader that it is more significant than it really is. The writer needs to be honest and remember that small-scale qualitative professional enquiry is not very likely to find anything of huge significance. It is more important to look at the data more deeply and try to understand it – to see if there is more to it if you look carefully. Remember, too, that sometimes research that did not turn out the way you expected can prove more interesting than the reverse.

Providing coherence in the text will help to make a better piece of writing. This means that the writer should provide explanations and make things clear for the reader; there is nothing worse than reading a piece of work that frustrates or is unfathomable. For example, research questions are decided early in the research process but may change as the research progresses. They help structure the work and so need to be constantly referred to and, if changed, the changes need to be consistent throughout the written work to ensure the focus and coherence of your work remain. In the spoken word, we often tend to repeat statements using different words to reinforce our points. In writing, however, subtly different terms can be ambiguous and get in the way of coherence; it is important to make clear whether two phrases mean exactly the same thing or not (e.g. midday assistants and midday supervisors; children and pupils; oracy and talk). If the two terms do, in fact, have the same meaning in your context, it is probably best to use only one. Writing can also be made more coherent through the use of subheadings to help structure the work, and by making sure the written report clearly reflects the methodology used in the professional enquiry/research. Finally, coherence is aided by using reading rather than merely quoting it. The researcher should try to tell a clear story without repetition of issues and themes.

Clarity of the written word is an important part of communication. The use of words which do not really say anything (sometimes called 'weasel' words) detracts from this. Words, such as 'basically', 'generally', 'nevertheless' pad out the work, but don't really say anything. Other examples include (PsyPAG, 2005: 48–49):

- 'It has long been known …' (I did not look up the reference)
- 'It is evident …' (someone might believe me)
- 'It is believed that …' (I think)
- 'Typically …' (I have not got a clue)
- Nevertheless …' (I am going to keep going).

Research should be written in plain English and clarify meanings. Most scientific reports are written in the passive tense but this does not have to be the case for educational research. It is more important that the researcher 'owns' the enquiry, so the use of active verbs in the first person (I found, we developed) can be appropriate and professional. It is important, however, not to move from one style to another and to maintain consistency of writing style.

Writing conclusions

The conclusions to written work are like an effective plenary, in that they should not simply repeat what has already been stated but should drive the implications forward and identify how the professional enquiry/research questions have been met. They should sum up the implications as outlined in the discussion of findings and identify the meaning of the findings for the professional and the wider educational community, being careful not to overstate the generalisability of the research results.

The conclusion for most professional enquiries should also reflect on the impact of the process on the personal and professional development of the professional and evaluate the process. In evaluating an enquiry, it is important to be objective and clear about how it might be improved. For example, in research this might mean discussing the appropriateness of the research questions and whether they needed adapting during the research process. It could be that there is an inconsistency between the research questions and the data collected and this could mean that the questions are adapted during the research process. In this way, research should not be seen as a predefined process, but rather as an iterative and developmental process. If the methodology is later found to be less appropriate than another methodology, this should be recognised and discussed. If the methods were not ones that supported the collection of rich data, or other methods would have enhanced the research, this too should be acknowledged. It should be hoped that researchers have developed their research skills through the process of researching and that, if they were to undertake the

Study Skills (*continued*)

research again, they would do it differently. This should also be acknowledged and the reasons discussed. In this way, researchers should identify how they have developed through carrying out the research (i.e. their personal and professional development).

Practical tasks

Review a piece of writing with a critical friend or a group of critical friends. Check your writing for:

- Composition – punctuation, grammar, sentence construction and accurate references
- Meaning – is it clear? Or does it leave unanswered questions in the reader's mind?
- Coherence – does the writing flow from one section/chapter to another and tell a full story?
- Criticality – can the reader understand the arguments? Are they persuasive and convincing?

Knowledge box

Light

Light is a disturbance of electric and magnetic fields that travels in the form of a wave. The light that we can see has a wavelength of about 1/2000 of a millimetre. Light of longer wavelengths that we cannot see includes infrared and radio waves and light of shorter wavelengths that we cannot see include X-rays and gamma rays. Light rays travel from a light source in straight lines and this is the cause of many effects of light that we see.

Shadows occur because when light hits an object it cannot travel around it. If the position of the light source changes, so will the position of a shadow. If the light source is above the object, the shadow will be short and fat (as when the Sun is above the object at midday), but if the light is at an angle to the object the shadow will be long and thin (as when the Sun is low in the sky early in the morning or late in the day). If some light can travel through the object (e.g. plastic bottles) then the shadow will be lighter than if the object lets no light through.

Reflection occurs when light hits a reflective surface, such as a mirror, a shiny spoon or another shiny object. The light will reflect off the surface at the same angle at which it hit the surface – hence, when we look in the mirror, light from one side of our image will be reflected at an angle so our image is laterally reversed. With flat/plane mirrors, images will be:

- the same size as the object;
- the right way up;
- as far behind the mirror as the object;
- a mirror image, so everything on the left is now on the right and everything on the right is now on the left.

If the mirror is not flat (e.g. concave or convex mirrors), the image is further distorted and so convex mirrors will see a larger part of the image but the image is smaller, and concave mirrors can make images larger or even appear 'upside down'.

When light travels through some objects (water, lenses, glass) it refracts or bends (Figure 8.3). If the lens is a strong convex lens, the light rays bend more and the focal point (the point where objects look focused when looking through the lens) is close to the lens. If the lens is a weak convex lens, then the focal point is further away. If the lens is concave then the light rays bend outwards and the light is spread out. If you look through old and distorted glass windows, you will see the effect of refraction of light.

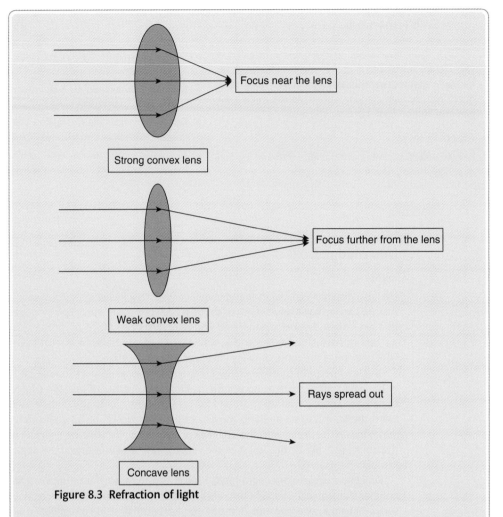

Figure 8.3 Refraction of light

Sunlight is made up of rays of different colours (the visible spectrum) and when it refracts, each colour refracts in a slightly different way. This was first demonstrated by Isaac Newton when he showed that light could be separated when it travels through glass. When light passes through a prism or droplets of water in rainstorms, the colours can be seen as rainbows or a spectrum of colour – red, orange, yellow, green, blue, indigo and violet.

When we see colours, this is because the white light from the light source hits a coloured object and absorbs all the light rays except the colour of the object, which is reflected back to our eyes. So a red object will absorb all other colours of the spectrum but reflect the red light. Black and white objects are seen because the white object reflects all the colours which together make the light look white, and black objects absorb all the coloured light and so reflect no light.

Mixing colours is slightly different because we are dealing with coloured pigments not light, but placing all the colours of the spectrum on a spinner makes it look whitish when it spins, while red and yellow mix to make the spinner look orange and so on.

When we see an object, this is because light travels from a light source and scatters. When this light reaches our eyes, it passes through the pupil (the hole in the iris which controls the amount of light entering the eyes by getting bigger or smaller depending on how bright the light is) **(see Figure 8.4)**. On reaching the lens, it refracts and focuses the image on the retina, at the back of the eye. This image is upside down because the light rays travel in straight lines and are refracted through the lens. Our brain sorts the image out and turns it the 'right way up'. If the lens is defective, so the person is short- or long-sighted (the image is not focused on the retina), or not a regular shape (the person has an astigmatism) then this means the person's vision will be blurred, but it can be corrected with glasses or contact lenses.

Anatomy of the eye

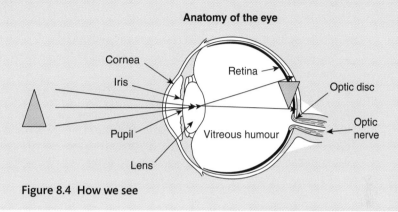

Figure 8.4 How we see

Knowledge box

Weather

The Earth's atmosphere is divided into fours main layers:

- the **exosphere**, where the atmosphere merges into space and there is no air present;
- the **ionosphere**, which is approximately 1,046 km from Earth and where the air is very hot and thin and full of electricity;
- the **stratosphere**, approximately 64 km from Earth – it is a calm part of the atmosphere that planes fly in;
- the **troposphere**, which is the narrowest layer of the atmosphere, stretching 10 km from the Earth –the further from the Earth, the colder it is. It contains 90 per cent of air and most weather conditions occur here.

Weather is a combination of air, water and Sun, and involves the transport of materials and input/reflection of solar radiation. The Sun give us warmth. Water gives us clouds, rain and snow. Pressure and temperature gradients cause wind.

Winds occur because of movements of warm and cold air throughout the Earth's atmosphere. Warm air rises because it is lighter than cold air (lower pressure) and cold air takes its place. Therefore, air is always moving from hot to cold regions of the world, but the movement is affected by the Earth's rotational orbit. Wind speed is measured on the Beaufort scale, invented by Admiral Sir Frances Beaufort in 1805. The scale goes from 0 (a wind speed of 0–1 km/hour, and seen as smoke rising vertically) to 12, which is a hurricane with wind speeds of over 118 km/hour.

Water from the Earth evaporates and rises into the air. Warm air can carry more moisture and, as it rises, it condenses into water droplets or ice crystals that group together to form clouds. The shapes of clouds can give us clues as to the weather, with fluffy cumulus clouds indicating warm sunny weather, cirrus clouds indicating that warmer weather is coming, dark cirrocumulus clouds indicating rain and cumulonimbus clouds indicating thunderstorms. In stormy weather, the water droplets in the clouds are forced together because of strong winds and rub together to form static electricity which is discharged as lightning **(see Chapter 6)**; this heats up the surrounding air, which in turn rises up and is replaced quickly by cold air in a clap of thunder.

The Earth is made up of three parts:

- The **crust** is a thin layer of solid rocks and soil and can be only 6 km thick in places.
- The **mantle** is a thick layer of 3,000 km and consists of hot molten rock which flows around the Earth like treacle.
- The **core** is the metallic centre of the Earth and the hottest part.

Material in the mantle is slowly circulated in a 'convection' current and can reach the crust through erupting volcanoes or earthquakes. Material in the crusts is also circulated in the rock cycle – rocks are worn down by weather and fragments are washed into the rivers and the sea; debris from the sea is collected as sediment and drawn in to the Earth's mantle.

References

Alexander, R. (2008). *Towards Dialogic Teaching: Rethinking Classroom Talk*, 4th edn. York: Dialogos.

Alexander, R. (ed.) (2010). *Children, their World, their Education: Final Report and Recommendations of the Cambridge Review.* London: Routledge.

Atherton, J.S. (2005). Academic practice: writing at master's level. Online: at: http://www.doceo.co.uk/academic/m_writing.htm. Accessed: 1 August 2012.

Bassey, M. (1999). *Case Study Research in Educational Settings.* Buckingham: Open University Press.

Bruner, J.S. (1991). 'The Narrative Construction of Reality', *Critical Inquiry*, 18, (1), 1–21.

Carle, E. (1996). *Little Cloud.* London: Penguin.

Cloke, R. (1989). *Tales of Oaktree Wood. Mandy's Umbrella.* London: Award Publications.

Clough, P. (2002). *Narratives and Fictions in Educational Research.* Buckingham: Open University Press.

Creative Little Scientists (CLS) (2012). Conceptual Framework and Literature Reviews as addenda. Online at: http://www.creative-little-scientists.eu/content/deliverables. Accessed 28/5/12.

Cosgrove, M. & Osborne, R. (1985). Lesson frameworks for changing children's ideas. In: Osborne, R., & Freyberg, P., eds. *Learning in Science: The Implications of Children's Learning.* Auckland, New Zealand: Heinemann.

Cremin, T., Burnard, P. & Craft, A. (2006). Pedagogy and Possibility Thinking in the Early Years. *Journal of Thinking Skills and Creativity*, 1(2), 108–119.

Department of Education and Science (DES) (1967). *Children and their Primary school. A report of the Central Advisory Council for Education (England) Vol. 1: Report.* London: HMSO.

Department for Education (DfE) (2012a). *Statutory Framework for the Early Years Foundation Stage. Setting the Standards for Learning, Development and Care for Children from Birth to Five.* London: DfE.

Department for Education (DfE) (2012b). *National Curriculum for Science. Key Stages 1 and 2 – Draft.* London: DfE.

Department for Education and Science (DfES) (2003). *Excellence and Enjoyment. A Strategy for Primary Schools.* London: DfES.

Elliott, J. (1991). *Action Research for Educational Change.* Buckingham: Open University Press.

Henn, M., Weinstein, M. & Foard, N. (2006). *A Critical Introduction to Social Research*, 2nd edn. London: Sage.

Hidi, S. & Harackiewicz, J.M. (2000). Motivating the academically unmotivated: a critical issue for the 21st century. *Review of Educational Research*, 70(2), 151–179.

Johnston, J. (2004). The Value of Exploration and Discovery. *Primary Science Review*, 85, 21–23.

Johnston, J. (2005). *Early Explorations in Science*, 2nd edn. Buckingham: Open University Press.

Johnston, J. (2009). What is creativity in science education. In: Wilson, A., ed. *Creativity in Primary Education*, 2nd edn. Exeter: Learning Matters.

Johnston, J. & Halocha, J. (2010). *Early Childhood and Primary Education; Readings and Reflections.* Maidenhead: Open University Press.

Moscovitch, I. (1988). *The Magic Cylinder Book.* Norfolk: Tarquin Publications.

Neville, C. (2007). *The Complete Guide to Referencing and Avoiding Plagiarism.* Maidenhead: Open University Press.

PsyPAG Quarterly June 2005: 48–49.

Shayer, M. & Adey, P. (eds.) (2002). *Learning Intelligence. Cognitive Acceleration Across the Curriculum from 5 to 15 Years*. Buckingham: Open University Press.

Siraj-Blatchford, I. (2009). Conceptualising progression in the pedagogy of play and sustained shared thinking in early childhood education: a Vygotskian perspective. *Educational & Child Psychology*, 26(2), 77–89.

Thody, A. (2006). *Writing and Presenting Research.* London: Sage.

Trafford, V. & Lesham, S. (2008). *Stepping Stones to Achieving Your Doctorate by Focussing on your Viva from the Start.* Maidenhead: Open University Press.

Vygotsky, L. (1962). *Thought and Language.* Cambridge, MA: MIT Press.

Vygotsky, L., & Cole, M. (ed) (1978). *Mind in Society, The Development of Higher Psychological Processes.* Cambridge, MA: Harvard University Press.

Walter, M. (1996). *The Mirror Puzzle Book.* Norfolk: Tarquin Publications.

Wilde, O. (1978). *The Selfish Giant.* London: Penguin.

Chapter 9

Scientific investigations and problem-solving

Introduction

Investigations are practical activities where children take increasing responsibility for the enquiry. It involves them in making decisions about the focus, resources, recording and handling variables involved in a systematic way (National Research Council of the National Academies, 2012). As a result, investigations are more suitable for older children in the early and middle years. We do, however, use the term investigations when we talk about other forms of practical scientific activity and this can be confusing.

A key feature of investigation is the presence and handling of variables. In an investigation, key variables are ones that are changed to see what happens (the independent variable) and the result of that change (the dependent variable). So if children are investigating what happens if they water a seed a lot, a little or not at all, the seed is the independent variable and what happens to the seed (if it grows, goes mouldy or does nothing) is the independent variable. In an investigation to see how compost decomposes in different conditions (above the ground in a dustbin or buried underground), the independent variable is the different places the compost is put in and the dependent variable is what happens to the compost (as it is dependent on the independent variable). In an investigation into vehicles rolling down a ramp (see the following case study), the different cars are the independent variables and how far the cars roll down the ramp or how fast they roll down it are the dependent variables.

In an investigation there may be other variables that need to be the same (controlled), so that the investigation is 'fair'. These are called the control variables. Simple investigations for younger children would have only one thing they are changing and not have too many other control variables to control. So a simple investigation that looks at how your pulse changes when you exercise will ask children to take their pulse before exercise and again after 5 minutes of running or jumping. A slightly more complex investigation would compare the results of different children's pulse rate after exercise but make sure that each child did the same 5 minutes of exercise.

Investigations can also be made more or less difficult by the complexity of the variables. The simplest variables are categoric ones, such as the colour, shape or person. More complex variables require measuring of some sort. So while investigating 'ourselves', children may investigate how many marbles they can pick up in one hand and so have to count the marbles (see Chapter 2). In an investigation to see how many marbles will go into a plasticine boat before it sinks, the marbles will likewise need to be counted, whilst in an investigation to see how the children's pulse rates change after 5 minutes of exercise, both the pulse and the time for exercise will need to be measured. Other measurements could include:

● Distance (How far do different toy cars travel after going down a ramp?). Measurement can be in non-standard measures such as lengths of string, or using cubes or a tape measure

● Temperature – this could be qualitative temperature (Which of the three bears' porridge gets cold quickest? Which glove keeps your hand warmer?) and/or quantitative temperature, using temperature probes or thermometers (Does salt dissolve better in water at different temperatures?)

● Weight/Mass (Do heavy cars go further down a ramp than light cars?).

Some investigations may include more than one measurement, such as how different layers of insulation make a difference to temperature. Some investigations require complex derived variables and a number of measurements. So a complex investigation might look at how the height of a ramp and the increase in weight/mass (with an increase of 10 g each time) of a toy car make a difference to the distance the car travels and the speed of the car. In this case there will be two independent variables; the height of the ramp (measured in cm) and the weight of the car (measured in g and in multiples of 10 g). There will also be two dependent variables: the distance the car goes (measured in cm) and the speed (measuring the distance and the time and calculating the speed, i.e. distance divided by time). This actually makes the investigation too complex for most early years children.

In order to be able to recognise and understand variables, children need to be able to see the differences between objects and variables. This means that they need to have a well-developed skill of sorting and classifying (see Chapter 1). The youngest children in the early years will not be able to recognise variables and find similarities and differences difficult to fully comprehend. This will mean that investigative approaches are not suitable for them. As they develop and begin to recognise variables, they can undertake simple investigations, with few and simple variables, and where the teacher controls the variables, that is to say, a highly structured investigation. As children develop they will be able to use their explorations as a step towards planning simple investigation (see Figure 1.1) but may still need scaffolding to help them handle the variables involved, especially to help children focus on variables that make a difference and not to become confused by variables that do not affect the results of the investigation, e.g. not to focus on the weight of a pendulum as it does not affect the swing of a pendulum (National Research Council of the National Academies, 2007). This is important, because, if children become frustrated in their scientific enquiry, it will adversely affect all areas of their development (skills, understandings and attitudes). However, even at an advanced stage of development children will need to explore first to identify avenues for investigation.

CASE STUDY

Investigating bouncing balls

A group of Year 1 children aged 5 and 6 years explored a range of different balls (a soft sponge ball, a tennis ball, a blow-up beach ball, a table tennis ball, a plastic ball and a rubber ball). They played with the balls and explored how they rolled, bounced and even put them in the water trough to see if they floated. Jamal and Maddison explored the bounce of the ball and they asked 'Which ball bounces best?' The class teacher sat down with them and together they discussed how they could investigate this. The teacher guided them to ensure that the investigation was productive, could be undertaken by children of this age and would produce findings that helped their understanding of forces.

The resulting investigation used the different balls (independent variables) to see how high they bounced (dependent variables). The children had to make sure that each ball was dropped from the same height and Maddison took charge of this, while Jamal had to see how far up a metre stick the balls bounced. When they had completed the investigation, Jamal and Maddison told the rest of the class what they had done and what they found out about the balls, concluding that it was the material the ball was made out of that made it bounce, so the rubber ball had the best bounce and the blow-up beach ball had the worst bounce.

When Hadiya and Naomi explored the collection of balls, they decided to investigate the rubber ball and see if it bounced just as well on all surfaces. The teachers helped them to choose the different surfaces and they decided to investigate the bounce on the carpet and lino in the classroom and on the sand pit and concrete outside in the play area. They also told the rest of the class what they did and found out, which was that the concrete and lino were equally good for bouncing surfaces but that the sand was 'awful'. They also said that the ball had

Photograph 9.1 Investigating bouncing balls

not bounced in the sand pit but that it left a crater in the sand. This led Paulo and Jake to take a different range of balls of similar sizes but different weights (a large marble, a ball-bearing, a table tennis ball and a small rubber ball) and see what happened if they were dropped in the sand. They concluded that the heavier the ball, the bigger the crater left on impact.

Case study (*continued*)

Reflective tasks

Early career professional

- How did the teacher support the planning for the investigation?
- How could the teacher support the children during the investigation?
- How can you move children from exploration to investigation?

Developing career professional/teacher

- How did the teacher use whole class discussion and dialogic teaching (Alexander, 2008) to help the next group plan an investigation (**also see Chapter 5**)?
- How could the teacher have extended the investigations by increasing the complexity of the variables involved?

- How can you support children in your own context to move from simple to more complex investigations?

Later career professional/leader

- How are investigations used as a pedagogical approach in different classes in your school/setting?
- How can you support professionals to develop understanding of investigations?
- How can you move from exploration to simple and more complex investigations?

Study skills reflections

How could you present your reflections on the case study to:

- a group of peers;
- A senior colleague;
- Parents as part of a parents' evening?

STUDY SKILLS

Presenting research

Oral presentations can be good ways to communicate research findings but can also help to articulate understandings and ultimately help with written communication. All professionals need to be able to articulate their findings, just as children need to be able to articulate their findings from investigations.

The professional who seeks out opportunities to speak out and articulate ideas is likely to advantage their personal and professional development. Groups of critical friends, action learning sets and informal presentations as part of staff meetings and development days can provide opportunities for small and larger group discussions and help to clarify ideas. Formally presenting research at conferences and in assessed presentations helps researchers to articulate ideas coherently, although, of course, the audience at a conference or in an assessed presentation is different from an audience at a staff meeting or within your setting and so the presentation style needs to be adapted to take this into account (Grey, 2009; Thody, 2006). Oral presentation requires the professional to engage with the audience and it is better to make eye contact, ocassionally referring to notes, rather than to reading from them – alternatively, use notes only as a prompt. An excellent visual and oral presentation will motivate and engage the audience and it should also have a clear sense of purpose. It is easy to spend considerable time making the visual part of oral presentations striking and even engaging, but if you fail to have a clear objective and do not engaging the reader orally it is likely to fail in its purpose.

The structure of the presentation needs to be carefully considered. It is better to have main bullet points that are expanded upon, rather than a huge amount of data that the audience cannot fully comprehend. Grey (2009) considers that it is best to present two or three key messages clearly than to overload the audience with dense slides of data than cannot possibly be explored deeply in a short space of time. Grey (2009) also identifies that engagement is enhanced through the use of personal stories or metaphors. Multimedia enables quality visual cues to engage, but the resource is likely to fail if:

Study skills (*continued*)

- there are too many slides;
- the slides are too densely packed;
- the writing on the slides is too small to be read from a distance;
- the researcher reads from the slides;
- the researcher looks at the screen and not the audience.

Poster presentations can use the available technology to create a poster that conveys the research findings succinctly and visually. They can be particularly useful if the data collected includes images, diagrams or simple tables. They are less useful if the research has complex data and analysis that cannot be displayed succinctly and clearly. As with oral presentations that use visual resources, poster presentations cannot contain everything the researcher has done; indeed, the worst ones are simply a written paper stuck on a wall. They need to convey the message in an A1 format, using pictures, diagrams and a few words. Poster presentations can also involve an element of oral presentation, helping the professional to communicate the findings to a wider audience.

Reflective tasks

Presenting informally to colleagues or critical friends
This could be preliminary to a more formal presentation or an opportunity to disseminate some initial findings or ideas that may support personal and professional development. You may ask them to consider whether:

- you clearly articulated the research, both orally and visually;
- you engaged the audience;
- the research design, analysis and findings were clear.

Preparing to present at a staff meeting
This may be a form of staff development for you and for your colleagues. Your presentation will need to consider:

- how to present your enquiry clearly and succinctly;
- how to present the findings clearly;
- how to engage the audience in a discussion of your findings and the implications of the findings on their practice;
- what questions they might ask.

Preparing to present at a conference
You can use published criteria from conferences to review your own oral or poster presentation synopsis before submitting it to a conference. Consider the following:

- Have you addressed the conference aims?
- Is the rationale for the research clear?
- Are the methodology and methods clearly linked to the research questions?
- Is the analytical framework clear?
- Have you identified the main implications of the research?
- Can the implications be tracked to the analysis?

Investigations as a pedagogical approach

Investigations are part of a portfolio of pedagogical approaches available for professionals to enhance development and learning in science. If used together with other approaches, such as play, exploration and discovery, children will be advantaged, as different approaches will support different children as well as different aspects of scientific development and learning **(see Chapters 7 and 8)**. Good teaching involves using different pedagogical approaches to the benefit of children and, as Alexander (2010: 279) has said, 'good teaching makes a difference. Excellent teaching can transform lives'. However, excellent teaching is complex and involves a number of elements as identified by Alexander (2010) and the Teaching and Learning Research Programme (TLRP), which undertook nearly 70 projects from 2000 to

2008 (James & Pollard, 2010). From an investigative approach in science, good teaching and learning should:

- Be well planned (Alexander, 2010), so that professionals start with learning outcomes and do not make the mistake of starting with activities (Feasey, 2011). This is a common and fundamental error in teaching and learning and very odd in an educational system that has focused on learning outcomes since the introduction of the National Curriculum **(see Chapter 5)**. When planning investigations professionals could start by identifying the learning outcomes before they consider the type of investigation that will achieve the outcomes. The National Research Council for the National Academies (2007) have identified that sustained investigations have the advantage of developing knowledge and explanations/interpretations of the natural world, but emphasise that this cannot happen without good planning, so as to avoid investigations that are mindless, fun activities with no link to scientific ideas. If the link with science is tenuous so the adult cannot see it, it is likely that children won't see it either.

- Recognise the importance of prior experience and learning (James & Pollard, 2010), even with the youngest children, and demonstrate an understanding of children's developmental needs (Alexander, 2010). This may mean that investigations will start from play or exploration, which helps children to raise their own questions (Campbell, 2012; Glauert, 2009; **see also Chapter 1**). This questioning can start with 3- and 4-year-olds and Blake and Howitt (2012) identify that it should be a pedagogical approach used by professionals. Questions raised should be real and important to the children, as this will give them greater autonomy in the investigation (Harlen & Qualter, 2009).

- Require professionals to have good subject knowledge (Alexander, 2010) and also good pedagogical subject knowledge, so they understand not just the science underpinning the learning outcomes but also the types of investigations that can be effectively used as a vehicle to achieve them. This will require effective teacher learning from initial teacher education through to continuing professional development (James & Pollard, 2010).

- Enable children to have the opportunity to carry out different types of investigations, increasingly making decisions for themselves and starting from their own hypotheses (National Research Council for the National Academies, 2012). Harlen and Qualter (2009) have identified different types of investigations with different learning purposes. The information-seeking investigation is where children see what happens and can be the forerunner to the hypothesis-generating investigation, where children generate 'why' questions, formulate hypotheses and test them out. Although children in the early years can generate hypotheses (see the research box that follows; **see also Chapter 1**), hypothesis-generating questions may be too complex for all but the oldest in the early years, as would comparing/fair-testing investigations. Other appropriate investigations include pattern-finding investigations, which help children see associations and cause-and-effect relationships, and 'how to do it' investigations (Harlen & Qualter, 2009), which are more directed and may involve technological problem-solving (see the section on 'Problem-solving as a pedagogical approach' below **and Chapter 3**).

- Be creative, recognising that creative science (such as inquiry-based science education) has a synergy with creative approaches (CLS, 2012) and that creative teaching will support creative learners (DfES, 2003) by inspiring children (Alexander, 2010).

- Facilitate learning (Alexander, 2010; Johnston, 2005) rather than impart knowledge, so that the professional scaffolds learning (James & Pollard, 2010; Vygotsky, 1978) and encourages increasing independence in investigations. In early investigations, children should be supported to help them to define variables, see patterns in data and begin to suggest causal relationships (National Research Council for the National Academies, 2012), rather than following instructions, as this will not help future development.

- Provide opportunities for children to discuss their findings with others and so embed learning. This acknowledges the importance of classroom dialogue (Alexander, 2008; Eccles & Taylor, 2011) as discussed in previous chapters **(see, in particular, Chapter 5)**.

As children play and explore, they may notice how rain splatters on the ground or the pattern that a dripping paintbrush makes on the floor or on the painting paper. This can be encouraged by the professional and extended into an investigation that looks at 'splats' – drops of liquid paint. Children could start by exploring splats and making splat pictures by dropping liquid paint from a pipette onto paper. They may note that the splat is round in shape with radiating spikes of different lengths and could begin to raise questions about splats that can be investigated, such as 'How does the height of the drop affect the splat?'; 'How does the size of the drop affect the splat?'; 'How does the thickness of the paint affect the splat?'; 'How does the type of paper affect the splat?' This might then lead to investigations that involve children looking at the size of the splat and the number of radiating spikes as a result of: the height the splat is dropped from; the liquidity/thickness of the paint; the type of paper (e.g. absorbent, shiny); and the size of the drop (by having different size pipettes).

In such an investigation, the professional needs to support the children to ensure that they do not try to find out too much (have too many dependent variables), or handle too many or too complex variables for their conceptual ability or age, or do not control other variables. The professional also needs to ensure that children do not lose interest, if the resulting investigation were to become too adult-led and less their own idea, and also that children have the time and space to discuss their findings and so consolidate their learning.

ACTIVITIES AND KEY QUESTIONS

To promote understanding of energy

These activities may also be used to promote other areas of scientific conceptual development, such as understanding the environment, weather, forces, magnetism or electricity, as described in other chapters.

Early Years Foundation Stage

- Start with the story *Wonderful Earth* (Butterworth & Inkpen, 1991) and use it as stimulus to discuss why we should look after energy resources in our world.
  Key question: How can we save energy?
- Observe wind energy using toy windmills and explore the strength of the wind.
  Key question: How do you think we can use wind energy?
- Explore a range of moving toys (e.g. electrical, magnetic, wind-up).
  Key question: What energy do the toys use to move?
- Explore energy when baking chocolate-covered cakes. Observe and discuss the energy used to bake the cakes and to heat the chocolate to cover the cakes.
  Key questions: Where does the energy come from to heat up the oven? Why do you think the chocolate melts?

Activities and key questions (*continued*)

- Use the book *Can You Move Like an Elephant?* (Hindley & Stojic, 2004) to stimulate exploration of the way we move and the energy we use when moving.
  Key question: Do you think you use more energy when you move like an elephant or move like a horse?

Key Stage 1

- Use the story *Where the Forest Meets the Sea* (Baker, 1987) to explore the effects of wasting energy and identify five ways we can save energy in school, e.g. by using energy-saving devices, switching off energy-using devices, recycling.
  Key question: What are the best ways to save energy?

- Investigate composting of vegetable waste by setting up two compost bins, one left alone and one with tiger worms (composting worms). Use the compost on a vegetable or flower plot to help growth. You can also investigate the effect of compost or no compost on growth.
  Key question: What difference do the worms make to the composting?

- Feel the energy release in the form of heat when plaster of Paris is mixed with water.
  Key question: What do you think is happening?

- Explore solar toys and investigate the effect of different lights on the movement; use torches of different brightness.
  Key question: What difference do you think the torches make?

- Make your own toy that uses energy from magnetism, electricity or a wind-up mechanism.
  Key question: How does your toy work?

Key Stage 2

- Recycle paper by tearing up paper and liquidising with a small amount of wallpaper paste (with no fungicide in). Investigate recycling paper by seeing whether particular paper or mixed paper makes the strongest recycled paper.
  Key questions: What else is used to make paper? Why should we recycle paper?

- Observe water being brought to the boil and boiling.
  Key question: Where does the energy come from to boil the water? What happens when the water starts to boil?

- Explore pulleys and investigate what difference one or two pulleys makes to lifting things.
  Key question: What difference does one or two pulleys make to lifting things?

- Investigate the effect of the length of the string on a pendulum swing. You could set up two pendulums (with different length of string and a ball of plasticine) suspended from a door frame. Alternatively, you could make two pendulums using two empty washing-up liquid bottles with the bottoms cut off and filled with liquid paint **(see Figure 9.1)**. Put paper on the floor underneath the pendulum and, as it swings, the liquid paint will drip out and make a pattern. The different patterns made by pendulums with different lengths of string can be compared.
  Key question: What difference does the string make to the pendulum?

- Undertake a collaborative problem-solving activity to design and make a 'mousetrap game' which, when triggered, sets off a series of energy changes. The game must contain at least four energy changes and can involve gravitational potential energy,

Activities and key questions (*continued*)

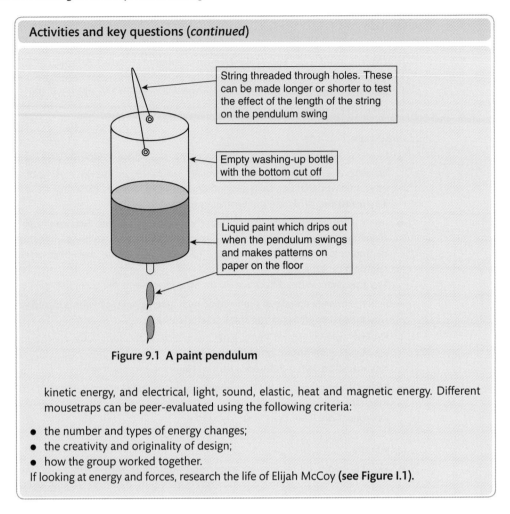

String threaded through holes. These can be made longer or shorter to test the effect of the length of the string on the pendulum swing

Empty washing-up bottle with the bottom cut off

Liquid paint which drips out when the pendulum swings and makes patterns on paper on the floor

Figure 9.1 A paint pendulum

kinetic energy, and electrical, light, sound, elastic, heat and magnetic energy. Different mousetraps can be peer-evaluated using the following criteria:

- the number and types of energy changes;
- the creativity and originality of design;
- how the group worked together.

If looking at energy and forces, research the life of Elijah McCoy **(see Figure I.1).**

Problem-solving as a pedagogical approach

Problem-solving is a child centred approach (Campbell, 2012) which inspires and motivates children. In Chapter 3 we looked at problem-solving as a vehicle to develop positive attitudes to science and promote scientific enquiry. In the research box later in this chapter, problem-solving is seen as an effective pedagogical approach to support the development of prediction and hypothesis in young children **(see also Chapter 1).**

Problem-solving is part of the portfolio of pedagogical approaches available to professionals and should be seen as one pedagogical tool in the armoury. There is not one approach that is 'best' or even 'better'; what is important is to choose the approach that best suits the child or children and the identified learning outcomes. As the National Research Council of the National Academies (2007) concluded in their review of learning and teaching in science in the early years, children need a variety of pedagogical approaches for full development. The Creative Little Scientists project identified problem-solving within inquiry-based science education as a highly collaborative, creative approach

(CLS, 2012) and that there is a synergy between the problem-solving and creativity approaches. Both problem-solving and creative approaches can encourage ownership of learning and the development of self-determination and control. The literature on creative approaches (Craft *et al.*, 2012; Cremin *et al.*, 2006, 2009) suggests that problem-solving encourages creative engagement, in that children identify their own problems.

As a pedagogical approach, problem-solving facilitates scientific skill development by encouraging children to raise their own questions from their observations and to use these to structure their enquiry **(see Chapter 1)**. It can also develop emergent ideas about scientific concepts in a meaningful and motivating context, thus developing positive scientific attitudes and providing children with opportunities to develop socially through shared, meaningful, scientific experiences **(see Chapters 2 and 3)**. In order for this development to occur, professionals need to have trust in and show interest and respect for the problems children choose to solve, i.e. the questions they raise that can lead to problem-solving. Remember that children are usually best placed to identify their learning needs and will, with support and encouragement from the teacher, move their learning forward themselves. Professionals should be able to scaffold the learning environment to enhance children's development and allow children increasing autonomy so that they begin to take ownership and control of their enquiry. In an open-ended exploration, professionals can scaffold learning to encourage children to raise questions and move to answering them through problem-solving **(see Chapter 8)**. So that, rather than structuring learning or leading children through an enquiry, professionals can work with children to plan and resolve cooperative or collaborative enquiry. This is a difficult approach for professionals who, for many years, have limited autonomy and opportunities for risk-taking in children (McWilliam, 2008). Joubert (2001) identifies that creative professionals:

- prioritise learner agency;
- expect high degrees of independence of even the youngest learners;
- encourage problem-solving and problem-finding activities;
- employ reverse questioning, passing the problem back to the learners to foster their decision-making.

CASE STUDY

Drinks can dragster

A class of 8-year-old children were shown a drinks can dragster/vehicle **(see Figure 9.2)** and asked to design one with their friends that would travel the furthest across the school hall. The vehicles work by having a cylindrical container threaded with a rubber band, which, when wound up, moves the vehicle by 'rubber band power'. The children were given 30 minutes to plan what they were going to use for their vehicle and to make a list of resources they would need, including things they could bring from home, if the school did not have them;

the next day they would have the afternoon to make their vehicle which would be tested at the end of the day.

The following morning, Matthew, with his friends Sam and Joe, arrived in school pushing a large reel that had been used for cables that were being put under the pavement outside the school. On the way home from school the previous day, Matthew had stopped to chat to the workmen and they offered him the reel (probably thinking the teachers would not know what to do with it!). Matthew asked his parents

Case study (*continued*)

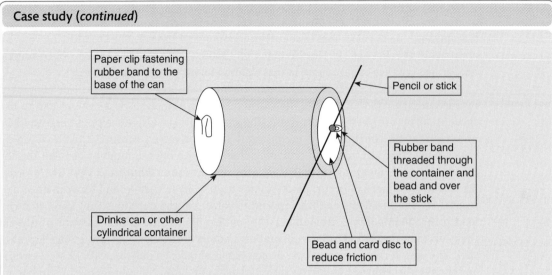

Figure 9.2 A drinks can vehicle

and they agreed that he could collect it on the way to school. When Matthew, Sam and Joe rolled it into the class, the other children looked aghast. The class discussed what the boys could use for a stick and a rubber band. They decided to ask the school caretaker if they could borrow a broom handle for the day and they found some thick elastic in a cupboard and set about making their vehicle. Some other children replicated the drinks can vehicle the teacher had shown the class, whilst other groups used a cylindrical crisp container and a pop bottle.

At the end of the day, Matthew, Sam and Joe's vehicle was very impressive and did roll but it did not go the furthest and it moved very slowly. Some of the vehicles went in circles and one went very fast but quickly stopped. A few went slowly but surely across the school hall and the children decided that they needed the stick to be 'longer on one side than the other' to make it go straight and 'not to be too tightly wound up' to make it go slowly and far.

Reflective tasks

Early career professional
- What do you think were the planned learning outcomes for the problem-solving activity?
- How did the activity promote autonomy and motivate the children?

- How can you use scientific problem-solving activities to motivate children's learning in science?

Developing career professional/teacher
- How did the teacher encourage autonomy and collaboration?
- How do you think the problem-solving approach aided learning?
- How can you develop and extend cognitive, affective and social development through collaborative learning?

Later career professional/leader
- What skills do professionals need to successfully use problem-solving as a pedagogical approach?
- How can you support colleagues in developing these pedagogical skills?
- How can you improve the use of problem-solving activities in your school/setting?

Use the case study and reflective questions with a group of colleagues or in a staff meeting and present your reflections to the rest of the group using either:

- a poster;
- a PowerPoint presentation;
- a discussion document.

Research

The effect of exploratory and problem-solving pedagogies on the skills of prediction and hypothesis

Jane Johnston

Research questions

- What do the skills of prediction and hypothesising look like in young children?
- How do the skills of prediction and hypothesising develop from initial observations?

Research design

Evidence to answer the research questions was collected during a day of science activities with 60 children aged 6 years. There were 10 activities (five that involved exploration or exploratory play and five that were problem-solving activities) and each one provided opportunities for the children to observe scientific phenomena that could lead to prediction and hypothesis. Adults moved around the activities, interacting with the children, recording spontaneous predictions and hypotheses and providing prompt questions to encourage prediction and hypothesis. The children's responses to the prompt questions and other predictions and hypotheses were recorded by the adults working with each group on prompt sheets with each activity; the part played by the adult interaction was not part of this study and whilst this would have had an impact on results, this would have been minimised by the adults interacting equally with each group.

Sample

The research was carried out with two classes of 6-year-old children. There were 60 mixed-ability children in total, 25% of whom had statemented special educational needs. The researcher, two class teachers and two teaching assistants supported the activities and the data collection, moving around the groups of children and activities, so that each activity and group of children had similar adult interaction. Permissions to carry out the research were obtained from the school, the parents and the children.

Activities and prompt questions to promote prediction and hypotheses

1 **Ice balloon exploration**

   What do you think will happen when you... put salt on the ice balloon/put the ice balloon in water?

2 **Which gloves will keep the ice hands cold?**

   What will happen if you put the different gloves on the ice hands?

3 **What clothes does Teddy need for his holidays?**

   Why does Teddy need these clothes for his holiday?

4 **Seasonal play-dough exploration**

   What do you think will happen when you ... mix the play-dough/add the stars?

5 **What wrapping paper is strongest?**

   Which paper do you think will be the strongest? Why?

6 **Exploring materials and mixing materials**

   What do you think will happen when you ... touch/squeeze/add water to the materials?

7 **Make a box to protect a delicate present**

   What do you think will make a good box? Why?

8 **Seasonal water play**

   What do you think will happen when you ... put this in the water/stir the water?

   Why do you think that has happened?

9 **How can we stop Santa's sledge sliding off the roof?**

   Which sledge do you think will stay on the roof? Why?

   Why is this sledge the best?

10 **How can we free the bears/mini-beasts from the ice?**

   How do you think we can free the bears/mini-beasts?

Summary of findings

The following table outlines the findings, showing the activities, prompt questions and resulting number of predictions and hypotheses and examples of each.

Research (*continued*)

Activities and prompt questions	Predictions	Hypotheses
Ice balloon (**exploration**) *What do you think will happen when you... put salt on the ice balloon/put the ice balloon in water?*	25 'Salt will melt the ice' 'The salt will turn into ice' 'It will go harder, because I have done it before'	4 'The water makes the ice smooth and melty' 'Melted because the water is HOT!' 'Ice gets bigger when salt is added'
Which gloves will keep the ice hands cold? (**problem-solving**) *What will happen if you put the different gloves on the ice hands?*	34 with most containing some reasoning 'Rubber, because they are thin' 'Kitchen gloves, because they are warm and cold' 'Black woolly glove, warm and soft – melting when you put different gloves on'	24 – many following on predictions 'Because it is rubber and does not have much air in it' 'The purple glove will melt the ice because it's so warm' 'The thick rubber glove won't let any air get to it'
What clothes does teddy need for his holidays? (**exploratory play**) *Why does Teddy need these clothes for his holiday?*	14 'Going to Spain – needs sunglasses and shoes trainers, swimming outfit'	2 'Needs a coat (for North Pole) because it's cold' 'Jumper and gloves to keep hands warm'
Seasonal play-dough (**exploration**) *What do you think will happen when you...mix the play-dough/add the stars?*	25 'Adding stars will make the dough turn gold' 'It will go solid' 'It will go sticky'	1 'The liquid took the colour of the star and turned my dough green'
What wrapping paper is strongest? (**problem-solving**) *Which paper do you think will be the strongest? Why?*	29 most with explanations 'Shiny thick wrapping paper – you can't tear it' 'Thin wrapping paper - you can screw it up'	22 'It feels like it's really strong' 'Because if you compare it's the heavy one' 'Newspaper - because it's made of wood' 'Tin foil because it's like metal'
Exploring materials and mixing materials (**exploration**) *What do you think will happen when you... touch/squeeze/add water to the materials?*	28 'It will stay the same' 'It will smell different and turn yellow' 'It will go purple and be more soft'	0
Make a box to protect a delicate present (we used an egg and this affected the responses) (**problem-solving**) *What do you think will make a good box? Why?*	18 – most with explanations 'Cotton wool –makes it "safer" ' 'Wool makes it softer' 'Boxes are hard so they're better to protect'	15 'Lots of padding at the bottom' 'Four sides so it doesn't fall out' 'Needs a nest (keeps it warm)'
Seasonal water play (**exploration**) *What do you think will happen when you...put this in the water/stir the water Why do you think that has happened?*	30 'The water will turn orange' 'Float and dissolve' 'Dissolve, make water, smell nice'	7 'Because the object is like soap' 'Because it's allergic to the air' 'Because we stirred the water'

Research (*continued*)

Activities and prompt questions	Predictions	Hypotheses
How can we stop Santa's sledge sliding off the roof? **(problem-solving)** *Which sledge do you think will stay on the roof? Why? Why is this sledge the best?*	11 many with explanations but they did predict after playing 'This one – it has sticky stuff on the bottom' 'It has nothing on it and may go properly'	25 'Because sandpaper grips onto the bits of wood' 'The weights push it down a bit' 'Because it has a smooth surface'
How can we free the bears/mini-beasts from the ice? **(problem-solving)** *How do you think we can free the bears/mini-beasts?*	16 'Roll it down the street. If it hits something sharp it will break' 'Wait until the ice turns to water' 'Tip it upside down then smash the ice'	5 'Wave hands like a fan because it's like a fan making it warm' 'I stopped because I was waving cold air' 'Going to try and breathe and wave hand'
Total	230	105

The children produced many more predictions than hypotheses (2.2 times as many). All activities and prompt questions appeared to encourage predictions and to encourage and support explanations for the predictions and hypotheses. Some activities (e.g. 'Which gloves will keep the ice hands cold?', with 34 predictions, and 'Seasonal water play', with 30 predictions) appeared more than twice as successful at encouraging predictions than others (e.g. 'How can we stop Santa's sledge sliding off the roof?', with 11 predictions, and 'What clothes does Teddy need for his holidays?' with 14 predictions). Some activities and prompt questions appeared to encourage the production of hypotheses, e.g. 'Which gloves will keep the ice hands cold?' and 'What wrapping paper is strongest?' encouraged both prediction and hypothesis, whilst 'How can we stop Santa's sledge sliding off the roof?' appeared to encourage hypotheses rather than prediction (25 hypotheses and 11 predictions). Others appeared to encourage few hypotheses (Seasonal play-dough exploration,

25 predictions and one hypothesis; Exploring materials and mixing materials, 28 predictions and no hypotheses; Seasonal water play, 30 predictions and seven hypotheses). The problem-solving activities (see the previous table) were more successful in encouraging the generation of hypotheses (91 hypotheses generated in total) than the exploration and exploratory play (14 hypotheses generated in total), although both types of activity supported the generation of predictions equally (problem-solving activities generated 108 predictions and explorations and exploratory play generated 122 predictions).

Both the predictions and hypotheses were analysed to identify any links in the reasoning; links based on prior experience, tacit or implied links, or links that were weak and scientific causal links.

The following table shows activity, number of predictions and hypotheses with no links to reasoning, experiential links, tacit or weak links and scientific causal links, with examples of each.

Activity	No link	Experiential link	Tacit or weak links	Scientific causal links
Ice balloon exploration	24 predictions 'Turn soft' 'Melt'	1 prediction 'It will go harder (because I've done it before)'	3 hypotheses The water makes the ice smooth and melty Ice gets bigger when salt is added	1 hypothesis Melted because the water is HOT!

Research (continued)

Activity	No link	Experiential link	Tacit or weak links	Scientific causal links
Which gloves will keep the ice hands cold?	2 predictions Purple glove, not sure why	17 predictions and hypotheses 'Purple woolly glove because the glove is warm'	5 predictions and hypotheses 'Thick rubber glove, it's big' 'Because it is already in it'	7 predictions and hypotheses 'Because of the properties of the gloves' 'Because it is woolly' 'Because it is rubber'
What clothes does teddy need for his holidays?	7 predictions (mainly lists of clothes needed with no explanation)	6 predictions (based on holidays in Spain and experiences) 'Welly boots (so it's raining)'		2 hypotheses 'Needs a coat (for North Pole) because it's cold' 'Jumper and gloves to keep hands warm'
Seasonal play-dough exploration	25 predictions		1 hypothesis Adding stars will make the dough turn gold	
What wrapping paper is strongest?	9 predictions	5 predictions and hypotheses 'It feels like it's really strong' 'Because it's soft'	3 predictions 'Because it's long' 'You can screw it up'	16 predictions and hypotheses (based on the properties of the paper) 'Tin foil because it's like metal' 'Because if you compare, it's the heavy one'
Exploring materials and mixing materials	28 predictions (lists of different types of materials)			
Make a box to protect a delicate present (we used an egg and this affected the responses)		3 predictions leading to hypotheses 'Bubble wrap because it stops things smashing' 'Make it look like a castle because egg boxes look like castles'	7 predictions and hypotheses 'It needs a nest to keep it warm'	6 predictions and hypotheses 'Boxes are hard so they're better to protect'
Seasonal water play	12 predictions The water will change colour The object will sink	15 predictions and hypotheses 'Because the object was too heavy and bubbles float'	8 predictions and hypotheses 'Because it is like soap'	2 hypotheses It will dissolve
How can we stop Santa's sledge sliding off the roof?	7 predictions This one – I don't know	9 predictions 'Turn the ramp the other way round' 'Let's do it really high up so it will go down'	1 prediction 'It will go easier'	19 predictions and hypotheses 'The rough sledge was slowest because it was still' 'Because it has a smooth surface'

Research (continued)

Activity	No link	Experiential link	Tacit or weak links	Scientific causal links
How can we free the bears/mini-beasts from the ice?	6 predictions Put them in a warm place	8, mainly predictions 'Get cup and hold hairdryer underneath to melt ice'		7 predictions and hypotheses 'Wait until the ice turns to water' 'The heat from the hairdryer is melting it'
Total	120 (44%)	64 (24%)	28 (10%)	60 (22%)

This analysis indicated that these children made slightly more predictions and hypotheses with explanations (152, i.e. 56%) than without (120, 44%) and that these predictions and hypotheses had links equally based on experience and science. There was also evidence that the problem-solving activities and prompt questions generated significantly more predictions and hypotheses with scientific causal links (55) than the explorations and exploratory play (5).

Problem-solving activities appeared to lead to the generation of more hypotheses as the children's thinking became more relational-based (Gentner & Medina, 1998; Rattermann & Gentner, 1998). It thus appeared that the activity and prompt question were important factors in encouraging and supporting explanations for the predictions and hypotheses, supporting children in making the links between their observations, prior knowledge and in developing their ideas through discussion with peers and informed adults (Vygotsky, 1978) in the co-construction of ideas (Siraj-Blatchford et al.,

2002). This has implications for curriculum design, planning science experiences, interacting with children during these experiences and teacher training (Yip, 2007).

References

Gentner, D., & Medina, J. (1998). Similarity and the development of rules. Cognition, 65, 263–287.

Rattermann, M.J., & Gentner, D. (1998). More evidence for a relational shift in the development of analogy: children's performance on a causal-mapping task. Cognitive Development, 13, 453–478.

Siraj-Blatchford, I., Sylva, K., Muttock, S., Gilden, R., & Bell, D. (2002). Researching Effective Pedagogy in the Early Years. Nottingham: DFES.

Vygotsky, L., & Cole, M. (eds) (1978). Mind in Society, The Development of Higher Psychological Processes. Cambridge, MA: Harvard University Press.

Yip, D.Y. (2007). Biology students' understanding of the concept of hypothesis. Teaching Science, S3(4) December, 23–27.

Practical and reflective tasks

Practical tasks
Set up some different activities to explore the effect of different pedagogical approaches.

Early Years Foundation Stage
In the Early Years Foundation Stage these could be play activities and exploratory activities. Each activity should have the same learning outcomes:

- A story sack and play around *Kipper's Toy Box* (Inkpen, 1992) could be used to explore forces in additional moving toys in the toy box, as could an exploration of a collection of toys.
- Role-play on going on holiday could focus on materials and their properties by packing clothes suitable for the climate being visited **(see Figure 7.2)**. Exploratory activities could also focus on materials and their properties by looking at a range of fabric and their properties, e.g. how strong, waterproof, soft, warm.

Key Stage 1

In Key Stage 1, exploratory or discovery approaches can be compared with problem-solving approaches:

● An exploration of a collection of sycamore seeds or other 'helicopter seeds', collected from the environment, can be used to focus on the forces involved in dropping things (gravitational force and upthrust/air resistance). Children can make their own helicopters and explore the same forces **(Figure 3.5)**.

● Children can explore a range of mirrors to focus on understanding of reflection or they can try to use mirrors to make a periscope so they can see round corners.

Key Stage 2

In Key Stage 2 investigative and problem-solving approaches can be compared:

● Children can investigate simple circuits and switches and see what materials the electricity will pass through. Alternatively, they can make a question-and-answer board **(see Figure 6.3)**.

● Children can focus on understanding sound and how pitch changes by making a stringed musical instrument or investigating how the thickness, length or tautness of a rubber band makes a difference to the pitch when plucked.

Practical and Reflective tasks

For each set of activities evaluate the learning and teaching and produce a PowerPoint presentation of your findings:

● How did the different pedagogical approaches support achievement of the learning outcomes?

● How could you improve your role in the pedagogical approach?

● What pedagogical knowledge and skills do you need to widen your use of the different pedagogical approaches?

● How can you access support to improve your teaching?

ACTIVITIES AND KEY QUESTIONS

To promote problem-solving

Early Years Foundation Stage

● Problem-solving in the sand tray.
Key question: Can you build a big sand tower?

● Make a waterproof hat for teddy/make an umbrella.
Key questions: What material is best for teddy's hat/umbrella? Why?

● Make a balancing toy **(see Figure 3.4)**.
Key question: How do you get the toy to stand back up when pushed over?

● Make a Duplo bridge.
Key question: How can you make your bridge stronger?

● Make a water run for boats from the water tray using guttering.
Key question: How does your water run work?

Activities and key questions (*continued*)

Key Stage 1

- Make a climbing Teddy **(see Figure 5.1)**.
  Key question: Can you make your Teddy climb down the string?

- Write a secret letter with a black pen on blotting or other absorbent paper. The pen can be identified using chromatography; dip one end of the paper in water and the colours in the ink will separate. If you do this with other pens, you will see that each type of black pen has different patterns and can identify which one wrote the letter. This activity can be part of a science detective role-play.
  Key question: Can you find out which pen wrote this letter?

- Make a kaleidoscope using mirrors, card boxes and sequins/beads.
  Key question: How does the kaleidoscope work?

- Make a box to protect an egg.
  Key questions: Which is the best design? Why?

- Make a helicopter **(Figure 3.5)**. Try to make your helicopter fall slowly to the ground.
  Key questions: How does the helicopter work? How do you get the helicopter to fall more slowly?

Key Stage 2

- Make a marble maze. The marble must travel through a table top maze without being touched.
  Key question: How can you make the slowest marble maze?

- Make a burglar alarm which signals when someone enters the classroom.
  Key question: How does the burglar alarm work?

- Make an electrical/magnetic game **(see Figure 6.3)**.
  Key question: How does the game work?

- Make a steady hand game **(Figure 6.4)**.
  Key question: How does the game work?

- Make a ball sorter that sorts out different types of balls in three different ways, e.g. size, buoyancy, magnetic, weight, bounce (see Chapter 5).
  Key question: How does your ball sorter work?

Knowledge box

Energy

Physics involves the study of different types of energy:

- Electrical energy, which can be generated by use of energy in fossil fuels, solar energy (light energy), nuclear energy, as well wind and wave energy (kinetic/movement energy) **(see Chapter 6)**.

- Magnetic energy, through rearrangement of atoms in soft iron or steel permanently **(see Chapter 6)**. The Earth's core is magnetic and this exerts forces from the Earth to the Sun's solar wind (another energy field). Since the Earth's core is molten, the poles are not static and the magnetic core fluctuates, probably due to the interaction with solar magnetism. The magnetic energy in the Earth affects daily life on Earth (e.g. it affects weather and humans, and birds navigate using the Earth's magnetic core).

- Sound energy, which is the type of energy associated with vibrating waves **(see Chapter 5).**

- Light energy, or energy emanating for a light source, in particular the Sun, which is a giant ball of energy **(see Chapter 8).** Solar/light energy can be collected using solar panels and used to generate electricity or heat energy.

- Heat energy is the energy used in heating and cooling (shown by a change in temperature), changing state or latent energy (shown when, for example, substances change state from solid to liquid or liquid to gas). Most energy transfers involve some heating and this heat energy is responsible for the global energy crisis and global warming, since it is difficult to capture the heat and transfer it to other forms of usable energy.

- Movement energy or kinetic energy is the energy in moving objects. When an object has the potential for movement, due to its position (an object teetering on the edge of a table, or a leaning post), it is said to have potential energy, i.e. it has the potential to move.

Our world (and the universe) contains a finite amount of energy, much of which is stored as chemical energy in organic matter, such as animals, plants and fossil fuels. The energy in the world is not used up but is transferred from one form to another, usually with some form of heat transfer involved. The energy crisis has not arisen because we are using up energy but because it is being transferred from accessible, stored forms into inaccessible forms.

References

Alexander, R. (2008). *Towards Dialogic Teaching: Rethinking Classroom Talk*, 4th edn. York: Dialogos.

Alexander, R. (ed.) (2010). *Children, their World, their Education: Final Report and Recommendations of the Cambridge Review*. London: Routledge.

Baker, J.(1987). *Where the Forest Meets the Sea*. London: Walker.

Blake, E. & Howitt, C. (2012). Developing pedagogical practices for science teaching and learning with 3 and 4-year old children. In: Campbell, C. & Jobling, W., eds. *Science in Early Childhood*. Sydney: Cambridge University Press.

Butterworth, N. & Inkpen, M. (1991). *Wonderful Earth*. London: Hodder and Stoughton.

Campbell, C. (2012). Teaching approaches. In: Campbell, C. & Jobling, W., eds. *Science in Early Childhood*. Sydney: Cambridge University Press.

Creative Little Scientists (CLS) (2012). Conceptual Framework and Literature Reviews as addenda. Online at: http://www.creative-little-scientists.eu/content/deliverables. Accessed 28/5/12.

Craft, A., McConnon, L. & Matthews, A. (2012). Creativity and child-initiated play: fostering possibility thinking in four-year-olds. *Thinking Skills and Creativity*, 7(1), 48–61.

Cremin, T., Burnard, P. & Craft, A. (2006). Pedagogy and possibility thinking in the early years. *Journal of Thinking Skills and Creativity*, 1(2), 108–119.

Cremin, T., Barnes, J. & Scoffham, S. (2009). *Creative Teaching for Tomorrow: Fostering a Creative State of Mind*. Deal: Future Creative.

Department for Education and Science (DfES) (2003). *Excellence and Enjoyment. A Strategy for Primary Schools*. London: DfES.

Eccles, D. & Taylor, S. (2011). Promoting understanding through dialogue. In: Harlen, W., ed. *ASE Guide to Primary Science Education*. Hatfield: ASE.

Feasey, R. (2011). Planning: elements of an effective lesson plan. In: Harlen, W., ed. *ASE Guide to Primary Science Education*. Hatfield: ASE.

Glauert, E. (2009). Research in early childhood science education: issues for early childhood curriculum design and implications for primary science education. *Lernen und Kindliche Entwicklung*, 41–57.

Grey, D.E. (2009) *Doing Research in the Real World*, 2nd edn. London: Sage.

Harlen, W. & Qualter, A. (2009). *The Teaching of Science in Primary Schools*, 5th edn. Abingdon: David Fulton.

Hindley, J. & Stojic, M. (2004). *Can You Move Like an Elephant?* London: Doubleday.

Inkpen, M. (1992). *Kipper's Toybox*. London: Hodder and Stoughton Children's Books.

James, M. & Pollard, A. (2010). Learning and teaching in primary schools: insights from TLRP. In: Alexander, R.J., Doddington, C., Grey, J., Hargreaves, L. & Kershner, R., eds. *The Cambridge Primary Review Research Surveys*. London Routledge.

Johnston, J. (2005). *Early Explorations in Science 2nd Edition*. Buckingham: Open University Press.

Joubert, M. M. (2001). The art of creative teaching: NACCCE and beyond. In: Craft, A., Jeffrey, B. & Leibling, M., eds. *Creativity in Education*. London, Continuum.

McWilliam, E. (2008). Unlearning how to teach. *Innovations in Education and Teaching International*, 45(3), 263–269.

National Research Council of the National Academies (2007). *Taking Science to School. Learning and Teaching Science in Grades K to 8*. Washington, DC: The National Academies Press.

National Research Council of the National Academies (2012). *A Framework for K-12 Science Education; Practices, Crosscutting Concepts and Core Ideas*. Washington, DC: The National Academies Press.

Thody, A. (2006). *Writing and Presenting Research*. London: Sage.

Vygotsky, L., & Cole, M. (ed) (1978). *Mind in Society, The Development of Higher Psychological Processes*. Cambridge, MA: Harvard University Press.

Glossary of terms and acronyms

Terms

Abstraction The ability to form a general concept.

Action research A cyclic research process of collecting data and analysing it before deciding the next research step. Each action step involves planning, doing and reviewing.

Affective attitudes Attitudes concerned with feelings.

Affective development The development of attitudes and attributes; feelings.

Analysis Breaking down ideas, reading or observations to understand them and their constituent parts.

Attachment Close bond; primary attachments are with main care-giver and secondary attachments with other close individuals.

Attitudes A stance or attribute arising out of a complex inter-relationship between the social (behaviour), affective (feelings/emotions) and cognitive (thinking/ideas).

Authoritarian Strict, controlling, severe, dictatorial.

Authoritative Showing high levels of warmth and achievement demands, with firm control.

Behavioural attitudes Attitudes concerned with actions and behaviour.

Classification Skill of sorting and ordering.

Cognition The construction of idea, knowledge and understanding.

Cognitive Concerned with cognition or thinking.

Cognitive attitudes Attitudes concerned with thinking or cognition.

Collaboration The act of working together.

Communication The skill of articulating ideas, thoughts or thinking to others.

Concept A big idea; a picture in the mind.

Constructivist The development of ideas or behaviours by experience or social interaction.

Cooperation The act of working alongside others.

Critical incidents Incidents that are critical in determining/developing reflection, ideas and action.

Curriculum The aspects of development and learning appropriate for children of a specific age.

Dialogic teaching Teaching approach that uses shared language to support development and learning.

Discovery A pedagogical approach where children follow their own lines of enquiry.

Early Years Foundation Stage From birth to 5 years of age.

Early years professional Generic professionals who work with young children on a daily basis and are responsible for their care and development.

Emergent science Science for children from birth to 8 years of age.

Enquiry What scientists do (e.g. investigating using scientific methods) sometimes termed inquiry (US). How children learn science (e.g. actively enquiring). A pedagogical approach in science.

Epistemic play Play where prior knowledge is used.

Ethics Moral principles/values.

Exploration A form of enquiry, where there is no set procedure.

Exploratory play Play that leads to exploration of scientific phenomena.

Hypothesis An explanation or set of possible explanations for observed scientific phenomena or events.

IBSE Inquiry-based science education; an approach to learning that emphasises children's understanding and skills in finding out and evaluating information around them.

Intelligence A measure of thinking ability as measured by intelligence quotients.

Interpretation The scientific skill of making sense of data.

Investigation A type of scientific enquiry, where variables are controlled and tested.

Key Stage 1 From 5 to 7 years of age.

Key Stage 2 From 7 to 11 years of age.

Ludic play Fantasy/imaginative play.

Metacognition To be aware and understanding your own thought processes.

Method Data collection tool; way of collecting data.

Methodology Type of research.

Misconception An incorrect idea or way of thinking; more correctly identified as an alternative conception.

Monocultural Involving a single culture.

Multicultural Involving a number of different cultures.

Multimodal A form of interaction using gestures and body language as well as speech.

National Curriculum The identified learning for children of compulsory school age.

Objectivity Being able to look at evidence without bias.

Observation The skill of using all senses in enquiry; the most important skill for early years children and in science.

Pedagogy The science of teaching.

Permissive Exercising limited control and being inconsistent about discipline.

Prediction Statement made about future events, usually based on prior knowledge.

Pre-school Before starting school.

Problem-solving A form of enquiry where a problem is posed and children attempt to solve it.

Reasoning Providing evidence or justification for a belief.

Reconstituted (or blended) family Where adults and children from different family groups combine to make a new family (or step-family).

Reflection The process of thinking and evaluating.

Reflective practice The process of reflecting on and evaluating professional practice.

Reliability The extent to which something (research) can be repeated with the same/similar results.

Scaffolding The pedagogical approach of supporting learning from individuals to support deeper learning.

Scientific process The range of processes involved in the development and testing of ideas in science in an inter-related way.

Social development The process of learning to live with others in a social learning environment.

Skills A learnt practical ability, may be generic (appropriate in a different areas of development and learning) or specific to an area.

Study skills Skills needed by professionals in order to develop their practice.

Synthesis To take analysis from a wide range of primary and secondary evidence and to combine the analysis in order to draw conclusions, make sense of the whole, draw inferences producing new ideas or models and identifying implications.

Transition The process of moving from one situation to another.

Validity The truth and honesty of data in research.

Variables Factors, components in a scientific investigation.

Acronyms

CLS	Creative Little Scientists
DfES	Department for Education and Skills (until 2007)
DfE	Department for Education (from 2010)
DfEE	Department for Education and Employment (from 1995)
DCFS	Department of Children, Families and Schools (from 2007)
ECM	Every Child Matters
EPPE	Effective Provision of Pre-school Education
ESERA	European Science Education Research Association
ESN	Emergent Science Network
EYFS	Early Years Foundation Stage
EYP	Early years professional
HE	Higher education
IBSE	Inquiry-based science education
ICT	Information and communication technology
JES	Journal of Emergent Science
PGCE	Post-Graduate Certificate of Education
PISA	Programme for International Student Assessment
QTS	Qualified Teacher Status
ROSE	Relevance of Science Education
SMART	Specific, measurable, analytical, relevant and time-related
SPACE	Science Processes and Concept Exploration
TIMSS	Trends in International Mathematics and Science Study
UK	United Kingdom

Index